EARLY CHILDHOOD EDUCATION AND CARE FOR SUSTAINABILITY

This innovative and timely book explores issues and concerns surrounding Education for Sustainable Development in early childhood, providing a range of perspectives on how we can live and promote more healthy, just and sustainable lives. It examines the professional responsibility of Early Years practitioners to embed sustainability into their everyday practice and to ensure that young children are acquiring the knowledge and skills they need to become effective agents of change, committed problem-solvers and system-thinkers.

Bringing together international examples of best practice, drawing on cutting-edge research and providing an array of practical examples, chapters focus on issues such as:

- the historical context of Early Education for Sustainability
- complexities and challenges involved in implementing sustainable approaches
- encouraging children to contribute to an enabling society
- adopting environmentally sustainable approaches in Early Years settings
- the future of sustainability in Early Years education.

This book offers essential support to Early Years educators, practitioners and students who are key players in shaping the fundamental attitudes and beliefs of our planet's future citizens, enabling them to assume their responsibilities, now and in the future, in regard to environmental, social and economic sustainability.

Valerie Huggins is Associate Director for Teaching and Learning and Associate Professor in Early Childhood Studies at the Institute of Education, Plymouth University, UK.

David Evans retired as Principal Lecturer and Director of the Integrated Masters Programme at Plymouth University, UK. He is currently involved in ECE curriculum development in Majority World contexts.

RESEARCH INFORMED PROFESSIONAL DEVELOPMENT FOR THE EARLY YEARS

TACTYC (Association for Professional Development in Early Years)

The books in this series each focus on a different aspect of research in early childhood which has direct implications for practice and policy. They consider the main research findings which should influence practitioner thinking and reflection and help them to question their own practice alongside activities to deepen knowledge and extend understanding of the issues. Readers will benefit from clear analysis, critique and interpretation of the key factors surrounding the research as well as exemplifications and case studies to illustrate the research-practice or research-policy links. Supporting the development of critical reflection and up to date knowledge, the books will be a core resource for all those educating and training early years practitioners.

Exploring the Contexts for Early Learning
Challenging the school readiness agenda
Rory McDowall Clark

Forthcoming titles:

Places for Two-Year-Olds in the Early Years
Supporting Learning and Development
Jan Georgeson and Verity Campbell-Barr

Young Children are Researchers
Building knowledge in early childhood
Jane Murray

Supporting Abused and Neglected Children in the Early Years
Practice, policy and provision
Sue Soan

Early Childhood Education and Care for Sustainability
International Perspectives
Valerie Huggins & David Evans

EARLY CHILDHOOD EDUCATION AND CARE FOR SUSTAINABILITY

International Perspectives

Edited by Valerie Huggins and David Evans

Routledge
Taylor & Francis Group

LONDON AND NEW YORK

First published 2018
by Routledge
2 Park Square, Milton Park, Abingdon, Oxon OX14 4RN

and by Routledge
711 Third Avenue, New York, NY 10017

Routledge is an imprint of the Taylor & Francis Group, an informa business

British Library Cataloguing in Publication Data
A catalogue record for this book is available from the British Library

Library of Congress Cataloging in Publication Data
A catalog record for this book has been requested

ISBN: 978-1-138-23943-2 (hbk)
ISBN: 978-1-138-23944-9 (pbk)
ISBN: 978-1-315-29585-5 (ebk)

Typeset in Bembo
by Taylor & Francis Books

CONTENTS

CONTRIBUTORS

Eva Ärlemalm-Hagsér is an Associate Professor in Early Childhood Education within early childhood teacher education at Mälardalen University and has a background as a preschool teacher. Her research focus is on early childhood education, education for sustainability and preschool children's participation and agency within policy and practices—indoors and outdoors.

David Evans retired as a Principal Lecturer and Director of the Integrated Masters Programme of the University of Plymouth. He had previously taught all ages of children and young people, from age two to 18, as well as being an ILEA Music Advisor, before moving into the fields of Early Years teacher education and the development of Children's Centres. Currently he is involved in ECE curriculum development in the Majority World, particularly in African countries.

Maria Assunção Folque is a lecturer on Early Childhood Education at the University of Évora in Portugal. She was a nursery teacher for 12 years and has been involved in the MEM (Modern School Movement)—a movement of teachers from all levels of education engaged in developing democratic schooling. Her research interests include quality in early years education, education for sustainable development, pedagogy and learning and teacher training, from a socio-cultural perspective.

Jan Georgeson is a Research Fellow in Early Education Development at Plymouth University and has a background in teaching young children with special educational needs. Jan was involved in supporting candidates for Early Years Professional Status from the pilot phase onwards and is currently investigating professional development for early years practitioners, especially in the context of multi-agency working and working with very young children.

Lucien Georgeson is a Doctoral Researcher in the Department of Geography, University College London. His principal research areas are the definition and measurement of the global green economy, climate adaptation, and the negotiation and implementation of the Sustainable Development Goals. He is a graduate member of the American Association of Geographers and a Postgraduate Fellow of the Royal Geographical Society. He is also a member of the Board of Trustees of Education Partnerships Africa, a grassroots international development charity that works in partnership with secondary schools in rural East Africa.

Sandra Hesterman is a senior lecturer at Murdoch University, Perth, Western Australia. She is a strong advocate for the provision of high quality early childhood care and education and has worked with various development projects on Education for Sustainable Development together with pre-service teachers and children in early learning centres. Sandra's research, grounded in postmodern theories, examines how a pedagogy of multiliteracies accommodates cultural and linguistic diversity, and promotes a culture of creativity and innovation.

Valerie Huggins is the Associate Director for Teaching and Learning at the Plymouth Institute of Education at Plymouth University, UK, where she lectures in Early Childhood Studies. Before taking up her current post she worked for several years as an Early Years teacher and consultant and spent some time with VSO, training teacher educators in Ethiopia. Her research interests centre on approaches to promoting Early Childhood Education and Care for Sustainability through the professional development of practitioners both in the UK and in Majority World contexts.

Sara Knight is a former Principal Lecturer in early years, education and playwork in the Department of Education at Anglia Ruskin University. Originally a nursery teacher in mainstream and special education, Sara contributed to the development of Forest School as an early years intervention across the UK. She has published articles and bestselling books on Forest School, and is in demand as a keynote speaker at conferences in the UK and internationally.

Paulette Luff is a Senior Lecturer in the Department of Education at Anglia Ruskin University where she leads the MA in Early Childhood Education and is convenor of the Early Childhood Research Group. Paulette has worked in the field of early childhood throughout her career and her specialist areas of teaching, writing and research are observation for learning and research; professional enquiry; early childhood education for sustainability; and creative and cultural learning.

Balázs Molnár is an associate professor in Early Childhood Education within early childhood teacher education at the Faculty of Child and Adult Education, University of Debrecen. His research focuses on Early Childhood Education, Play and Learning in Early Childhood and Virtual Learning Environments.

Alun Morgan taught Geography and Integrated Science in secondary schools in England and Wales for ten years before working as a teacher adviser in Education for Sustainability. From 2002 he has worked in higher education. His work focuses on the interface between geography and science education, environmental education and education for sustainability, place-based education and global citizenship. He is particularly interested in working across the formal–informal learning sectors, outdoor education and in the sphere of community outreach.

Kate Nash graduated from Liverpool University in 1983 and has worked overseas and in the UK. Throughout her life, Kate has been passionate about sustainability. Currently a head teacher in a primary school in the UK, as her leadership roles have developed she has been able to influence the curriculum so that sustainability is integral to the school ethos and community. Kate is married with three children and her passions include music, entertaining, gardening, chickens and bee-keeping.

Sándor Pálfi is Vice-Dean and Head of the Department of Child Education and Professor in Early Childhood Education within early childhood teacher education at the Faculty of Child and Adult Education, University of Debrecen. He has a background as a kindergarten pedagogue. His research focus is on Early Childhood Education, Principles of Project Pedagogy in Hungary, and the Interpretation of Child-based Education Approach in kindergarten and children's free play.

Ingrid Pramling Samuelsson is Professor in Early Childhood Education at the Department of Education, Communication and Learning, Gothenburg University in Sweden. She also holds a UNESCO Chair in Early Childhood Education and Sustainable Development. Her research interest is the conditions for successful learning and teaching in preschool.

John Siraj-Blatchford is an Honorary Professor at the University of Plymouth, and provides independent research, training and consultancy through the SchemaPlay partnership. He was recently commissioned by UNESCO to provide an early childhood review of the UNESCO Decade for Education for Sustainable Development, and he chaired the Early Childhood for Sustainable Development workshop at the 2014 UNESCO 'End of Decade' Conference in Nagoya, Japan.

Sándor Szerepi is Vice-Dean and Associate Professor in Early Childhood Education within early childhood teacher education at the Faculty of Child and Adult Education, University of Debrecen. His research focus is History of Education, Early Childhood Education and the Integration of Roma Children in Early Childhood.

Anikó Nagy Varga is a senior lecturer in Early Childhood Education within early childhood teacher education at the Faculty of Child and Adult Education, University of Debrecen. Her research focus is on Early Childhood Education, Comparative Education, History of Education, and Roma Children's Education.

Sue Waite is Associate Professor (Reader in Outdoor Learning) at Plymouth University, where she has been a researcher for the last 20 years, leading a series of studies about the impacts of outdoor learning on children and young people through Forest School, National Parks and curriculum-based activity.

Alice Warwick is an Early Years teacher at Shakespeare Primary School in Plymouth. Her practice interests include outdoor learning through Forest School approaches, pupil leadership development through school council participation and care for pupil well-being.

Paul Warwick is an Associate Professor in Sustainability Education and is the Centre for Sustainable Futures Lead at the University of Plymouth. His research and practice focus is on Sustainability Education, Active Citizenship Education, Global Learning, student voice and innovation in applied pedagogy.

FOREWORD

Professor Emerita Moyles and Professor Jane Payler

Welcome to the third volume in the inspiring TACTYC book series. As part of the Association for Professional Development in Early Years, TACTYC members believe that effective early years policies and practices should be informed by an understanding of the findings and implications of high quality, robust research. TACTYC focuses on developing the knowledge base of all those concerned with early years education and care by creating, reviewing and disseminating research findings and by encouraging critical and constructive discussion to foster reflective attitudes in practitioners. Such a need has been evident in the resounding success of events such as our conferences where speakers make clear connections between research and practice for delegates. Early years practitioners and those who support their professional development engage enthusiastically with research and understand how it is likely to impact upon, and enhance, practice. They acknowledge that research has a distinct role to play in effective work in early years education and care, and that they should be part of a research-rich education system.

TACTYC is an organisation with a specific focus on the professional development of all those involved in early childhood with the express purpose of improving practices to enhance the well-being of young children. Its reputation for quality research and writing includes its international *Early Years* journal. This book series is likely to be popular with those who value the journal as it will add to its range and scope. Our aim for the series is to help those who educate and train early years practitioners at all levels to understand the implications and practical interpretation of recent research, and to offer a rationale for improving the quality and reach of practice in early years education and care.

It is not always easy for busy trainers and practitioners to access contemporary research and translate it into informed and reflective practice. These books are intended to promote the benefits of applying research in an informed way to develop high quality pedagogical practices. Each individual book in this series will explore a range of different topics within a theme. This third book considers the issues involved in Education for Sustainability, which features increasingly in educational debate. Globally, there is growing recognition that we all have to address a wide range of issues and problems, often interlinked, if we are to avoid destroying ourselves and to create instead a more equitable and sustainable environmental, economic and social world. In this book, the writers aim to introduce and comment on some of the current debates about Early Childhood Education and Care for Sustainability (ECECfS), present some new research and provide ideas for practice, anticipating that this will help practitioners to introduce and develop ECECfS in an informed and ethical way and to adopt sustainable practices. Material with a strong international dimension is presented in order to avoid parochialism and to widen awareness of the rapidly increasing body of ideas in this field. The contributors also offer leads to some of the wider aspects of EfS, at present and in the future.

This book contributes significantly to our understanding of this field and reflects the general growing interest in this early years phase of education and care. There is now a rich source of early years research on which writers may draw. The claim is frequently made that policies are 'evidence-based' but this is not the same as rigorous, impartial research. Many policy and practice documents purport to be based on 'evidence', but this depends to a large extent on the political framework and ideology in place at different periods in time—few governments have the scope in their relatively short elected periods to give strategic consideration to the complex implications of different research outcomes for policies and practice. What is politically and economically expedient at the time is too often the driving force behind decisions about young children and their families.

All the writers in this series have been asked to present their particular focus, and to outline the issues and challenges within that framework that are relevant for early years practitioners. Exploring aspects of early years practice, based on research and sound theoretical underpinning, the writers will offer guidance on how findings can be analysed and interpreted to inform the continuing process of developing high quality early years practice. They will examine the research background to each topic and offer considered views on why the situation is as it is, and how it might move forward within the frameworks of imposed curricula and assessments. They will offer thoughtful advice to practitioners for dealing with the challenges faced within that particular focus and will suggest relevant follow-up reading and web-based materials to support further reflection, practice and curriculum implementation. Each book will also identify where further research is needed and will help tutors, trainers and practitioners to understand how they can contribute to research in this field.

Early years education and care is universally contentious, especially in relation to how far those outside the field (e.g. politicians and policymakers) should intervene in deciding what constitutes successful early years pedagogy, curriculum and assessment. The main focus of the series is on practice, policy and provision in UK, but writers will also draw on international research perspectives, as there is a great deal to learn from colleagues in other national contexts.

The series particularly targets readers qualified at Level 6, or students on such courses, preparing for roles in which they will be expected to educate and train other practitioners in effective early years practices. There will be many others who will find the books invaluable: leaders of early years settings, who often have an education, training and professional development role in relation to their staff (and may well be qualified at Level 6 or beyond), will similarly find the series useful in their work. Academics and new researchers who support the training and development of graduate leaders in early years will also appreciate the books in this series. Readers will benefit from clear analysis, critique and interpretation of the key factors surrounding the research as well as exemplifications and case studies to illustrate the links between research and policy as well as research and practice. The books will support the development of critical reflection and up-to-date knowledge, and will be a core resource for all those educating and training early years practitioners.

In summary, research-based early years practice is a relatively new field, as much of practitioners' work with young children over recent years has been based on the implementation of policy documents, which are often not grounded in rigorous, clear, unambiguous research evidence. The main aim of the TACTYC series is to help tutors and trainers to enable practitioners to become more informed advocates for provision of high quality services for children and their families. This will be achieved by promoting the benefits of applying research in an informed way to develop the quality of practice.

PREFACE

John Siraj-Blatchford

This book is written at a critical point in history. In January 2016, the seventeen United Nations Sustainable Development Goals (SDGs) came into force. The United Kingdom, along with all other nations of the world, have committed themselves to achieving these ambitious goals, by the year 2030, to reduce inequalities, eradicate extreme poverty, bring an end to hunger, improve health and education provisions, achieve gender equality, protect the environment and promote peace, justice and prosperity. These united efforts are being instituted in recognition of the fact that challenges that we currently face, in terms of climate change, environmental damage, natural resource depletion, conflict, diminishing biodiversity, and so on, are all global problems that cannot be solved by national policies alone. Their solution requires common efforts and shared understandings. It is important to recognise that if the UK, or, by some magical swipe of Harry Potter's wand, even the whole of Europe and the United States were suddenly to become 'sustainable' societies, the world would still be set on an inevitable path of ecological destruction. In the UK, and in other relatively wealthy countries, we need to set a good international example, adopt sustainable practices and reduce consumption and carbon emissions, but we also need to recognise that all round the world nations are in this together. We need to collaborate and communicate more effectively than ever before if we are to face the challenge. Nicholas Stern, a Former World Bank chief economist and UK government economic advisor, has described climate change as the 'greatest market failure in history', and he has estimated that in the absence of radical intervention it could reduce global gross domestic product (GDP) by 20 per cent by 2050 (cited in Sauven, 2015). An economic contraction on that scale would have a massive effect on the lives and welfare of us all, but as always, it would disproportionately affect those already most disadvantaged.

Governments around the world are addressing the issues and Education for Sustainable Development (ESD) is seen as fundamentally important in tackling these problems. As Irina Bokova, Director-General of UNESCO, has argued:

Education is the most powerful path to sustainability. Economic and technological solutions, political regulations or financial incentives are not enough.
We need a fundamental change in the way that we think and act.

(Bokova, 2012, p. 2)

Early Childhood Education and Care (ECEC) has been recognised as a significant
contributor to ESD (UNESCO, 2014). The SDGs include explicit aims to increase
early childhood educational provisions and to reorientate education at every level
towards sustainable development. Britto (2015) and Siraj-Blatchford et al. (2016)
have argued that ECEC is of crucial importance in achieving many of the other
SDGs. It is increasingly recognised, as Britto (2015) writes that:

Investments in ECEC are fiscally smart, given the multiplier effect of ECEC
across several goals. But, they are also scientifically credible and morally correct.
Let us affirm our commitment to the Global Goals by giving every child a fair
chance in life from the start.

(Britto, 2015, p. 1)

It is in the early years that many fundamental attitudes towards the environment,
towards consumption and waste and towards fairness and social justice are formed,
and this text makes an important contribution towards developing a better understanding of the kind of curriculum and approaches that may be adopted to support
sustainability. The authors' adoption of the term 'Education *for* Sustainability' (EfS)
in itself reflects a shared concern to promote the active involvement of the child in the
development of more sustainable futures. This emphasis upon the importance of
recognising the agency and rights of young children can be found echoed throughout
the text, and in my own recent writing (Siraj-Blatchford & Brock, 2017).

A controversial view adopted by a number of authors, and referred to in this
text, questions the very possibility of defining *any* effective global prescriptions for
EfS. The United States president apparently sees the whole sustainability agenda as
bad for business, and a threat to US sovereignty. But Donald Trump is not the
only critic, and the issues are also presented at times in stark dichotomous terms,
where EfS is defined as an unwarranted Minority World imposition upon the less
industrially developed Majority World. The very real and deadly excesses of cultural
imperialism in the past (Rodney, 1972) might sometimes blind us to the historical
reality that cultural exchanges have often had positive as well as negative consequences. For example, Barbara Rogoff (2003) has referred to the introduction of
farming from Mesopotamia 10,000 years ago, and the events that followed the
domestication of horses in the Ukraine about 5,000 years ago. While globalisation
has allowed transnational companies to build upon the colonial domination of the
past to exploit those least able to defend themselves (Chomsky, 2004), the same
features of globalisation have supported the United Nations (UN) in improving
global dialogue and have contributed significantly towards the achievement of
greater peace, environmental protection and human rights. The achievements of

the UN may be difficult to assess but, worldwide, fewer people died in conflict in the first decade of the 21st century than in any decade of the 20th. Whilst a great deal more needs to be done to end famine, this century has already seen massive reductions in the number of people who have died from hunger. Thanks in large part to UN efforts, the number of deaths worldwide for children under the age of five has also reduced from nearly 12 million in 1990 to 6.9 million in 2011. UN efforts to deal with HIV/AIDS and other epidemics have also been crucial. The UN Conventions on Climate Change and on Children's Rights are critically important in terms of sustainable development. World Heritage sites contribute to conservation. Refugees have been aided through UN agencies, the proliferation of atomic weapons has been reduced and war crimes tribunals have also been established. While there remains so much to be achieved, UNESCO's coordination of the Global Action Programme (GAP) on ESD[1] is set to make a substantial contribution to the implementation of SDG 4 and to its Target 4.7 in particular:

> By 2030, ensure that all learners acquire the knowledge and skills needed to promote sustainable development, including, among others, through education for sustainable development and sustainable lifestyles, human rights, gender equality, promotion of a culture of peace and nonviolence, global citizenship and appreciation of cultural diversity and of culture's contribution to sustainable development.

While all of these institutional efforts are essential, it is important to recognise that there are important global ideological struggles taking place that we are all, more or less, engaged in through our day-to-day democratic and cultural participation, in our purchasing decisions and in our economic assumptions and behaviour. The fact is, as suggested above, that sustainability can only be achieved through global collaboration. We should consider the agreement on a common core curriculum for sustainability in the same light. We need to recognise that there is a need for more dialogue between the Minority and Majority World and not less.

A related debate concerns the issue of 'readiness for school' or 'schoolification'. Moss (2013) and others have been extremely critical of those promoting the view that ECEC provisions should be considered as some sort of investment in children's later performance in school. Such arguments are often reduced to a simplistic binary opposition where the child's welfare is seen as being disregarded in efforts to gain economic advantage for the wider society. The more complex motives of those promoting greater investment in the early education of disadvantaged children are often ignored:

> Why should society invest in disadvantaged young children? The traditional argument for doing so is made on the grounds of fairness and social justice. It is an argument founded on equity considerations.
>
> There is another argument that can be made. It is based on economic efficiency. It is more powerful than the equity argument, in part because the gains

from such investment can be quantified and they are large. There are many reasons why investing in disadvantaged young children has a high economic return.

It is a rare public policy initiative that promotes fairness and social justice and at the same time promotes productivity in the economy and in society at large. Investing in disadvantaged young children is such a policy.

(Heckman, 2006, p. 2)

A central issue in this 'readiness' debate concerns the degree of emphasis placed upon literacy and numeracy in the early childhood curriculum. While recognising that an overemphasis on literacy and numeracy outcomes may sometimes serve as a barrier to the development of ECECfS, in these pages, Ärlemalm-Hagsér and Pramling Samuelsson sensibly suggest that literacy and numeracy on the one hand, and ECECfS on the other, can be seen as complementary, rather than as oppositional alternatives. They argue for a more balanced approach, and suggest that an EfS curriculum focused upon the development of 'collaboration and critical thinking, the development of self-confidence, and a sense of responsibility' may contribute significantly towards children being even more 'ready' for their future life challenges.

We know that high quality preschool education is effective in supporting young children who have been disadvantaged in their early years. If we consider this issue in terms of the Rights of the Child then it is clear that they should be given every opportunity possible to succeed in education and not suffer due to the 'accident of birth' in a disadvantaged family or community (Siraj-Blatchford et al., 2016). The very first of the UN's SDGs to be achieved by 2030 is to end poverty in all its forms (Goal 1), and the UN recognises that poverty is more than a simple lack of income or resources; it includes the lack of basic services such as education, health and nutrition, social discrimination and exclusion, and a lack of participation in decision-making. In many cases poverty must also be considered in terms of a poverty of aspirations that often exerts unnecessary limitations upon social mobility. An adequate view of ECECfS must therefore include those basic skills in literacy and numeracy that are absolutely necessary if the child is to actively participate in modern democratic civil society.

Often the 'readiness' discourse has also been reduced to a misleading binary opposition that is set between emphasising teaching or play. Both concepts are often presented as exaggerated caricatures, with an image of whole class didactic instruction on the one hand, and children given total freedom to play and express themselves away from adult influence on the other. Neither of these are a reality in UK early childhood practice and, just as long as play is given strong precedence, they may be seen as essentially synergistic (Siraj-Blatchford & Brock, 2016a, 2016b):

The promotion of totally 'free play' in early childhood doesn't put the curriculum in the hands of the child; inevitably they are playing in the cultural contexts and within the environmental constraints provided by the adults around them, and for good or ill they 'play out' the day to day realities of all those whose lives they observe around them.

(Siraj-Blatchford et al., 2016, p. 199)

Rogoff (2003) has contributed greatly to our understanding that play is of universal consequence to child development and learning. This is an aspect of quality practice that might usefully be encouraged through a global EfS programme which would also provide recommendations related the child's playful access to natural environments and their freedom to express themselves on issues of sustainability. In doing so we would also be supporting Article 31 of the UN Convention on the Rights of the Child (1989), which states that the child has a right to leisure, play and participation in cultural and artistic activities.

Educational practices are always informed most significantly by conceptions of what it is that constitutes the making of a 'good life'. Inevitably these conceptions change over time, and the curriculum changes with them. Processes of curriculum development always involve making choices, and in the interests of social justice all the members of any culture or society should be actively engaged in decisions about what should be preserved and what should be let go (Sen, 1999, p. 242). Sen argues that when it comes to deciding which capabilities should be prioritised we can never expect complete unanimity, but that a just 'working solution' may still be found in dialogue. This is an important principle. Curriculum change is just the same, and what we should be aiming for is the development of just 'working solutions' in free and unrestrained dialogue. Thus, while acknowledging the wide range of other important ideas and approaches in EfS, we should accept that in the 21st century, literacy and numeracy may also be considered essential to enjoy a life of 'genuine choices with serious options', enhancing 'the ability of people to help themselves and to influence the world' (Sen, 1999).

Nevertheless, seeking an appropriate balance does not mean that that educators should seek to be neutral; as Freire (1998), and Gramsci (1971, pp. xvii–xcvi) before him, argued, educators must always take a stand:

> We need to be clear that respecting a plurality of conceptions of the good life (and hence of how education is arranged) is not the same as endorsing all versions of the good life, and this has clear educational implications. The key issue here is that to count as education, processes and outcomes ought to enhance freedom, agency, and well-being by making one's life richer with the opportunity of reflective choice.
>
> *(Sen, 1992, p. 41)*

This book looks to support Early Childhood educators in laying the foundations for such reflective choice as children worldwide embark upon tackling the pressures and problems of the coming decades.

Note

1 http://en.unesco.org/gap

References

Britto, P. (2015). *Why early childhood development is the foundation for sustainable development.* New York: UNICEF. [Online resource.] Available at: https://blogs.unicef.org/blog/why-early-childhood-development-is-the-foundation-for-sustainable-development/. Accessed 25 August 2016.

Bokova, I. (2012). *Opening address on the occasion of the 'Educating for a sustainable future' Rio +20 side-event.* Rio de Janiero: UNESCO. [Online resource.] Available at: http://unesdoc.unesco.org/images/0021/002167/216708e.pdf. Accessed 22 May 2017.

Chomsky, N. (2004). *Hegemony or survival: America's quest for global dominance* (The American Empire Project). London: Owl Books.

Freire, P. (1998). *Pedagogy of freedom: Ethics, democracy and civic courage.* Lanham: Rowman & Littlefield Publishers.

Gramsci, A. (1971). *Selections from the prison notebooks.* New York: International Publishers.

Heckman, J. (2006). Skill formation and the economics of investing in disadvantaged children. *Science,* 312(5782), 1900–1902.

Moss, P. (2013). Beyond the investment narrative. *Contemporary Issues in Early Childhood,* 14(4), 370–372.

Rodney, W. (1972). *How Europe undeveloped Africa.* London: Bogle-L'Ouverture Publications.

Rogoff, B. (2003). *The cultural nature of human development.* Oxford: Oxford University Press.

Sauven, J. (2015). *A Greenpeace manifesto for change.* London: Greenpeace UK. [Online resource.] Available at: www.greenpeace.org.uk/sites/files/gpuk/Greenpeace_Manifesto.pdf. Accessed 22 May 2017.

Sen, A. (1992). *Inequality re-examined.* New York: Russell Sage Foundation.

Sen, A. (1999). *Development as freedom.* New York: Anchor Books.

Siraj-Blatchford, J., & Brock, L. (2016a). *Putting the schema back into schema theory and practice: An introduction to SchemaPlay.* Poole, Dorset: SchemaPlay Publications.

Siraj-Blatchford, J., & Brock, L. (2016b). *Wellbeing and sustainable development: The legacy of Maria Montessori.* Paper presented at the European Early Childhood Education Research (EECERA) Conference, Dublin, September 2016.

Siraj-Blatchford, J., & Brock, L. (2017). *Education for sustainable citizenship in early childhood.* Poole, Dorset: SchemaPlay Publications.

Siraj-Blatchford, J., Park, E., & Mogharreban, C. (Eds.) (2016). *International research on Education for Sustainable Development in Early Childhood.* London: Springer.

UNESCO (2014). *Shaping the future we want: UN Decade of Education for Sustainable Development 2005–2014* (Final Report). Paris: UNESCO.

ACKNOWLEDGEMENTS

Initially and most importantly, we want to express our gratitude as editors to all the colleagues across the globe, from South Korea to South America, from Sweden to Australia, who have been working for so many years, often as part of Organisation Mondiale pour l'Éducation Préscolaire (OMEP), to provide a solid theoretical and research justification for the crucial importance of Education for Sustainable Development in safeguarding our planet. They often battle against powerful vested interests which aim to discount, diminish and undermine their work. They have recruited us to this field, inspired us and supported our own subsequent efforts. We especially thank those of them who have contributed chapters to this book.

Similarly, we wish to thank the smaller (but no less important) group of UK colleagues, especially at Plymouth University, who have constituted a community of concern and shared interest in ESD, all of us looking to widen the perspectives of educators in the UK. Again, some are valued contributors to the book.

EfS is a global concern and project, not targeted at any continent or country. But we cannot avoid acknowledging how much as editors we each have learned about it through our involvements in Ethiopia, especially in the district of Nekemte, because of our engagement with the tiny charity Exeter Ethiopia Link and its voluntary workers, together with its dedicated Ethiopian team. Its effectiveness in changing many lives through targeted intervention and support contrasts with the relative ineffectiveness of some much larger charities.

In such an enormous field, listing individual acknowledgements can be invidious and often results in a lengthy list of names that is largely meaningless to the reader. But we must recognise the special contributions of three colleagues. Ingrid Pramling Samuelsson has been a central figure in OMEP and is an inspiration and support to colleagues across the world, including ourselves. Similarly, John Siraj-Blatchford has been a constant source of feedback and ideas (most of which we have agreed with) and has always been most generous and supportive on the very rare occasions when we have differed. Even closer to home, Jan Georgeson has always been on hand for us to bounce ideas off and to offer crucial help when things have been difficult for us. We offer them all our profound thanks.

We recognise that it may seem a conventionality to acknowledge the people involved in the practicalities of publication, but we must emphasise that their support for us as novice editors has been exemplary. From the series editors outwards, throughout the team, their positive and encouraging responses have helped us to battle through challenging times. Thank you all.

1

INTRODUCTION

Valerie Huggins and David Evans

Introduction

Within the now substantial literature on Education for Sustainability there is not a great deal that addresses direct approaches with the youngest children. In this book, we are looking to support the wide range of educators involved with young children in addressing some of the complex issues raised by Education for Sustainability (EfS). Such educators will naturally include parents and members of the community, but we are particularly addressing the wide range of Early Childhood Education and Care professionals in education, teacher education, health and social care. We need to stress from the outset that this volume is not a handbook, attempting to cover all aspects of ECECfS, theoretical and practical. Rather, we look to support new thinking about many key elements, based upon recent international research. This follows our belief and experience that ECECfS cannot be achieved by the delivery of a laid-down common curriculum, but must be very largely constructed by practitioners in response to local contexts and needs.

We are aiming to introduce and comment on some of the current debates about ECECfS, present some new research and provide ideas for practice, anticipating that this will help practitioners introduce and develop ECECfS in an informed and ethical way and to adopt sustainable practices. We present material with a strong international dimension in order to avoid parochialism and to widen awareness of the rapidly increasing body of ideas in this field. We also offer leads to some of the wider aspects of EfS, at present and in the future.

Education for Sustainability: A central concern for educators?

Education for Sustainability is featuring increasingly in educational debate. Globally, there is growing recognition that we all have to address a wide range of issues and problems, often interlinked, if we are to avoid destroying ourselves and to create instead a more equitable and sustainable environmental, economic and social world. Whenever we look at the news, there is an item on aspects of this task:

- Global warming has resulted in bleaching two thirds of the Great Barrier Reef
- The Indian government announcing that by 2030 every car sold will be electric
- Nuclear tests in North Korea
- 8 million tons of plastic dumped in the oceans every year
- Costa Rica mostly running on renewable energy
- Famine in East Africa and Yemen
- Refugee crisis in Syria

This sharply reminds us that countries have passed the point when such matters could be dismissed as not the concern of the ordinary person, much less as not the concern of educators.

We are also acutely conscious as grandparents that young people will all too soon find themselves engaging in decision-making about sustainability issues and encountering, possibly painfully, the consequences of earlier decisions. Even our youngest grandchildren, now in ECEC provision, will be first-time voters in the early 2030s and may well move on to be policy makers, leading experts in their disciplines, business leaders, politicians. What kind of world will they be aspiring to live in, socially, environmentally, economically, politically? And how will their education have prepared them for such a responsibility? How will we have supported and shaped, or denied and constrained, their aspirations? What future lives do we envisage for them? Will they be 'good lives'? As Siraj-Blatchford and Huggins (2015) argue, we need to engage now in the debate about what a 'good life' is and how we are preparing children for it. And for us, this requires underpinning all our work with the concerns and the principles of Education for Sustainability (EfS).

Widening our perceptions and definitions of EfS

In order to do this effectively we will all need to widen our consideration of EfS. Understandably, much of the previous discussion of sustainability has centred upon environmental aspects, and so educational responses, in the UK for example, have often focused solely upon providing environmental activities, as is acknowledged by Joyce (2012). Projects emphasising recycling, encouraging wildlife, gardening, Forest School experience and similar initiatives are clearly of enormous importance and educational value. However, Hedefalk, Almqvist and Östman (2015), in their review of the literature, clarify that this green-focused, holistic approach is increasingly being replaced by one that adds three further interrelated dimensions—economic, social and political. This is accompanied by a radical shift in the educators' purposes. As Hedefalk, Almqvist and Östman (2015) suggest,

During the period studied, the research has evolved from teaching children facts about the environment and sustainability issues to educating children to act for change. This new approach reveals a more competent child who can think for him- or herself and make well-considered decisions. The decisions are made by investigating and participating in critical discussions about alternative ways of acting for change.

(Extract from Abstract)

This challenges common assumptions that educators simply should give children experience of and knowledge about the environment, influencing their behaviour by acting as role models and by directing them to act in particular ways. Instead, it suggests that they should educate children to think critically, make value judgements about actions, engage in meaningful projects, participate in debates and look at perspectives. This approach emphasises children's potential for decision-making and problem-solving and is linked to children's rights and responsibilities. It requires a democratic approach and collaborative work rather than an emphasis upon individual learning and development. It sees children as competent, to be empowered to act as agents of change within society. It also asserts that even within the early years of life children have greater powers than have often been assumed, so that ECEC must look to increase their agency, both in educational settings and in the wider community. In order to achieve this and to support active transformation in thinking and action we need educators globally and locally to be well-informed about why EfS is vital, and confident in how to embed it in their practice, whether as parents, teacher educators, practitioners or policy makers.

For us, a central aspect of this is that the process is research-led and informed by debates at local, international and global level. We have therefore included examples from Australia and Sweden, leaders in this field, and have brought in new voices from Hungary, Portugal and Africa, as well as from the UK. But it is increasingly argued that EfS has powerful implications for action and change outside the narrowly educational focus of EY settings, and in our final chapter we address some of the tensions and issues inherent in promoting and implementing the Sustainable Development Goals (SDGs).

Preparing educators for EfS

Despite the challenges to sustainability highlighted every day by the media, and despite the publicity around the introduction of the Sustainable Development Goals (United Nations, 2015), many educators are not yet engaging in the debate or transforming their practices. In some countries, and indeed in some settings in many countries, concern for such matters is absent or at best seen as an optional additional aspect of the curriculum, to be addressed only after the perceived priorities of literacy and numeracy have been fully dealt with. For some educators the newer remit of EfS demands a difficult move from simply discussing recycling and giving children experience of natural environments (relatively uncontroversial areas) into the analysis of social issues in a critical way and the discussion of the connections between environment and society. Practitioners may be aware of the need to do this, but feel lost or uncertain when faced with the major issues involved. It is therefore easy for them to see EfS within a setting as needing to be the individual pursuit of an expert, a 'champion', an eco-warrior or human rights activist, rather than part of everyone's basic educational responsibilities.

Another area of uncertainty can be the belief that a wider definition of EfS will take them into areas which are 'political' and so not expected to be part of their remit as an Early Years (EY) educator. Thus they may use their genuine and powerful commitment to the narrowly environmental dimension of sustainability as a way of avoiding the complexity and potential controversy of the economic and socio-political dimensions. By contrast, we would argue that if as ECE practitioners we are to make EfS an essential part of mainstream thinking and practice we will have to be 'political', in terms of agreeing, asserting and advocating particular beliefs and values. If, as trainers and educators of EY teachers and practitioners we are preparing our students to be critically reflective in their practice, we have to be willing to challenge prevailing taken-for-granted views that may be limiting children's learning opportunities. At the same time we must acknowledge that in the international context there will be countries where such 'political' activity will place teachers at risk.

A further set of factors may affect those who work with very young children. It is not uncommon to find the argument made that issues of sustainability are irrelevant to such work because young children are cognitively and affectively unable to appreciate them and because they are not yet capable of taking action to make a difference in their world. Importantly, in this book we challenge such a blanket dismissal. In the first place our contributors give a number of examples from practice which refute such arguments. In the second place we have encountered situations where practitioners have not explicitly linked to a sustainability agenda aspects of their existing practice which are already successful with this age group. A close colleague of ours, who is a contributor to this book and who has researched in the field of outdoor learning for many years, only recently realised during a staff workshop on Sustainability in Higher Education (HE) that her work was closely related to EfS. We are all in danger of crouching in our silos of research and practice and not looking up or making such new connections unless we are willing to engage in dialogic spaces, as she clearly was. In the third place, we argue that as in many others areas of the ECEC curriculum the role of the practitioner is as much that of fostering underpinning dispositions, understandings and skills as that of engaging in full-scale activities characteristic of the curriculum area. For instance, fostering young children's love of books and stories is as important a literacy activity as the later decoding of print.

Duhn (2012) identifies yet another belief that can marginalise or prevent consideration of the issues of sustainability with young children. This belief is often triggered by the depictions of famine, environmental damage caused by climate change or the noxious rubbish dumps caused by our throw-away society. There is a strong tendency for adults to see young children as innocent, vulnerable and in need of protection from unpleasant experiences and harsh realities. Parents and ECEC practitioners often define themselves as largely being in a protective, caring role, sheltering children for as long as possible. We suggest that in doing so they fail to recognise the robustness of young children, who are from the beginning producers of complex meaning from their experiences (Christensen, 2004) and that concerned adults may not sufficiently acknowledge that, as Siraj-Blatchford and Huggins (2015, p. 3) note, '[I]t is in the early years that fundamental attitudes towards the environment, towards consumption and waste and towards fairness are formed.'

In this book we argue that educators have the responsibility to make ECEC a significant contributor to EfS, and we reason that young children are well able to engage in appropriately chosen areas of this field and to take action to make a difference in their world. It is important of course not to overload them or to make inappropriate demands, and this means we have a delicate professional responsibility. As Davis and Elliott (2014) warn, we have to avoid burdening young children with a role of saviours for sustainability, charged with repairing the damage done to the world by their predecessors. We have to avoid pressuring them into becoming 'worriers' or 'warriors' (Davis & Elliott, 2014), instead supporting them in developing the ability to make considered and informed responses to the challenges that we know they will face but that we cannot define with any precision.

This requires practitioners who are knowledgeable and passionate about EfS and who wish to promote it in their work with children and families, but who are also sensitive to the complexities of work with young children. In order to underpin ECEC with sustainability, there need to be significant shifts in many practitioners' mind-sets, involving them in critical reflection upon existing values and beliefs, in an opening up to the ideas of ECECfS, in giving them opportunities for safe dialogical spaces and in developing a new understanding of how ECECfS can enhance their practice and benefit children's lives. It is also important for educators to be exposed to the work of colleagues working in this field in Africa, Australia and Europe. Such an international dimension is powerful because the disequilibrium caused by learning about approaches in a different country can force us to evaluate our taken-for-granted ways of working (Huggins, 2013) and so provoke the shifts in thinking needed for transformative learning (Mezirow, 1990) and for the generation of new ways of taking action. In a global context of accelerating change educators cannot afford to be rooted in the past, or bounded by taken-for-granted practices derived almost entirely from their own local experiences and traditions. This process of reorientation takes time; hopefully, this book will provide a catalyst towards new ways of conceptualising ECECfS and so support changes in practice. Dyment et al. (2014), in their research on the professional development of teachers, argue that to change teachers' thinking and pedagogies and to ensure that ECECfS is valued, understood and implemented, we need strong communities of practice, partnerships between environmentalists and ECEC settings, new resources and system-wide pre-service and in-service teacher education. This text is one such resource as we build such active communities of practice in ECECfS.

Embedding EfS in ECEC

But even if we accept the central importance of EfS with young children there still needs to be a reorientation in ECEC content and pedagogy in order to embed sustainability in ECEC curricula and practices. Such orientation remains very patchy. Aspects of a sustainability approach are included in some ECEC curricula and practice—for example, in Australia (ACARA, 2010; DEEWR, 2009), in Sweden (Ärlemalm-Hagsér, 2014) and South Korea (Yoo et al., 2013)—but in many countries this approach is only just emerging. For instance, Duhn (2012) notes that in New Zealand ECEC is virtually untouched by EfS, and in the Majority World there is at present little direct involvement, perhaps because very many governments do not yet offer pre-primary provision (for children aged 4–6), and in those that do there is still a major emphasis upon the teaching and resourcing of basic literacy and numeracy. Again, where EfS does figure in EY settings it is often restricted to the environmental dimensions, excluding the wider economic and socio-political aspects. As previously noted, this is a common pattern in the UK.

A top-down, determinist schooling system, such as that currently operating in the UK, would probably see this as requiring the imposition upon settings of a Sustainability Curriculum, with the associated activities, assessments and standards. We would argue that whilst this might be partially effective with older children, its impact upon ECEC would be limited and potentially negative. This is because a prescriptive curriculum is likely to divert educators' focus towards the sustainability content—the environmental, economic and socio-political ideas and knowledge—which are inevitably complex and therefore difficult for young children to appreciate and so difficult for EY practitioners to incorporate in educational activities. Implementing such a curriculum would deflect us from a key aspect. ECECfS is a socially transformative approach (Davis, 2015) and requires a curriculum and pedagogy that is holistic, encourages critical thinking and creative responses to solutions, and promotes collaborative engagement. Thus, whilst constantly keeping in mind the vital issues and knowledge central to the Sustainability agenda, the key question is how what we do prepares children to live and work within a sustainability context. We would argue that effective early years pedagogy already does a good deal of this, in contrast to later schooling which can be too focused on subject-based knowledge and the pursuit of individual academic achievements. But there does need to be a reorientation in ECEC content and pedagogy so that it is consciously underpinned by EfS, and it is vital that this reorientation is research-led and informed by debates at both global and local level. It will require practitioners who are 1) passionate about EfS and their role in promoting such work with children and families; 2) knowledgeable about the issues; and 3) skilled in providing project-based activities that engage children in collaborative and/or independent inquiry and problem-solving.

This does not demand any one particular pedagogical approach. Educational approaches depend upon the values and ideologies that underpin them, so those of us who value play will provide more play-based opportunities (Moyles, 2010), and those who believe in the benefits to be gained from learning outside the classroom will privilege outdoor environments (Waite et al., 2014). Education systems, such as some in the Majority World, where both tradition and limited resources impose constraints upon classroom practice, may adopt a more adult-centred, didactic approach. Rather, it requires that educators think consistently about how their chosen approaches are currently fostering the qualities and understandings necessary if children are to act for sustainability, both now and as they take more mature responsibilities, and so look to expand their provision in ways that strengthen such development.

Existing research into pedagogical approaches to EfS (e.g. Summers & Cutting, 2016; Peterson & Warwick, 2015) and key texts on EfS in ECEC (e.g. Siraj-Blatchford et al., 2012; Davis, 2015) identify problem-solving, systems thinking and creativity as key to this, rather than the transmission of knowledge about sustainability issues. This fits well with the traditional approach to ECEC in most Minority World contexts that envisages children as active learners, being supported to follow their own learning through exploration and experimentation and to create their own meaning from processing their experiences. This approach assumes that children are natural problem-solvers, keen to resolve the challenges they meet in their everyday lives and environments, and so require us to provide them with enabling environments, as advocated by Wickett and Selbie (2015), to promote their learning and development. Over the past three decades, ideas from Scandinavia, Reggio Emilia in Italy, the Early Years Foundation Stage in England and Te Whariki in New Zealand have circled the globe, shaping and evolving practice in local community-based settings. Many Minority World educators now use topic-based approaches, such as the project work advocated by the *pedagogistas* in Reggio-inspired settings (Piccinini & Giudici, 2011), where children work collaboratively to address real-life situations, looking at systems and connections. Underpinning much of what we do are the relational pedagogies, such as those promoted by Papatheodorou and Moyles (2009), influenced by New Zealand's Te Whariki (Dalli, 2010). We teach children to respect each other, to listen to the perspectives of others and give them the understanding that they have a voice, that they will be listened to and they can change things in their lives. Thus we need to emphasise to practitioners that many aspects of the social, cultural and political dimensions of EfS implicitly underpin their everyday routines, in the way they encourage children to relate to each other, manage conflict and appreciate diversity (Siraj-Blatchford & Huggins, 2015). As an example, providing project-based activities that engage children in collaborative and/or independent inquiry and problem-solving, marshalling evidence, negotiating, making a case for their own position, but learning to be sensitive to the force of more effective argument, must be a crucial preparation for an informed response to issues of sustainability in the community. But it is clear from the research cited above that these are often not explicitly linked in practitioners' minds to a sustainability agenda.

Promoting EfS with young children throws up a further complexity for ECEC educators, especially for those concerned with the two- to five-year-old age group. As identified earlier, children in this age group may have difficulty in appreciating complex sustainability ideas and in taking direct independent action. Unfortunately, this has sometimes led those who claim to be writing about 'the Early Years' to slip into considering only possibilities and activities for children aged six to eight. We would argue that EfS for two- to five-year-olds involves not only developing appropriate aspects of the qualities and understandings discussed above but also reconceptualising the scope of the sustainability curriculum. Alongside major, fully fledged elements such as recycling, educators must value other obviously related activities such as the avoidance of waste, caring for living things, tidying up and so on, all tackled within the familiar trajectories of provision for early learning and development. They must also analyse and understand how a range of knowledge, attitudes and skills that are not in themselves part of the sustainability 'subject' may be vital in underpinning children's later learning about it. In particular, ECEC educators may take inspiration from the notion of the early 'emergence' of a subject, and may use the ideas of Europeans such as Norling et al. (2015) on emergent literacy, Sundberg et al. (2016) on emergent science and Kaartinen and Kumpulainen (2012) and Worthington and van Oers (2016) on emergent mathematics to construct a model of emergent sustainability as a basis for their provision.

Once again, we are not arguing that current and proven ECEC practices should be abandoned or replaced; rather we are inviting educators to engage in a clearer, better informed analysis of how these practices, and the relational pedagogies advocated by Papatheodorou and Moyles (2009), support sustainability and the child's developing powers. And, above all, we would want such educators to reassert the argument that the early years are fundamental in shaping lifelong attitudes, awareness and actions.

The structure of the book

We are delighted to be able to offer in the book a range of up-to-date and stimulating chapters with a strong international focus, offering a wide-ranging picture of ECECfS. The book falls into five sections. In the first Eva Ärlemalm-Hagsér and Ingrid Pramling Samuelsson, in Chapter 2, draw upon their very considerable experience in the field of EfS to set the context by providing an overview of current understandings and approaches. They consider developments over the past 20 years and identify challenges we face in enabling EfS, and particularly ECECfS, to make positive contributions to a sustainable world.

The second section looks at some important underpinning ideas and perspectives on ECECfS. In Chapter 3 Paul Warwick and his colleagues acknowledge the all too frequent tendency for EfS to be framed in terms of discourses of crisis and disaster, potentially dispiriting and even alienating. Instead, they articulate a 'pedagogy of hope' in which the EY practitioner plays a vital role in nurturing the positive attitudes and dispositions of young children to undertake caring and compassionate roles in society. Paulette Luff follows in Chapter 4 by emphasising the role of creativity, and especially of the expressive arts, in ECECfS. She reviews three Australian projects in which researchers used approaches and activities from the expressive arts to work on sustainability issues with practitioners, with children aged 2–4, 3–5 and in an all-age primary school, and with EY student teachers. From these studies she identifies four themes which she discusses in relation to a UK preschool project on bat conservation. In Chapter 5 Alun Morgan and Sue Waite widen the theme of positivity. They recognise that EfS is always rooted in physical realities and physical locations and so examine the concept of 'place' as the context for human development, considering how to support young children in building a powerful affection for, an understanding of and a sense of agency within their expanding world. In discussing these processes, they explore the fascinating concept of 'nestling into the lifeworld' and in doing so reinforce Warwick's argument that EfS should start at a very early age.

The third section widens our focus in three chapters, each of which locates aspects of EfS within a specific geographical and cultural setting, so illustrating that EfS approaches will necessarily vary according to local traditions, expectations and demands. In Chapter 6 Maria Assunção Folque uses a Portuguese context to challenge the common idea that EY children are too young to engage critically and actively in EfS issues. She shows that practitioners employing pedagogies that encourage a problem-based, participatory approach can enable young children to take a role within their community as active democratic citizens. She illustrates how to put these pedagogical approaches into practice through referring to research-based case studies. Chapter 7 on EfS in Hungary, by Anikó Nagy Varga and colleagues, offers a rare insight into an EfS approach in Eastern Europe, describing ways in which Hungarian preschool education deliberately develops and shapes children's responses to sustainability in accordance with Hungarian approaches and principles. It illustrates how indigenous knowledge and folk traditions meet with sustainable development in the context of the Hungarian kindergartens, but questions whether this will continue to be enough to promote sustainability for future generations. This is followed in Chapter 8 by Valerie Huggins, who picks up the threads of place, cultural context and the role of indigenous knowledge in an analysis of processes of developing ECECfS in a Majority World situation. Using her considerable experience of life and schooling patterns in Ethiopia, she illustrates features of ECECfS in low-income, low-resource communities, identifying some of the financial and cultural constraints upon its implementation. She suggests processes within schools, the local community and teacher education that may enable the development of EfS in ways that fit with local beliefs and ambitions whilst remaining cognisant of wider global agendas and of wider knowledge about children's learning and development that have been established by a substantial body of international research.

The next section contains three chapters that pick up on the importance for EfS of professional development for the EY workforce, whether through positive leadership strategies within ECEC settings, through Continuing Professional Development whilst in post or through initial training. In Chapter 9 Sara Knight and Paulette Luff locate this theme in the context of Forest School provision in England. They argue that now that Forest School has become integrated into many settings, with many practitioners familiar with its principles and approaches, it has the potential to be extended from its original narrowly environmental focus to promote some of the wider aspects of EfS. As an example, they illustrate how Forest School practices can promote the 7Rs of Sustainability and suggest that experienced Forest School practitioners can take a lead in making other practitioners within the EY setting active in expanding and backing up sustainability activities. Jan Georgeson takes up this theme in Chapter 10 by focusing on the role of leadership in an ECEC setting, drawing on the seven principles of Hargreaves and Fink (2006). At a time of reduced resourcing, when the ECEC sector is becoming increasingly market-driven, pressuring leaders into becoming more entrepreneurial and business-minded, she argues that leaders must be creative and positive in their thinking, since they sit at an interface between entrepreneurship, education and sustainability. Thus, they have a responsibility to embed the principles of sustainability through all aspects of setting life, maintaining a strong and agile business sense whilst avoiding exploiting the human resources as an expendable commodity. Finally, in Chapter 11 Sandra Hesterman turns our attention to the place of the teacher-educator in training new practitioners in ECECfS, illustrating this by describing and discussing a recent online Australian university course which enabled participants to share their ideas about sustainability at a distance and to collaborate in designing 'provocations', activities to use with young children in promoting 'sustainability in action' and in offering them ideas on how to live, work and play sustainably.

The concluding section directs attention forward. In Chapter 12 Lucien Georgeson recognises that the establishment of the Sustainable Development Goals, together with the concomitant global expansion of ECE, have offered us all a 'window of opportunity' for the development of a wider, holistic approach to ECECfS worldwide, potentially not only enhancing EfS through the development of a shared global vision but also raising the quality of ECE. He picks up on the earlier arguments that this must involve widening the definition of EfS from its frequently narrow focus on protecting the environment to a broader concern with social, economic and even political challenges. He therefore endorses the opinion of several other contributors that this is not chiefly a matter of 'teaching sustainability' but from the earliest years a concern to develop in children critical thinking allied to meaningful problem-solving and an active awareness of their roles and responsibilities in influencing social and environmental change in sustainable directions. But he stresses that the 'window of opportunity' is narrow and is narrowing rapidly—so full engagement with EfS is a matter of urgency for all ECEC practitioners.

In a short Afterword we as editors suggest four broad themes that we have seen emerging from the chapters. You may wish to use them to guide further exploration/ discussion, whether as an individual or as part of the staff team of an EY setting, in making ECEC provision more compatible with the principles and aims of EfS.

References

Ärlemalm-Hagsér, E. (2014). Participation as 'Taking Part In': Education for sustainability in Swedish preschools. *Global Studies of Childhood*, 4(2), 101–114.

ACARA (2010). The Australian Curriculum. Sydney: Australian Curriculum, Assessment and Reporting Authority. [Online resource.] Available at: www.australiancurriculum. edu.au/.

Christensen, P. H. (2004). Children's participation in ethnographic research: Issues of power and representation. *Children & Society*, 18(2), 165–176.

Dalli, C. (2010). Towards the emergence of a critical ecology of early childhood profession in New Zealand. *Contemporary Issues in Early Childhood*, 11(1), 61–74.

Davis, J. (Ed.) (2015). *Young children and the environment: Early education for sustainability* (2nd ed.). Port Melbourne: Cambridge University Press.

Davis, J., & Elliott, S. (Eds.) (2014). *Research in early childhood education for sustainability*. Abington: Routledge.

DEEWR (2009). *Belonging, being and becoming: The early years learning framework for Australia*. Canberra: Department of Education Employment and Workplace Relations.

Duhn, I. (2012). Making 'place' for ecological sustainability in early childhood education. *Environmental Education Research*, 18(1), 19–29.

Dyment, J. E., Davis, J. M., Nailon, D., Emery, S., Getenet, S., McCrea, N., & Hill, A. (2014). The impact of professional development on early childhood educators' confidence, understanding and knowledge of education for sustainability. *Environmental Education Research*, 20(5), 660–679.

Hargreaves, A., & Fink, D. (2006). *Sustainable leadership*. San Francisco, CA: Jossey-Bass.

Hedefalk, M., Almqvist, J., & Östman, L. (2015). Education for sustainable development in early childhood education: A review of the research literature. *Environmental Education Research*, 21(7), 975–990.

Huggins, V. (2013). Widening awareness of international approaches: An imperative for 21st century early years practitioners? In J. Georgeson & J. Payler (Eds.), *International perspectives on early childhood education and care*. Maidenhead: Open University Press.

Joyce, R. (2012). *Outdoor learning: Past and present*. Maidenhead: Open University Press.

Kaartinen, S., & Kumpulainen, K. (2012). The emergence of mathematising as a culture of participation in the early childhood classroom. *European Early Childhood Education Research Journal*, 20(2), 263–281.

Mezirow, J. (1990). How critical reflection triggers transformative learning. In J. Mezirow & E. W. Taylor (Eds.), *Fostering critical reflection in adulthood*. San Francisco, CA: Jossey-Bass.

Moyles, J. (Ed.) (2010). *Thinking about play: Developing a reflective approach*. Maidenhead: Open University Press.

Norling, M., Sandberg, A., & Almqvist, L. (2015). Engagement and emergent literacy practices in Swedish preschools. *European Early Childhood Education Research Journal*, 23(5), 619–634.

Papatheodorou, T., & Moyles, J. (Eds.) (2009). *Learning together in the early years: Exploring relational pedagogy*. Abingdon: Routledge.

Peterson, A., & Warwick, P. (2015). *Global learning and education*. Oxon: Routledge.

Piccinini, S., & Giudici, C. (2011). Reggio Emilia: A transforming city. In C. Edwards, L. Gandini, & G. Forman (Eds.), *The hundred languages of children: The Reggio Emilia experience in transformation*. Westport, CT: Greenwood Press.

Siraj-Blatchford, J., & Huggins, V. (2015). Sustainable development in early childhood education and care. *Early Education Journal*, 76 (Summer2015).

Siraj-Blatchford, J., Smith, K. C., & Samuelsson, I. P. (2012). *Education for sustainable development in the early years*. Sweden: OMEP.

Summers, D., & Cutting, R. (Eds.) (2016). *Education for sustainable development in further education: Embedding sustainability into teaching, learning and the curriculum*. London: Palgrave Macmillan.

Sundberg, B., Areljung, S., Due, K., Ekström, K., Ottander, C., & Tellgren, B. (2016). Understanding preschool emergent science in a cultural historical context through Activity Theory. *European Early Childhood Education Research Journal*, 24(4), 567–580.

United Nations (2015). Sustainable development goals. New York: UN Web Services Section, Department of Public Information. [Online resource.] Available at: www.un.org/sustainable development/sustainable-development-goals/ (Accessed 11 April 2016).

Waite, S., Huggins, V., & Wickett, K. (2014). Risky outdoor play: Embracing uncertainty in pursuit of learning. In Maynard, T., & Waters, J. (Eds.), *Exploring outdoor play in the early years*. Maidenhead: Open University Press.

Wickett, K., & Selbie, P. (2015). Providing an enabling environment. In R. Parker-Rees & C. Leeson (Eds.), *Early childhood studies*. London: Learning Matters.

Worthington, M., & van Oers, B. (2016). Pretend play and the cultural foundations of mathematics. *European Early Childhood Education Research Journal*, 24(1), 51–66.

Yoo, Y. E., Kim, E. J., Shin, E. S., & Park, E. H. (2013). Analysis of the Korea educational policy and current curriculum based on the education for sustainable development. *Early Childhood Education Research & Review*, 17(3), 319–341.

2

EARLY CHILDHOOD EDUCATION AND CARE FOR SUSTAINABILITY

Historical context and current challenges

Eva Ärlemalm-Hagsér and Ingrid Pramling Samuelsson

Introduction

It is widely acknowledged that social, economic, environmental and political challenges are affecting young children's lives all over the world. This chapter discusses Early Childhood Education and Care for Sustainability (ECECfS) from two perspectives: 1) placing ECECfS in its recent historical context; and 2) identifying the challenges early childhood education is in striving to contribute to a sustainable world.

As the concept of 'sustainability' is ambiguous and, to some extent, normative, with important theoretical (Jickling & Wals, 2014) and ideological tensions (Sandell & Öhman, 2013), it is necessary to clarify our understanding of the concept. We agree with Davis's (2014) understanding of sustainability as an 'alternative progress' striving for an ecologically sustainable world, for respect and care for the non-human world, and for social, economic and political justice for all humans. We here want to stress that the definition we make is a considerably broader definition/agenda for EfS than the commonly held perceptions that sustainability is mainly concerned with environmental issues. As previously has been stated by Pramling Samuelsson (2016), sustainability in early years is related to two different levels: 1) access for all preschoolers to Early Childhood Education and Care (ECEC); and 2) the work in practice with children. These two levels represent policy as well as everyday life in ECEC with children.

Let us begin with a short glimpse of the policy level. Education for Sustainability has been on the political agenda for the last thirty years. The United Nations Education, Scientific and Cultural Organization's (UNESCO) 2015 document on the United Nations' (UN) Decade of Education for Sustainable Development (DESD) gives perspective on Education for Sustainable Development, and discusses among other things that it is of importance to integrate the three dimensions—environmental, social/cultural and economic, an approach which calls for a more holistic view in education—and to look at the world from an intergenerational perspective (UNCED, 1992). In the final DESD report (UNESCO, 2014) the role of early childhood education in creating sustainable futures is recognised:

> Young children are both current and future citizens with already existing capabilities to shape sustainable societies. Investments to build their awareness, values, knowledge and capacity for sustainable development will serve to set the world on more sustainable pathways now and into the future.
>
> *(UNESCO, 2014, p. 78)*

One of the UN Sustainable Development Goals (SDG) for 2016–2030 is access for all children to quality early childhood development, care and pre-primary education. Goal 4.2 states: 'By 2030, ensure that all girls and boys have access to quality early childhood development, care and pre-primary education so that they are ready for primary education' (United Nations, 2016). Focus is here on preparation for subsequent schooling, but we should recognise that ECEC in itself contributes to sustainability factors since research shows that the community, the family and the child benefit from children's experiences in ECEC (see e.g. Heckman, Pinto, & Savelyev, 2012; Pramling Samuelsson & Siraj-Blatchford, 2015; Pramling Samuelsson & Wagner, 2012). However, readiness for school should not be considered purely in terms of intellectual and academic skills. The 'readiness for school' discourse has rightly been strongly criticised (Moss, 2013), especially the 'schoolification' of ECEC curricula, whose learning objectives and instructional methods in many countries are viewing ECEC as an investment for children's later performance in school. Instead, it is increasingly argued that children should also be 'readied' by engaging in collaboration and critical thinking, by strengthening their self-confidence and by developing their sense of responsibility. Even more fundamentally, according to White and Pramling Samuelsson (2014), the point of departure—readiness for primary education—is that children have good health due to health care and nutrition, as well as having been taken care of by adults who respect children as well as providing them with stimulus and intellectual challenges.

To make sure that all children get access to ECEC is, however, a challenge in itself, since ECEC is unequally distributed around the globe, with more or less full access in Europe, some Asian countries and the US, and very limited access in many parts of Africa. Ban Ki-Moon (2015), UN General Secretary, put education as the first priority for sustainability, including three aspects: 1) put every child in school; 2) improve the quality of learning; and 3) foster global citizenship. A key point here is the emphasis upon learning, since it has been shown in developed as well as in developing countries that not all children learn well in school, and also that the quality of preschool gives children different starts in life (Sheridan, Pramling Samuelsson, & Johansson, 2009). With learning and children's meaning-making instead of 'normative' schooling as the focus for sustainability, children must be seen as active agents who create meaning by making sense of experience and who explore cultural domination, identity, difference and diversity. Of further importance here is that the work with sustainability in ECEC over the world must be handled with culture sensitivity (see e.g. Davis & Elliott, 2014; Gupta, 2013) if it is to make the desired impact.

Within the last twenty years ECEC has been accepted as an important societal institution, and many more children have gained access (OECD, 2015) although there is still much to do, both in terms of access and of quality in ECEC, all over the world. But in this chapter, we will mainly focus on the policy and practice within ECEC, how it has changed and what the challenges are for teachers in their everyday life with young children. We will specifically focus on what Ban Ki-Moon talks about as global citizenship, and how ECEC can contribute to this. We here follow the philosopher Peter Kemp's (2005) definition of 'world citizens' as humans that are part of, and so need to take responsibility for, at least two levels of society: the local/national and the global. The resulting questions for ECEC are how every child can become a local and global citizen with awareness of sustainability issues based on their own experiences, and how practitioners can build educational practices where children develop care for themselves, others and the world as well as possibilities and skills for critical thinking and action competence. This can become reality when the participation of children, together with adults, in the wider society is a central aspect of pedagogical practice. This requires that children are being empowered to be active in their daily life for local and global sustainability and, together with the teachers, to challenge unsustainable everyday lifestyles and inequality, both in preschool and in the nearby local society, so making a proactive contribution to a more peaceful, tolerant, inclusive, secure and sustainable world.

The last twenty years and onwards

With this as a starting point we claim that ECEC has a long tradition of working in the context of social, economic, ecological and political sustainability issues (Ärlemalm-Hagsér, 2013; Dahlbeck & Tallberg Broman, 2011). This can be seen in the pedagogical work that already took place during the formation of preschools in the mid-1850s in many European countries, the remit of which included individual health, lifestyle issues and individual competence, with children viewed as key actors shaping a better future society characterised by social stability, health and economic progress.

On the individual level ECEC has been based upon wholeness as a key position—developing the whole child, not only their academic skills and knowledge, and seeing children as individuals developing within a collective setting. Other characteristics, such as creativity and play, have also been key corners of ECEC, which means that children's creation and inventions are more appreciated than a correct answer (Pramling Samuelsson & Asplund Carlsson, 2014/2003). Because of this the curricula of ECEC have never been organised in subjects, as is the norm in schooling systems, and which unfortunately many countries today are introducing into ECEC. From Fröbel's (1995/1826) time until very recently a major emphasis has been to teach children to care for the environment, the animals and plants and the world around them. Fröbel's ideas thus have led to a strong focus on nature and on moral aspects of life, and through the whole history of ECEC the environmental and social/cultural aspects have been a major focus in ECEC programs, at least in many European countries, using a thematic or projects approach to topics drawn from real life. This was the case long before anyone talked about sustainability issues. On the other hand, economic aspects have seldom been a dimension of the work with children in ECEC.

The concepts of sustainability and of education for sustainability have only been made explicit in ECEC practices for a short period of time. Looking back twenty years to the middle of the 1990s, according to Elliott and Davis (2009), sustainability questions were not on the agenda in ECEC to any large extent, and even now early childhood educators are struggling to handle the complexity and ambiguity of sustainability issues (Ärlemalm-Hagsér, 2014; Hedefalk et al., 2015).

That the ECEC sector was slow in embracing sustainability issues can be explained by several factors. Firstly, a common view of children has been that they are innocent, passive, immature and vulnerable recipients. In this model, children should be protected from hard reality—for example, from environmental, social and economic problems. Even today this view is not totally extinct amongst ECEC practitioners. Secondly, the theoretical view of children's learning has often been that they were not capable of understanding such difficult questions. Thirdly, children were not considered competent to be active agents in this field.

In the 1990s, children and childhood were problematised in research (Sommer, Pramling Samuelsson, & Hundeide, 2010), seen as limited in their capability and agency as learners. Slowly, a changing view of children as competent, active and willing to learn has been established. Young children are now understood and viewed as social agents with the ability to contribute ideas, experiences and creativity, and also to influence change, both as unique individuals and collectively as a group (Davis, 2014; James & Prout, 1997). However, even today, depending on the theoretical perspectives of the adults involved, children can be considered to be competent or not (Pramling Samuelsson, 2011), and children's right to participation is still constrained, both in research and in practice, by ambiguity and divergent views of how such participation is to be defined and to be enacted (Ärlemalm-Hagsér, 2014).

Placing ECEfS on the agenda for policy and research

In the work of introducing sustainability to ECEC the non-governmental organisation Organisation Mondiale pour l'Éducation Préscolaire has been a driving force. OMEP is an international, non-governmental and non-profit organisation, involving both practitioners and researchers, with a focus on all aspects of ECEC. OMEP in 2007 organised the first international workshop on sustainability, which resulted in a publication by UNESCO called *Early Childhood Education's Role for a*

Sustainable Society (Pramling Samuelsson & Kaga, 2008). OMEP subsequently took it as a main priority to work for getting young children on the agenda for sustainability. Every year since 2009 OMEP has initiated world projects about sustainability: 1) an interview study, involving teachers and children, about a logo of the world where children are cleaning the globe; 2) a topic-based thematically organised work with children centred upon the 7Rs of sustainability (respect, reflect, rethink, reuse, reduce, recycle and redistribute); 3) a thematic work in ECEC in combination with older generations, called *Intergenerational Dialogues for ESD*; and 4) thematically organised work in ECE on the topic *Equality for Sustainability*. Around 45,000 children and their teachers all over the world have been involved in all four world projects of OMEP.[1]

When the UN's DESD came to an end in 2014, UNESCO (UNESCO, 2016, June 30) changed the focus to develop five partner networks for scaling up education for sustainable development (ESD). The Partner Networks[2] have the role to 'scale up and drive implementation' of the Global Action Program (GAP) (UNESCO, 2014). They serve as global communities of practice and exist for each of the five priority action areas, of which one is 'building capacities of educators and trainers' (UNESCO, 2016, June 30). OMEP is the only organisation invited in this network focusing on ECEC teachers and staff for young children. A reason may be that OMEP has developed a rating scale called the ECE rating scale for environment education. It is a scale inspired by the Early Childhood Education Rating Scale (ECERS) developed in the USA about quality in ECEC by Harms, Clifford and Cryer (1998). The structure from ECERS is used but the content is the three dimensions of sustainability (Siraj-Blatchford, Mogharreban, & Park, 2016). The scale is also piloted in nine different countries and translated into many different languages. OMEP has promised to disseminate findings by distributing good examples both from practice with young children and from in-service and pre-service training for ECEC staff – laudable intention as the work is in progress without any financial support from UNESCO. Sustainability questions for ECEC are increasingly being raised by different stakeholders, as discussed earlier. Nevertheless, there is still a long way to go before sustainability is fully embedded in ECEC policy.

Recent research in the area of sustainability in ECEC

Research into sustainability questions in ECEC has also taken off. Davis (2009) made a meta-study of the field between 1996 and 2007, showing that the focus in teaching EfS in ECE had been mainly related to environmental questions, which she describes in terms of education *in* nature, education *about* nature and education *for* nature. Barratt Hacking, Barratt and Scott (2007) and Davis (2009) also argued at that time that few studies in early ECEfS recognised children as competent participants and agents of change in connection with sustainability. Since then, the research field of ECEfS has been considerably expanded and several research overviews and research studies have developed our knowledge in the field (Davis &

Elliott, 2014; Green, 2015; Hedefalk et al., 2015; Somerville & Williams, 2015). For example, Somerville and Williams (2015) have replicated Davis's (2009) meta-study by investigating contemporary dominant theoretical discourses in research with focus on ECECfS and environmental education (EE). Their findings showed that three categories appeared in different theoretical orientations: connection to nature; children's rights; and post-human frameworks. The category of connection to nature clearly reflected the EE tradition, focusing on children's connection to the natural environment, teaching and learning about nature, promoting values, establishing how to behave in natural settings and supporting nature conservation. The children's rights category focused on the nature of such rights and the children's ability to speak and act on issues of sustainability. Finally, the category of post-human frameworks dealt with a philosophical and theoretical perspective that goes beyond the binary opposition of nature and culture; this theoretical perspective was rare.

Another research overview, this time of the field between 2006 and 2013, was carried out by Hedefalk et al. (2015) using Davis's (2009) three notions: in, about and for sustainability. This showed that two different definitions of EfS were found in the research. One was a three-part interrelated approach focusing on education in, about and for the environment; the other treated the economic, environmental and social domains as interrelated. This makes clear how recent is the growing view that these need to be integrated in educational practice.

A study by Green (2015) of 36 articles published between 2004 and 2014 examined children's participation in EE and EfS. This study showed that children mostly were positioned by adults as 'human becomings', not yet able to be fully active; this was interpreted as 'research on children'. In some studies, children were seen as important participants, and their voices and perspectives were used; this was 'research with children'. In only one of the articles was 'research by children' used. In 2014 Davis and Elliott (2014) published a book where the focus was on children's capabilities and potential as critical thinkers and agents for sustainability changes. Other studies have highlighted children's experiences and perspectives, and their competence and capacity to get involved and participate in action leading toward a sustainable future (Hägglund & Johansson, 2014). This is an important and developing aspect of EfS.

Several studies have focused on teachers' and practitioners' perceptions of ESD in ECEC (Ärlemalm-Hagsér & Sandberg, 2011; Ärlemalm-Hagsér & Sundberg, 2016; Hedefalk et al., 2015). In a current survey Park and Pramling Samuelsson (2016) have studied Swedish and South Korean teachers' perceptions of ESD in ECEC. There are many similarities, but also differences of which we just mention a few here. ESD is expanding in ECEC in both countries, but culture is strong in both the teachers' perceptions and what they say they can do with children. In Korea the focus is on growing awareness, while in Sweden the focus is on actions related to topics interesting for children. A higher percentage of the Korean teachers say they have reasonable knowledge of ESD (80 per cent) while only half of the

Swedish teachers say so (50 per cent). When teachers are asked about their work in practice with children, Swedes claim they work most with human rights, while the Korean teachers claim they work more with environment questions. Last but not least, the Korean teachers identify lack of awareness of ESD, while the Swedish point out the lack of appropriate teaching materials for this age group.

From all this it is obvious that most research in the area of sustainability is still related to environment questions. Even in networks like Early Urban Environment Education, the main focus is on finding nature in the city (Derr, Chawla, & Pevec, 2016), even though at the same time they identify creativity, self-expression, collaborative learning, experiential play-based learning and development of empathy as key factors for the pedagogical approach to environment questions. A better balance still needs to be found.

Current challenges for ECEfS policy, practice and research

It is a remarkable paradox that, at the pinnacle of human material and technical achievement, we find ourselves anxiety-ridden, prone to depression, worried about how others see us, unsure of our friendships, driven to consume and with little or no community life.

(Wilkinson & Pickett, 2009, p. 3)

Identifying the challenges in ECEfS policy

We do not have all the answers, and do not and cannot know what the most sustainable way of living is, as aspects that might be seen as sustainable now may not be in the long run. Moreover, our environment is not something we can remove ourselves from, so climate change and inequality affect people throughout the world differently. But most politicians and researchers now agree that there is a need to scale up the work toward a sustainable future as there are deep concerns about both the state of the planet and existing unsustainable systems and lifestyles (United Nations, 2016).

Since the 1990s education for sustainability has been seen as a tool in an international political effort to ensure a sustainable future (UNCED, 1992). In the UN SDGs for 2016–2030 (United Nations, 2016) and the implementation of the GAP and ESD (UNESCO, 2016, June 30), children and quality ECEC are seen as important stakeholders for a sustainable future. There are increasingly strong arguments that education for sustainability now needs to move forward to be systematically integrated into national educational polices, steering policy documents and curricula, not as a vehicle for implementing the 'right' values or the 'right' knowledge but as a necessary challenge to how ECEC is practiced in actual pedagogical contexts, in this era of uncertainty, instability and rapid change. As an alternative, EfS in ECEC should enhance critical thinking, participation and taking moral responsibility for actions affecting present and future humans and non-humans (including to challenge domineering interactions between humans and the natural world).

This suggests that the first challenge is the need for support for providing children with quality education with a powerful emphasis on sustainability issues. In talking about quality education for young children it is of great importance to keep the intentions and values from ECEC about developing children's skills and capabilities, but also to let children and their world of play, creativity and agency get space, and not fall into pure academic preparation for school subjects.

Secondly, in implementing EfS in ECEC over the world, there is a need for culture-sensitive education. Gupta (2013) stresses that 'western concepts cannot be readily and easily implemented within the practical context of culturally-diverse worldviews' (p. 223). She argues for a hybrid pedagogical approach that holds alternative practical and theoretical interpretations and opens possibilities to acknowledge both the local and the global, and the coexistence of diverse educational approaches, so supporting anti-colonisation policies and practices for avoiding new ways of colonisation (Gupta, 2013). As part of achieving this Serpell and Nsamenang (2015) point toward three important ways of using the richness of the culture of children: 1) building children's early education on their native languages; 2) using the African conception of child development; and 3) using traditional games and songs, since they distribute the culture. We broadly agree with Serpell and Nsamenang, but at the same time one should bear in mind that not everything in a specific culture is good for children. If we use spanking and hostility as an example, that is a way of fostering children in many countries, but we would argue strongly that it is not good for children. Cultures have to change, and do change, or we would still have spanking in Sweden. The same goes for countries where siblings take a major share of the care of their younger sisters and brothers, a pattern that easily leads to girls taking care of siblings, and so not receiving school education.

Thirdly, there is a need in ECEC policies to problematise any consensus that neglects individual ambivalence, structural barriers and social conflicts. This is crucial in order to acknowledge and work against the injustices that have been entrenched in the political/economical construction of the society, leading to economic and social marginalisation (Fraser, 2009). For example, questions should be raised about what kind of early childhood education and care are provided and for whom. Research has shown that the vulnerable children benefit most from ECEC (Sylva et al., 2004), and that ECEC can be one important actor in educating for social justice, social responsibility and social inclusion—against racism, prejudice and oppression.

Identifying the gaps and challenges in ECEfS practice

Reviewing and reconceptualising ECEC practice is therefore needed today as perhaps never before. As Moss (2010) puts it: 'I want to argue that we, humankind, are in a period of crisis and peril … that we must review fundamentally the purposes of all education and, therefore, the values, qualities and practices needed of all educators, whether working with 15-month-olds or 15-year-olds' (p. 9).

There are both barriers and possibilities in current ECEfS practice. These result from the fact that children are dependent on what objectives and issues practitioners in early childhood education perceive as important in the everyday life of the preschool, as well as their views of children and childhood (Elliott, 2012). This can block or shape EfS, but as Elliott (2012) states:

'Through an awareness of the potential of aligning early childhood philosophy and pedagogy with the principles of education for sustainability, educators can more effectively understand and lead transformative processes for sustainability'.

(p. 161)

Nevertheless, to reflect upon your own practice is difficult and especially on sustainability in early childhood education. Research has shown that preschool educators are struggling to handle the complexity and ambiguity of sustainability issues (Ärlemalm-Hagsér, 2014; Park & Pramling Samuelsson, 2016). Certainly it is easier to work with conserving resources, such as saving electricity and water, and with recycling rubbish or composting than with equity, ethics and values (Ärlemalm-Hagsér & Sundberg, 2016).

The challenge is to create opportunities and time for reflection on concrete situations in practice, including giving time for teachers and children together. Hägglund and Johansson (2014) argue that the value conflicts existing in everyday early childhood education can offer opportunities to challenge practices and explore value dilemmas. These are essential to human relations and can be utilised as spaces for learning and transformative change of injustices, power structures and hierarchies as well as everyday preschool practices. Also powerful is Gupta's (2013) pedagogical approach, where inclusion, diversity and equity are seen as important parts for building basic democracy and developing transformative places for diversity and minority perspectives.

Another barrier is that if early childhood education is seen from a perspective of developing readiness for school (Moss, 2013), then education for sustainability may be seen as taking time away from more important, academic activities. But the fact is that there are also other ways for children to learn to read and write in contexts and during thematic work/project work than entirely through practice of the basic subjects (Pramling Samuelsson & Asplund Carlsson, 2014). Understanding children as active agents and creators of meaning right from the beginning of life, and respecting early childhood as the most important stage of experiences for further life and learning, are key factors in creating a sustainable future. As Taylor (2013, p. 117) puts it, '[T]wenty-first century children need relational and collective dispositions, not individualistic ones, to equip them to live well within the kind of world they have inherited'.

A key challenge for practice, among other things, is to develop 'cultures of sustainability' in order to generate transformative thinking, practices and relationships in early childhood education about sustainability (Davis, 2014). This holistic approach demands much more than the introduction of a range of 'sustainability activities'. It requires that ECEC integrate a sustainable long-term design into the preschool management, physical environment, approaches to teaching and learning as well as community involvement, all aiming to promote social, economic, political and environmental sustainability. This changing of the culture in an organisation requires, according to Davis (2005), small but persistent steps, based on constructing clear vision, building local capacity and competence and developing skills amongst the practitioners and among the director and the professional leadership of the setting. This means organising systems and pedagogical ways of doing to assure that transformative change takes place in ECEC, so that children's rights, respect and trust permeate the curriculum and everyday practice.

The final challenge that we want to highlight for ECEC practice is to provide opportunities for professional development about the theory and practice of sustainability generally as well as specifically about early childhood education for sustainability. Research shows that preschools supported by in-service training about the wide range of sustainability issues have a broader understanding of the concept and work more actively with environmental and sustainability issues with the children (Ärlemalm-Hagsér & Sundberg, 2016).

Identifying the gaps and challenges in ECEfS research

There is now a growing body of literature about early childhood education and sustainability from different theoretical and methodological perspectives (Davis & Elliott, 2014; Green, 2015; Hedefalk et al., 2015; Somerville & Williams, 2015) and the research into ECEfS has come to a new stage. Davis's study from 2009 identified a number of issues to be addressed in research in the field of early childhood education for sustainability including children's active participation, professional practices, leadership and in-service and pre-service training. Some of these issues, such as children's active participation and professional practices, have been scrutinised since then. The other aspects are areas that need further research.

Further areas that need to be explored have emerged since 2009. Examples, with reference to researches already conducted, include the following: critical perspectives that challenge the relationship between humans and nature (Davis, 2014; Ritchie, 2016; Somerville & Williams, 2015); alternative conceptualisations, drawing on post-humanist and indigenous theorising (Ritchie, 2016; Somerville & Williams, 2015); processes of children's active learning in focus (Hedefalk, Almqvist, & Lidar, 2014); how children can be seen as co-researchers (Green, 2015); equality and multilingual and intercultural practices in relation to social sustainability (Ärlemalm-Hagsér & Engdahl, 2016; Hawkins, 2014); and, finally, quantitative studies of education for sustainability in ECEC from different perspectives, which are important to understand what actually is happening in practice (Davis, 2009; Davis & Elliott, 2014; Inoue, 2014).

Conclusion: ECEC and children as global citizens

The field of EfS shows broad agreement that a key element must be educating children from the beginning as global citizens. Such expectations are challenging on many levels and for many people. Obviously, politicians and other stakeholders have first to create opportunities for all children to have a safe and stimulating childhood in their families and in ECEC programs but it also involves developing curricula including education for sustainability and where teachers are educated to take care of young children and to provide for them in ways that take account of both research and of cultural sensitivity (Pramling Samuelsson, Sheridan, & Williams, 2006).

To be a global citizen means to have necessary skills and knowledge for taking responsibilities for the environment, for other human beings and for the economy if we are to develop justice in the local and global world. Since human rights are basic for democracy, children both have to be involved in an education built on this, and also to learn about democracy. The same goes for the environment: children have to learn about the environment, but they must also learn how to live in a sustainable environment. It further requires that children must learn about the economy as an aspect of everyday life in the family and in ECEC.

Multicultural issues and issues of cultural difference have to be made visible to children, perhaps by the ECEC program having preschools in other cultures to communicate with. Children also have to learn early on to take part in helping and caring for other people, both within their preschool setting and inter-generationally within their family and the local community. All these aspects have emerged as essential elements in an ECECfS approach, requiring not only that we teach children about sustainability but that we model sustainability in our values, our actions and the organisation and practice of our settings.

But many obstacles remain. We have to learn to bypass the gatekeepers who defend the status quo in education and to overcome substantial barriers if we are to change our lives and those of the children we represent in order to contribute to a more sustainable world. Moreover, we do not have a precise prescription of how to make this happen. Nevertheless, we already know a very great deal that young children will benefit from in their future lives, as they relate themselves as citizens to the local and global world. Our challenge is to play our part now in making that happen.

Questions for you to consider

1. How would you from your personal, professional and national experiences place ECEfS in its recent historical context?
2. What do you identify as the challenges in ECE in your own professional context in striving to contribute to a sustainable world?

Notes

1 For an extended version of these OMEP projects see Engdahl, 2015, and for an example of economic aspects from the equality projects see Hammond, Hesterman and Knaus, 2015.
2 There are five Partner Networks, one of which is about teacher education and in-service training, and they consist of NGOs from all over the World.

Further reading

Farrell, A., & Pramling Samuelsson, I. (Eds.) (2016). *Diversity in the early years: Intercultural learning and teaching*. South Melbourne: Oxford University Press.

This book is a valuable resource for practitioners and teacher educators. It raises awareness of diversity and helps us to develop our approaches to working with diverse populations.

Engdahl, I., & Ärlemalm-Hagsér, E. (2014). Education for sustainability in Swedish preschools: Stepping forward or out-of-step? In J. Davis & S. Elliott (Eds.), *Research in Early Childhood Education for Sustainability: International perspectives and provocations* (pp. 208–224). London: Routledge.

This chapter provides a useful insight into EfS practice in Swedish preschools.

References

Ärlemalm-Hagsér, E. (2013). *'An interest in the best for the world'? Education for sustainability in the Swedish preschool* (Doctoral thesis, Gothenburg Studies in Educational Sciences 335). Gothenburg: Acta Universitatis Gothoburgensis.

Ärlemalm-Hagsér, E. (2014). Participation as 'Taking Part In': Education for sustainability in Swedish preschools. *Global Studies of Childhood*, 4(2), 101–114.

Ärlemalm-Hagsér, E., & Engdahl, K. (2016). *Social sustainability: Language as an arena for democracy in Swedish preschools*. Paper presented at the OMEP World Conference, Seoul, 5–7 July.

Ärlemalm-Hagsér, E., & Sandberg, A. (2011). Sustainable development in early childhood education: In-service students' comprehension of the concept. *Environmental Education Research Journal*, 17(2), 187–200.

Ärlemalm-Hagsér, E., & Sundberg, B. (2016). Nature experiences and recycling: A quantitative study on education for sustainable development in Swedish preschools. *Nordina*, 12(2), 140–156.

Barratt Hacking, E., Barratt, R., & Scott, W. (2007). Engaging children: Research issues around participation and environmental learning. *Environmental Education Research*, 13(14), 529–544.

Dahlbeck, J., & Tallberg Broman, I. (2011). Ett bättre samhälle genom pedagogik: Högre värden och barnet som budbärare [A better society through education: Values and the child as a messenger]. In P. Williams & S. Sheridan (Eds.), *Barns lärande i ett livslångt perspektiv* (pp. 202–214). Stockholm: Liber.

Davis, J. (2005). Education for sustainability in the early years: Creating cultural change in a child care setting. *Australian Journal of Environmental Education*, 21, 47–55.

Davis, J. (2009). Revealing the research 'hole' of early childhood education for sustainability: A preliminary survey of the literature. *Environmental Education Research*, 15(2), 227–241.

Davis, J. (2014). Examining early childhood education through the lens of education for sustainability: Revisioning rights. In J. Davis & S. Elliott (Eds.), *Research in early childhood education for sustainability: International perspectives and provocations* (pp. 21–37). London, New York: Routledge.

Davis, J., & Elliott, S. (2014). *Research in early childhood education for sustainability: International perspectives and provocations*. London: Routledge.

Derr, V., Chawla, L., & Pevec, I. (2016, June 19). *Early childhood urban environmental education* [Online resource]. Available at: www.thenatureofcities.com/2016/06/09/early-childhood-urban-environmental-education/

Elliott, S., & Davis, J. (2009). Exploring the resistance: An Australian perspective on educating for sustainability in early childhood. *International Journal of Early Childhood*, 41(2), 65–77.

Engdahl, I. (2015). Early Childhood Education for Sustainability: The OMEP World Project. *International Journal of Early Childhood*, 47(3), 347–366.

Fraser, N. (2009). *Scales of justice: Reimagining political space in a globalizing world*. New York: Columbia University Press.

Fröbel, F. (1995/1826). *Människans fostran [Die Menschenerziehung]*. Lund: Studentlitteratur.

Green, C. J. (2015). Toward young children as active researchers: A critical review of the methodologies and methods in Early Childhood Environmental Education. *The Journal of Environmental Education*, 46(4), 207–229.

Gupta, A. (2013). Play: Early childhood pedagogies and policies in a globalizing Asia. In O. F. Lillemyr, S. Dockett, & B. Perry (Eds.), *Varied perspectives on play and learning: Theory and research on Early Years Education* (pp. 213–230). Charlotte, NC: Information Age Publishing.

Hägglund, S., & Johansson, M. (2014). Belonging, value conflicts and children's rights in learning for sustainability in early childhood. In J. Davis & S. Elliott (Eds.), *Research in early childhood education for sustainability: International perspectives and provocations* (pp. 38–48). London: Routledge.

Hammond, L., Hesterman, S., & Knaus, M. (2015). What's in your refrigerator? Children's views on equality, work, money and access to food. *International Journal of Early Childhood*, 47(3), 367–384.

Harms, T., Clifford, R., & Cryer, D. (1998). *The Early Childhood Environment Rating Scale—Revised edition* (ECERS-R). New York: Teachers College Press.

Heckman, J., Pinto, R., & Savelyev, P. (2012). *Understanding the mechanisms through which an influential early childhood program boosted adult outcomes*. NBER Working Paper No. 18581 [Online resource]. Available at: www.nber.org/papers/w18581

Hedefalk, M., Almqvist, J., & Lidar, M. (2014). Teaching for action competence in preschool education. *SAGE Open*, 4, 1–8.

Hedefalk, M., Almqvist, J., & Östman, L. (2015). Education for sustainable development in early childhood education: A review of the research literature. *Environmental Education Research*, 21(7), 975–990.

Inoue, M. (2014). Perspectives on early childhood environmental education in Japan: Rethinking for a sustainable society. In J. Davis & S. Elliott (Eds.), *Research in early childhood education for sustainability: International perspectives and provocations* (pp. 79–96). London: Routledge.

James, A., & Prout, A. (Eds.) (1997). *Constructing and reconstructing childhood* (2nd ed.). London: Falmer Press.

Jickling, B., & Wals, A. E. J. (2008). Globalization and environmental education: Looking beyond sustainable development. *Journal of Curriculum Studies*, 40(1), 1–21.

Ki-Moon, B. (2015). *Global Education First Initiative* [Online resource]. Available at: www.globaleducationfirst.org/about.html

Kemp, P. (2005). *Världsmedborgaren: Politisk och pedagogisk filosofi för det 21 århundradet [World Citizen: Political and Educational Philosophy for the 21st Century]*. Gothenburg: Daidalos.

Moss, P. (2010). We cannot continue as we are: The educator in an education for survival. *Contemporary Issues in Early Childhood*, 11(1), 8–19.

Moss, P. (2013). *Early childhood and compulsory education: Reconceptualising the relationship*. London: Routledge.

OECD (2015). *Starting Strong IV: Monitoring quality in early childhood education and care*. Paris: OECD Publishing.

Park, E., & Pramling Samuelsson, I. (2016). *A study of Swedish and Korean early childhood teachers' perception and attitude on education for sustainability.* Paper presented at the OMEP World Conference, Seoul, 5–7 July.

Pramling Samuelsson, I. (2011). Why we should begin early with ESD: The role of Early Childhood Education. *International Journal of Early Childhood*, 43(2), 103–118. Available at: www.springer.com/education+%26+language/journal/13158

Pramling Samuelsson, I. (2016). What is the future of sustainability in early childhood? In A. Farrell, S. L. Kagan & E. K. M. Tisdall (Eds.), *The SAGE handbook of early childhood research* (pp. 502–516). London: SAGE.

Pramling Samuelsson, I., & Asplund Carlsson, M. (2014/2003). *Det lekande lärande barnet—i en utvecklingspedagogisk teori* [*The playing learning child—in a developmental pedagogical theory*]. Stockholm: Liber.

Pramling Samuelsson, I., & Kaga, J. (2008). *The contribution of early childhood education to a sustainable society.* Paris: UNESCO.

Pramling Samuelsson, I., Sheridan, S., & Williams, P. (2006). Five preschool curricula: Comparative perspective. *International Journal of Early Childhood*, 38(1), 11–30.

Pramling Samuelsson, I., & Siraj-Blatchford, J. (2015). *Education for sustainable development in Early Childhood Care and Education: A UNESCO Background paper.* (Unpublished manuscript for UNESCO).

Pramling Samuelsson, I., & Wagner, J. (2012). Open appeal to local, national, regional and global leaders to secure the world's future. *International Journal of Early Childhood*, 39(2). doi:10.1007/s13158-13012-0071-0

Ritchie, J. (2016). Qualities for early childhood care and education in an age of increasing superdiversity and decreasing biodiversity. *Contemporary Issues in Early Childhood*, 17(1), 78–91.

Ritchie, J., Duhn, I., Rau, C., & Craw, J. (2010). *Titiro Whakamuri, Hoki Whakamua. We are the future, the present and the past. Caring for self, others and the environment in early years learning.* Wellington: Teaching and Learning Research Initiative.

Sandell, K., & Öhman, J. (2013). An educational tool for outdoor education and environmental concern. *Journal of Adventure Education & Outdoor Learning*, 13(1), 36–55.

Serpell, R., & Nsamenang, B. (2015). The challenge of local relevance: Using the wealth of African cultures in ECCE programme development. In P. T. M. Marope & Y. Kaga (Eds.), *Investigating against evidence. The global state of Early Childhood Care and Education* (pp. 231–247). Paris: UNESCO.

Sheridan, S., Pramling Samuelsson, I., & Johansson, E. (Eds.) (2009). *Barns tidiga lärande. En tvärsnittsstudie om förskolan som miljö för barns lärande.* Göteborg: Acta Universitatis Gothoburgensis.

Siraj-Blatchford, J., Mogharreban, C., & Park, E. (Eds.) (2016). *International research on education for sustainable development in early childhood.* Dordrecht: Springer.

Somerville, M., & Williams, C. (2015). Sustainability education in early childhood: An updated review of research in the field. *Contemporary Issues in Early Childhood*, 16(2), 102–117.

Sommer, D., Pramling Samuelsson, I., & Hundeide, K. (2010). *Child perspectives and children's perspectives in theory and practice.* New York: Springer.

Sylva, K., Melhuish, E., Sammons, P., Siraj-Blatchford, I., & Taggart, B. (2004). *The effective provision of pre-school education project: Findings from the early primary years.* London: Institute of Education.

Taylor, A. (2013). *Reconfiguring the natures of childhood.* London: Routledge.

UNCED (1992). *Promoting education and awareness and public training, Agenda 21.* United Nations Conference on Environment and Development. Conches, Brazil: UNCED.

UNESCO (2014). *Shaping the future we want: UN Decade of Education for Sustainable Development (2005–2014) Final Report.* Paris: UNESCO.

UNESCO (2015). *Incheon Declaration: Education 2030.* Paris: UNESCO. [Online resource.] Available at: http://en.unesco.org/world-education-forum-2015/incheon-declaration

UNESCO (2016, June 30). *Global Action Programme on Education for Sustainable Development: Preliminary monitoring report, focusing on the GAP key partners.* Paris: UNESCO.

United Nations (2016). *Global follow-up and review of the 2030 agenda for sustainable development.* New York: United Nations. [Online resource]. Available at: https://sustainablede velopment.un.org

White, J., & Pramling Samuelsson, I. (2014). Global crisis: Local reality? An international analysis of 'crisis' in the early years. *Educational Philosophy and Theory,* 46(9), 1036–1051. Available at: http://dx.dio.org/10.1080/00131857.2014.931007

Wilkinson, R., & Pickett, K. (2009). *The Spirit Level: Why more equal societies almost always do better.* London: Allen Lane.

3

TOWARDS A PEDAGOGY OF HOPE

Sustainability education in the early years

Paul Warwick, Alice Warwick and Kate Nash

Introduction

Education for Sustainability (EfS) is increasingly being recognised as an essential dimension of quality education in the 21st century. However, it is common for EfS to be framed around a narrative relating multiple points of global crisis. This stems from an awareness that our children today are growing up in the midst of manifold threats to well-being, in both human and environmental terms, as articulated by the United Nations' (UN's) Sustainable Development Goals (SDGs). Whilst recognising this problem-based and challenge-led imperative for EfS, our chapter argues for the importance of an alternative starting point in the early years. EfS, we propose, needs to be appropriately scaled to the lifeworlds of our children and to be agency-based and appreciation-led. The Early Years practitioner has a vital and exciting role to play in helping to nurture in young citizens ways of being that enable them to participate in the creation of more sustainable futures in their everyday lives. This needs to be contextualised in a sense of wonder and awe at the beauty of the natural world of which they are a part. This chapter will therefore present an approach to EfS that seeks to highlight the importance of providing a pedagogy of hope, with compassion and creativity at its heart. In so doing we draw from a case study of a pioneering primary school that is seeking to embody such an approach and that is highlighting the leading role early years practitioners can play in this vital area of educational reform.

The end is nigh: Common narratives of crisis driving EfS

The Education for Sustainability (EfS) movement has stemmed from an increasing understanding of multiple and global points of crisis that threaten the ability of humans, other species and ecosystems to flourish and thrive (Hart, 1997; Hicks,

2014; Sterling, 2001). More so, these narratives of crisis place cause and blame at the feet of humankind and our modern ways of living. Articulated by seminal texts such as Rachel Carson's (1962) *Silent Spring*, what has proceeded since have been countless scientific reports and commentaries observing a situation of peril and plight that current dominant patterns of societal development are framed as driving us towards.

Consequently, children today are growing up in the midst of a sense of crisis, exposed to an array of mind-boggling sustainability challenges with spatial dimensions of global complexity and temporal dimensions of far-reaching future generational consequence. The roots of these anxiety-inducing challenges are systemic and enmeshed within the adult worlds of cultural, economic, technological and political spheres that our children are still in the early stages of inheriting. Today such global issues of crisis include climate change, environmental degradation, biodiversity loss, pollution and waste, fresh water scarcity, extreme poverty, inequality, food and nutrition insecurity and disease and health risks.

These and other interlinked sustainability challenges highlight that we are living in times of unprecedented global challenge that together present a web of threat to our quality of life. As a result, calls for sustainable change at a societal level remain prevalent. Most recently this has led to the UN articulating a series of SDGs (United Nations, 2015). Covering both environmental stewardship and social justice agendas of radical reform, these 17 goals, to be achieved by 2030, are as follows:

Goal 1	End poverty in all its forms everywhere
Goal 2	End hunger, achieve food security and improved nutrition and promote sustainable agriculture
Goal 3	Ensure healthy lives and promote well-being for all at all ages
Goal 4	Ensure inclusive and equitable quality education and promote lifelong learning opportunities for all
Goal 5	Achieve gender equality and empower all women and girls
Goal 6	Ensure availability and sustainable management of water and sanitation for all
Goal 7	Ensure access to affordable, reliable, sustainable and modern energy for all
Goal 8	Promote sustained, inclusive and sustainable economic growth, full and productive employment and decent work for all
Goal 9	Build resilient infrastructure, promote inclusive and sustainable industrialisation and foster innovation
Goal 10	Reduce inequality within and among countries
Goal 11	Make cities and human settlements inclusive, safe, resilient and sustainable
Goal 12	Ensure sustainable consumption and production patterns
Goal 13	Take urgent action to combat climate change and its impacts
Goal 14	Conserve and sustainably use the oceans, seas and marine resources for sustainable development

Goal 15   Protect, restore and promote sustainable use of terrestrial ecosystems, sustainably manage forests, combat desertification, halt and reverse land degradation and halt biodiversity loss

Goal 16   Promote peaceful and inclusive societies for sustainable development, provide access to justice for all and build effective, accountable and inclusive institutions at all levels

Goal 17   Strengthen the means of implementation and revitalise the global partnership for sustainable development

Crucially this agenda for transforming our world raises not simply the need for education for all, but asks much deeper questions around what *kind* of education is necessary?

In search of a hopeful starting point in the early years

The recent global interest in EfS can therefore be traced back to a growing awareness of multiple threats to present and future well-being. These systemic points of crisis lie across the environmental, social, economic and political spheres and bring into question the role, function and form of an education system that is fit for transforming such a reality, rather than replicating it.

Whilst we can see the merit of a global set of sustainable development goals being utilised as focal points within a problem-based, challenge-led approach to EfS, we would argue that in the early years setting a more apt starting point needs to be constructed. The sheer enormity, complexity and seriousness of these global narratives of peril can induce an array of emotional responses including anxiety, despair, denial and fear (Hicks, 2014). Whilst it is impossible and arguably not beneficial for early years practitioners to try and protect their children from this burden, a deficit and crisis narrative does not represent in our view the appropriate starting point for EfS.

Instead, we would argue that the vital role of early years practitioners is to playfully engage children with a sense of appreciation and value of the natural and social world by nurturing a sense of compassionate connection, convivial relationship and civic capacity. The early years setting needs to be a nurturing ground for children to develop their sense of wonder and innate curiosity about their life-worlds. It is also where they can actively experiment with their sense of collaborative agency and capacity to steward and serve the well-being of themselves, each other and the landscapes they inhabit. This frames EfS in the early years as seeking to innovate towards pedagogies of hope.

This position is very much in alignment with recent EfS research at an international level that recognises the effectiveness of learner-centred, active, participatory and experiential pedagogies (UNESCO, 2012). These applied learning approaches in EfS actually build upon many pre-existing pedagogical traditions within the early years context. For example, in the UK they mirror the characteristics of effective learning, as stated within Development Matters in the Early Years Foundation Stage, such as creating and thinking critically, playing and exploring and active learning (Early Education, 2012). Similarly, in New Zealand the Te Whāriki curriculum policy emphasises the critical role of socially and culturally mediated learning in the early years and the importance of space for collabora- tion, exploration and reflection (Ministry of Education, 1996). This all supports early years practitioners in employing a variety of creative activities in EfS such as storytelling, simulations, role play and place-based learning. EfS can be seen as advocating child-centred approaches in order for learning to be provided in ways that are personally accessible, locally relevant and culturally appropriate. It promotes concepts of learning beyond the classroom with flexible and natural spaces for learning coming to the fore, such as is advocated by Forest Schools (Constable, 2015). Similarly it encourages young learners to engage with values that underpin notions of social justice, such as is advocated by UNICEF's Rights Respecting Schools Award (UNICEF, 2015). This pedagogical approach also recognises the importance of early years education being centred on nurturing children's collaborative creativity. With the very real possibility that many of our early years children could live to see the turn of the next century, it is impossible for us as educators to foresee entirely how global challenges are going to play out in their lifetimes and the solutions they need to be educated about (Scott & Gough, 2004). Instead their ability to flourish as future citizens requires in the first instance a sense of appreciation and connection to the places where they live and a playful curiosity to explore together how they can start to create their own lives and landscapes.

Through this appreciation-based active learning process, early years children develop and exercise the values, skills, knowledge and convivial relationships that EfS ultimately seeks to nurture. This frames children as active social agents with the rights and capacities to participate in decision making about matters affecting them, as endorsed in the United Nations Convention on the Rights of the Child (United Nations, 1989). Engaging children in the process of conceptualising, planning, acting and reflecting helps them to develop the collective will, courage and wisdom necessary for the pursuit of more sustainable futures.

Reframing the sustainable development goals for the early years

The direction of travel of EfS in adopting an agency-based and appreciation-led starting point in the early years encourages a framing of EfS as essentially being centred on an active concern for well-being. EfS encourages extending this relational care across three dimensions:

The biosphere dimension   Appreciative care for people and planet
The spatial dimension   Appreciative care for the local and global
The temporal dimension   Appreciative care for the present and future

Applying this relational and compassionate value-based lens to the Sustainable Development Goals framework enables this translation for the early years setting:

The Love Living Goals:

Goal 1	We're taking care of each other's needs
Goal 2	We're checking we have all got enough to eat today
Goal 3	We're looking after our head, heart and hands
Goal 4	We all love learning here
Goal 5	We're treating boys and girls as equally precious
Goal 6	We treasure water that keeps us well and clean
Goal 7	We use wind and sun energy for having fun
Goal 8	We're making a safe space to learn and grow
Goal 9	We're creatively imagining new and kinder futures
Goal 10	We're playing fair
Goal 11	We're guardians of where we live
Goal 12	We refuse, reduce, reuse, recycle and rot
Goal 13	We're sky minders
Goal 14	We're sea carers
Goal 15	We're land keepers
Goal 16	We're peacemakers
Goal 17	We're making friends around the world

Putting this approach into practice: The story of Silverhill

Within nurseries and primary schools, implementing an educational approach that embodies these love living goals requires an integrated systemic leadership approach. It requires that school leaders, staff, pupils and parents all play a part in carefully considering how EfS can be infused across the curriculum, campus, community and culture of the school. Outlined below is an example of one school's efforts to put this into place.

Silverhill Primary School is an example of a leading sustainable school within the UK. The love living goals outlined above are very much embodied in the ethos and culture of the school today. The school's EfS work began by using the Department for Children, Schools and Families' (DCSF's) Sustainable Schools Framework (DCSF, 2008). This framework proved valuable in supporting the school's overarching well-being agenda and its conceptualisation of education in helping children to learn the following: 1) care for oneself; 2) care for each other (across cultures, distances and generations); and 3) care for the environment (both near and far) (DCSF, 2008, p. 4).

As a result of its pioneering work in this area, in 2013 Silverhill Primary School became one of the first schools in England to be awarded Eco-Schools Ambassador status by Keep Britain Tidy (www.eco-schools.org). Here is an account of the school told from the perspective of its Headteacher, Kate Nash.

As the Headteacher of Silverhill Primary School I have over the past decade endeavoured to harness my passion for sustainability and have driven the transformation of the school campus, creating a variety of EfS learning spaces in our school grounds. Moore (1997, p. 32) writes, 'Natural spaces and materials stimulate children's limitless imaginations and serve as the medium of inventiveness and creativity observable in almost any group of children playing in a natural setting.' My vision has been to create a land-scape of opportunity that enables children to develop their communica-tion and play in purposeful and diverse learning spaces. The curriculum has been designed to integrate themes that enable children to learn through their experiences and utilise the campus to ignite imagination and make connections with the natural world that inspire an appreciation of what we have and a hope for the future.

The values-based approach to EfS by the school is captured by the 'Spirit of Silverhill' wooden tower displayed in the school entrance. This tower is made of blocks each illustrating a core value. Integrity, loyalty, passion, honesty, pride, strength, perseverance, initiative, respect, independence and tolerance are some of the tenets that bind our community together and make it strong. If we do not adhere to these values some of the building blocks are lost; the tower, and therefore the strength and spirit of our community, crumbles. Our vision is to teach our children to embrace and internalise these values and become resilient, responsible, sustainable and global citizens.

We have sought to nurture an appreciation, sense of wonder and con-nection with the natural world both near and far through a variety of approaches. Previous twinning projects with schools in Africa and India have brought a wealth of understanding and knowledge about different cultures, landscapes and our own lives and have ensured some amazing first-hand experiences for the children and staff. As part of our Polar Region theme, links with the Polar Foundation have enabled Skype sessions with a scientific research station in Antarctica. The children were fascinated as they were taken on a guided tour of the Princess Elizabeth Station and gained a huge insight from speaking with the Norwegian scientist. A major highlight was seeing flags the children had designed for Antarctica Day flying outside this impressive building surrounded by crystal white snow and turquoise blue skies. These activities certainly heightened the awareness of all children of the beauty as well as fragility of the Polar Regions and our children are passionate about doing all they can to protect these amazing habitats.

The school environment, and particularly our Early Years, demonstrates much of Elizabeth Jarman's doctrine of Communication Friendly Spaces using natural colours and materials (Jarman, 2013). These purposeful spaces and calming, natural décor are set up to allow the children to explore new experiences without being distracted from the immediate environment. The reading and writing dens are cosy places filled with high quality resources that promote communication and storytelling. The mud kitchen is a carefully considered environment which promotes independence, organisation and working together whilst having great fun in the mud!

I fully subscribe to Sir Ken Robinson's principle that it is hard to have new ideas if you grow up in an education culture that is fixated with standardisation (Robinson, 1999). Rather than adopting pre-designed schemes of work, our curriculum is bespoke and fluid in its construction. It has flexibility and space and is very much tailored to the interests of our pupils, focusing on the key skills they need to develop to enable them to flourish. We have created a learning environment where children feel emotionally and physically safe in a stimulating, inclusive and supportive environment.

An important element of our EfS curriculum involves giving the children the opportunity to really take time to awaken their senses through their surroundings. Spending time in the den listening to stories or watching birds, walking through the woodland, sitting in the wildflower meadow, dipping in the pond, collecting the chicken eggs, picking fruit in the Forest Garden, wandering through the willow dome, cooking marshmallows or singing round the fire pit, digging up the vegetables or planting flowers for the bees—all this allows the children space to think and reflect and develop a strong sense of connection and well-being. Each year the children become stewards of a tree, to learn about the different features, observe the changes and decorate it as the seasons dictate. These carefully constructed, diverse areas throughout the campus ensure children have a personal space within and beyond the classroom walls.

Aspiration and the pursuit of excellence is a key component of our EfS vision and our young children learn from the outset the value of listening to the critiques of their peers in order to improve upon what they are trying to achieve (Berger, 2003). The assessment process of 'peer critique' follows the format of being kind, specific and helpful and has shaped pupils who are proud of what they do and proud of how they respect both themselves and others.

Fisher (2016) stresses the importance of quality interaction that is not totally led by the practitioner, but by the child, something which more accurately indicates the child's level of understanding and then allows the adult to guide the child in their 'next steps' on their learning journey. The children have autonomy over many of their activities and discover much through their self-directed play. Whether in the mud kitchen, the wood or around the fire pit the EfS practitioner needs to think closely about the words, prompts and questions used in order to enable each child to develop their language and thinking rather than their learning being 'hijacked' by the adult.

Talking and Thinking Floor Books (Warden, 2012) provide a channel for creating a closer match between the child and the EfS curriculum they are experiencing. The books are often used to support topic work, posing questions such as 'Does everything grow?' and 'Would a dinosaur make a good pet?' The children get the opportunity to share their ideas in relation to the questions posed as well as identifying what they would like to learn more about. This in turn helps to guide their own learning. They provide the opportunity for building self-esteem and positive attitudes as the learner is involved in the decision-making process. The process of being involved in their own learning increases inherent motivation that stays with the child throughout their life. Books can be created around any sustainability topic, such as *Autumn: The Leaf Man*. We believe that children have the right to be respected as individuals and we can afford them respect by valuing their thoughts, opinions and demonstrate to them that their ideas are important. Making these books available and treating them with respect are fundamental to the learning process.

The involvement of community is central to the ethos of our school. Parents and grandparents are encouraged to interact on a daily basis with the school's EfS work through, for example, helping to maintain our outside learning spaces or supporting the children in their learning adventures. The school's annual Food Fayre is always a popular event with community members. Harvest lanterns carved from pumpkins and a variety of apple- and pumpkin-based dishes help ensure everyone has the opportunity to learn about food and farming through creative, play-based activities whilst socialising, interacting and eating a range of homemade, delicious dishes!

Pupil voice is fundamental to the Spirit of Silverhill. Our youngest pupils are involved in shaping ideas through class discussion which ensures they are involved in the EfS decision-making processes and know their views are treated with respect. Pupils are rewarded for demonstrating the Spirit of our school and supporting our Environmental Promises and Eco Code.

A fundamental component of the integration of EfS into the curriculum is the involvement and engagement of all staff. Teachers lead on specific EfS themes such as global dimension, food and farming or energy and water. The teachers have a team to assist them in organising different activities such as the energy-based Green Day. A Community of Practice was established nine years ago; this has provided a forum whereby teachers gain inspiration and encouragement from each other. Throughout the year, time is allocated for the teams to come together to plan cross-curricular themed activities. This approach has enabled us to develop a cohesive strategy that has embedded EfS into the curriculum. An example would be the whole school project based on *The Tin Forest* (Ward & Anderson, 2001) which enabled us to explore the topic of 'waste' for a week, in a cross-curricular and innovative way.

'Come forth into the light of things, let nature be your teacher', wrote William Wordsworth in 1888, and in today's interactive virtual world I believe it is the time to re-engage children with the natural world so that they do not become victims of 'nature-deficit disorder' (Louv, 2005) but are enthused, empowered and stimulated to learn through the enjoyment of their surroundings.

The aspirational vision and ethos of our school very much mirrors the Love Living Goals outlined above and is encapsulated in our school prayer which is recited on a daily basis:

Imagine a world where all people are at peace and have food and shelter.
Where every child is loved and educated to develop their talents.
Where love is more important than money.
In this world everyone is treated equally and fairly.

Imagine a world where we care for our environment and all that lives in it is treated with respect and kindness.

Life is filled with happiness and laughter.

May I play my part in sharing love, understanding, wisdom and courage to help the world live in harmony.

Conclusion

The stance we have taken here is that the early years practitioner has the important task of translating EfS goals into the lifeworlds of their children—playing with learning spaces that are congruent with the values of care and compassion and that embrace a sense of curiosity and appreciation of where the children live. This, we argue, involves resisting the tendency in EfS to frame everything around pre-existing narratives of crisis and deficit.

Returning to the work and words of Rachel Carson, she herself pointed towards a way that we feel apt for the early years—highlighting the importance of immersion and reflection on the beauty of Planet Earth:

Those who contemplate the beauty of the earth find reserves of strength that will endure as long as life lasts.

(Carson, 1965, p. 100)

The more clearly we can focus our attention on the wonders and realities of the universe about us, the less taste we have for destruction.

(Carson quoted in Lear, 1999, p. 94)

As our children grow up surrounded by narratives of trouble on their streets and screens, we would argue that in these formative years it is vital that they are given the space to be immersed in the natural beauty of this world and engaged in creating their own narratives of hope. The early years of school need to begin the adventure of children collaborating within their communities to make a positive difference—to realise the power of compassion in action. For this to take root, the early years practitioner needs to embody this relational and appreciative approach in their daily practice.

Adopting such a hopeful and appreciative stance will provide the very foundations upon which intellectual curiosity, resilient relationships and emotional agility can flourish in all its diverse forms. A growing body of work is helping to highlight the importance of EfS in representing a pedagogy of hope and the leading role early years practitioners can play in this approach (Siraj-Blatchford et al., 2010). Taking up this challenge in many national educational policy contexts means much needs to be rethought and redesigned in early years education (Elliott et al., 2017). It therefore represents an approach that requires early years practitioners to receive specialised training and support, drawing from the insights of international research in the field (Davis & Elliott, 2014) as well as from organisations set up to offer practical support to educators across all sectors, such as the charity SEEd in the UK (www.se-ed.co.uk/edu/).

But we would also wish to argue that early years practitioners already have much to offer the field of EfS, due to their familiarity with and expertise in the creative, experiential and learner-centred pedagogies that much of the EfS research points towards as good practice for engaging learners of all ages. As demonstrated by the story of Silverhill Primary School, early years practitioners have a vital contribution to make in EfS being put into practice in relationally informed ways that are apt and life affirming, placing well-being at the heart of how a school is structured and led. This is where children learn through a playful exploration of their life-world and act as active citizens, constructing in the classroom, school grounds and neighbourhood their own preferable futures.

Questions for you to consider

1. If you were to apply the Love Living Goals (as set out in section 4 of this chapter) to your educational setting/practice, what aspects of what you currently do would this affirm and what initial changes do you think this would prompt?
2. Could collaborative leadership of EfS be developed in your setting through a Community of Practice?
3. This chapter has suggested that there is value in an approach to EfS that combines an appreciation of the world with a sense of agency, regardless of the person's age. What might be alternative perspectives to this position?

Further reading

Davis, J., & Elliott, S. (2014). *Research in early childhood education for sustainability*. London: Routledge.

A provocative and challenging read with chapters from a range of international researchers that offer new dimensions for more deeply informed practices in EfS.

Jarman, E. (2013). *The communication friendly spaces approach*. Kent: Elizabeth Jarman Publishing.

This focuses on the role of the environment in supporting communication skills, emotional well-being, physical development and general engagement, offering advice on how to develop truly effective learning environments where the child is at the centre of the learning.

References

Berger, R. (2003). *An ethic of excellence: Building a culture of craftsmanship with students*. Portsmouth, NH: Heinemann.

Carson, R. (1965). *The sense of wonder*. New York: Harper and Row.

Carson, R. (1962). *Silent spring*. London: Hamish Hamilton.

Constable, K. (2015). *The outdoor classroom in practice, ages 3–7*. London: Routledge.

Davis, J., & Elliott, S. (2014). *Research in early childhood education for sustainability*. London: Routledge.

Department for Children, Schools and Families (DCSF) (2008). *S3: Sustainable school self-evaluation: Driving school improvement through sustainable development*. Nottingham: DCSF.

Early Education (2012). *Development matters in the Early Years Foundation Stage (EYFS)*. London: Early Education.

Elliott, S., Carr, V., Ärlemalm-Hagsér, E., & Park, E. (2017). Examining curriculum policy and pedagogy across borders: Re-imagining socially transformative learning in early childhood education. In P. Corcoran, J. Weakland, & A. Wals (Eds.), *Envisioning futures for environmental and sustainability education* (pp. 205–216). Wageningen: Wageningen Academic Publishers.

Fisher, J. (2016). *Interacting or interfering? Improving interactions in the Early Years*. Maidenhead: Open University Press.

Hart, R. (1997). *Children's participation*. London: Earthscan.

Hicks, D. (2014). *Educating for hope in troubled times*. London: Institute of Education Press.

Jarman, E. (2013). *The communication friendly spaces approach*. Kent: Elizabeth Jarman Publishing.

Lear, L. (1999). *Lost woods: The discovered writing of Rachel Carson*. Boston: Beacon Press.

Louv, R. (2005). *Last child in the woods*. London: Atlantic Books.

Ministry of Education (1996). *Te Whāriki Early Childhood Curriculum*. Wellington, NZ: Learning Media Ltd.

Moore, R. (1997). *The need for nurture: A childhood right*. Amsterdam: World Options Press.

Robinson, K. (1999). *All our futures: Creativity, culture and education*. London: DfES.

Scott, W., & Gough, S. (Eds.) (2004). *Key issues in sustainable development and learning*. London: RoutledgeFalmer.

Siraj-Blatchford, J., Smith, K., & Pramling Samuelsson, I. (2010). *Education for sustainable development in the early years*. Gothenberg: Organisation Mondiale Pour L'Education Prescolaire (OMEP).

Sterling, S. (2001). *Sustainable education*. Totnes, UK: Green Books.

United Nations (1989). *Convention on the Rights of the Child. United Nations General Assembly, Treaty Series*, 1577, 3.

United Nations (2015). *Transforming our world: The 2030 agenda for sustainable development.* Resolution adopted by the General Assembly on 25 September 2015. Available at: http://tinyurl.com/od9mens.

UNESCO (2012). *Shaping the education of tomorrow.* Paris: UNESCO.

UNICEF (2015). *UNICEF UK: The Rights Respecting Schools Award: A quick guide.* London: UNICEF.

Ward, H., & Anderson, W. (2001). *The tin forest.* Hampshire, UK: Templar Publishing.

Warden, C. (2012). *Talking and thinking floor books: An approach to consultation, observation, planning and children's learning.* Crieff, Scotland: Mindstretchers.

4

THE PLACE OF EXPRESSIVE ARTS IN EARLY CHILDHOOD EDUCATION AND CARE FOR SUSTAINABILITY

Paulette Luff

(WITH THANKS TO ZOE LAVIN-MILES, ANGELA HIBBERD AND THE STAFF AND CHILDREN OF ALDERHOLT SUNBEAMS PRESCHOOL IN DORSET)

Introduction

This chapter arises from an ongoing professional enquiry and self-study, through which I seek to understand more about the relationship between expressive arts and sustainability. It stems from long-held beliefs about the importance of expressive arts in early childhood education and throughout life, and a personal commitment to work for peace and sustainability. Initially, I expected this task to be a simple one of making links between these two areas of learning and research. As with many topics, as I investigated I became aware of the vastness of the potential field of knowledge and the complexity of my chosen subjects. There is rich theory, history, research and practice literature in the areas of arts and arts education (for specific art forms and for arts in general), of culture and heritage, of creativity and imagination, of curriculum and pedagogy, of peace education and of sustainability and early childhood education for sustainability. Many philosophical and practical questions are raised about the purpose of expressive arts in early childhood education and about the use of arts in exploring, responding to and communicating topics and issues relating to sustainability. In short, I have begun a fascinating and engaging quest that goes far beyond the scope of a single book chapter! After much deliberation, the contribution that I am making here is a review of the research of those who have already accepted the challenge of bringing together expressive arts and early childhood education and care for sustainability (ECECfS). This is followed by a reflection on themes from this work, linked with discussion of an integrated curriculum project. The overall aims are as follows: 1) to identify the pedagogical potential of the arts in ECECfS; 2) to provide possibilities for practice; and 3) to identify areas for further research.

Five papers are explored, covering projects by three authors. The papers are those found from a search within the body of existing ECECfS literature and selected because specific reference is made to both arts and sustainability. All the research is from an Australian context. This can be attributed to the fact that there is explicit mention of sustainability in the Australian Early Years Learning Framework (EYLF) (Department of Education, Employment and Workplace Relations, 2009). For example, it makes the following statements: 'Environments and resources can also highlight our responsibilities for a sustainable future and promote children's understanding about their responsibility to care for their environment' (p. 16); two learning outcomes are associated with sustainability—'children are connected with and contribute to their world' and 'children become socially responsible and show respect for the environment' (p. 29); and educators are required to embed sustainable practices in daily routines and procedures. In this chapter the projects are briefly described and then findings from across all the projects are used as the basis for a discussion in which four key themes are drawn from the papers and links are made to a contemporary project undertaken within the Early Years Foundation Stage curriculum in England (Department for Education, 2017).

Research into arts in ECECfS

Kumara Tarr (2008) conducted an action research project, *Enhancing Environmental Awareness through the Arts*, in which she worked with practitioners in a day nursery in Sydney, Australia, to facilitate their use of arts-based approaches to enhance children's awareness of their natural environment. The argument presented in her paper is that a sense of positive connection with the natural world can be fostered and observed in arts activities and free play. The workshops for staff began with storytelling as a means to introduce concepts relating to flora and fauna (linked with two- and three-year-old children's current interests and levels of understanding). Stories about plants and animals were made up, set in the locality, and told using props that were later incorporated in play—natural materials, open-ended resources such as coloured silk scarves and toy animal characters. The stories were extended in subsequent workshops with the use of music, movement and verse, with visual arts (painting, drawing and sculpture) and with crafts using natural materials.

In a follow-up project, Kumara Ward (2013) extended this arts-based, creative approach to ECECfS, writing about the experiences of ten educators who worked with three- to five-year-old children attending four different preschools in Sydney. They participated in a workshop-based arts and sustainability project, and associated action research, throughout one academic year. This involved developing and using creative arts experiences to support children aged three and four to connect with and learn about the natural environment. For example, in one preschool the topic of rainbows was introduced through a story about water droplets and sunrays and further investigated with light tables, prisms, drawing, paintings and songs. Through the processes the educators themselves learned to understand and respect the natural environment and the ways that things grow and live, and they found new ways to engage children with flora and fauna in the locality.

The medium of story also provided a starting point in the work of Georgina Barton and Margaret Baguley (2014). Their study was not solely focused upon early childhood, as they report on a project undertaken in a small, multi-age school in Australia with 18 children from Prep to Year 7. The children studied a book, Graeme Base's *The Sign of the Seahorse*, with a message about conservation of a coral reef and marine life. The children then developed their understanding of this text and the roles of the sea creature characters through shared reading and multi-modal arts practices, before creating and staging a performance in which the story was retold through drama, dance and music, using costumes, stage sets and props. The principal emphasis of Barton and Baguley's work is on literacy learning and understanding story. Nevertheless, because the picture book chosen as a stimulus carries a message about environmental sustainability, it offers important insights about developing understandings through the arts.

The multiple languages that the arts afford for engaging with and expressing ideas about sustainability are also explored by Lyndal O'Gorman (2014), who reports on a study of student teachers' engagement with sustainability in a cross-curricular arts and humanities programme during their teacher education course. The aim of the programme was to assist the student teachers in Queensland, Australia to appreciate the transformative potential of the arts and education for sustainability through an integrated cross-curricular approach. The cross-curricular learning in arts and humanities experienced by the students mirrored holistic, integrated approaches to sustainability in the national curriculum that they would teach in early childhood services and schools. A wide variety of face-to-face and online learning activities and resources were utilised, including an online discussion forum. Drawing upon critical theory and identity theory, the student teachers were provided with opportunities to challenge their own attitudes towards local and global sustainability and to consider how their identities shaped and were shaped by the prevailing social, environmental and political context. Their ideas were expressed via self-portraits and shared with peers and tutors; some of these displayed links between identity and sustainability and changed perceptions of the relationships between themselves and the natural world.

O'Gorman (2014, 2015) stresses the potential of the arts for consciousness-raising in relation to controversial social issues. With examples from contemporary visual arts, she shows how artists use different media to provoke responses to environmental, social and political issues. In a further article (O'Gorman, 2015) she also points out that children's drawings have been used to communicate powerful messages about their views of the world. She demonstrates the potential for rich learning from combining visual arts with education for sustainability by using a case study of five-year-old Ava's drawing project. Ava expresses her interest in birds, and particularly spoonbills, via a visual journal in which, over a sustained period of time, she experiments with observing and drawing creatures from the natural environment and especially birds, inspired by favourite picture books. Supported by her mother, who draws attention to colours around her and assists in selecting pencils, crayons and paints in natural colours, Ava shows knowledge of birds in the creation of a wonderful collage. Ava's picture is used to illustrate the front cover of a book (see Davis, 2015).

Seeking insights from the research

The work of the three researchers whose work is outlined above offers many exciting ideas, insights and inspirations for practice that can be applied in other contexts. In the discussion that follows, I have taken four themes from the reported research in order to draw out key points about the place and potential of expressive arts for ECECfS. In linking work within the EYLF in Australia with opportunities in the Early Years Foundation Stage (EYFS) in England, I have used as an exemplar the work of environmental educator Zoe Lavin-Miles and her collaboration with Alderholt Sunbeams Preschool in Dorset on a bat conservation project (Luff et al., 2015; Nikiforidou et al., 2015). The bat project was a three-week integrated curriculum project designed with an explicit focus upon sustainability. It was not designed as an arts project but it has relevance here as 'expressive arts and design' was one of seven areas of learning covered during the planning and implementation of project activities. Below, four themes are explored in turn: 1) learning through story and imagination; 2) knowledgeable, confident educators; 3) making and strengthening connections; and 4) the further potential of expressive arts for sustainability.

Learning through story and imagination

In four of the five examples presented above, books and stories were used as a stimulus and point of reference for arts and sustainability learning. This was also the case in the bat project, where the book *Bat Loves the Night* by Nicola Davies (2015) was used as an introduction and as a point of reference throughout the topic. The story follows a night in the life of a mother Pipistrelle bat from when she wakes at dusk, through a night of searching and hunting for food, until her return to the roost to feed her batling and sleep through the day.

Children are seen to develop and deepen their understandings of the natural world through the telling and retelling of the stories and by re-presenting the stories and information in different modes (Barton & Baguley, 2014; Tarr, 2008; Ward, 2013). In Ward's (2013) project, stories about the natural world were followed by setting up themed play areas in the preschool rooms, providing play props, engaging in drama, music and movement activities and also offering painting, drawing and modelling visual arts experiences. Ward (2013) reports, 'This multi-modal creative arts activity reflected a significantly intensified and detailed understanding of the local natural environment in each of the preschool settings' (p. 173). Similar learning and teaching strategies were used in the bat project where children developed and reinforced knowledge when they drew and then made bats and bat habitats from recycled materials, role-played wearing bat cape wings and living in a bat cave, acted out echolocation in a bat and moth game (in which blindfolded 'bats' listened out for, chased and captured 'moths') and sang songs about bats (Luff et al., 2015; Nikiforidou et al., 2015).

Using picture books, there is also scope for art appreciation as children look closely at and talk about the illustrations and perhaps engage in their own visual artwork in response to that of illustrators. This is seen in O'Gorman's (2015) account of Ava's creation of the bird collage where a particular picture book inspires Ava's depiction of the spoonbills. In the *Bat Loves the Night* book, too, the beautiful, detailed and lifelike illustrations by Sarah Fox-Davies provide children with opportunities to revisit the pictures in the text and glean information from the realistic images that they may then use in their own representations of bats and bat habitats in their play, drawings and model making.

It can be argued that stories, expressive arts and imagination are keys to learning in the early years. Kieran Egan (1986, 1988) presents a view of the early years as a stage of life where children are inherently imaginative and skilled in fantasy. O'Gorman (2014) agrees, suggesting that 'the human capacity for art-making, for the flourishing of imagination, ingenuity, flexibility of thought and attraction to fiction, is at its peak in early childhood' (p. 267). This ability to learn about and make sense of the world through fantasy provides a basis for ECECfS that is grounded in storytelling and invites creative, artistic, cognitive and affective engagement with important topics and issues.

Knowledgeable, confident educators

In all the studies reported above, young children's learning was enabled by knowledgeable educators. Indeed, O'Gorman (2014) stresses the importance of initial teacher education in advancing education for sustainability. Continuing Professional Development is also important, as the educators who took part in the storytelling and arts workshops benefitted from expert guidance that enabled them to experiment with ideas that they could develop for use in meaningful ways with children in their settings (Tarr, 2008; Ward, 2013). In the bat project in Dorset, there was mutual learning whereby the preschool staff gained knowledge about bats plus ideas for outdoor and environmental education whilst also sharing their expert knowledge of the children and of the EYFS curriculum.

The practitioners in Dorset could draw upon Zoe's expertise to learn about local bat populations and habitats (Luff et al., 2015). Yet not all practitioners have expertise to hand and they may have to work independently to gain knowledge and understanding of the sustainability topics that they plan to investigate with the children. In the projects to enhance environmental awareness through the arts, outlined above, the educators had support with the arts element of the project but needed to do research in textbooks and online to ensure accuracy in their narrative representations of animal, bird and insect characters and contexts (Tarr, 2008; Ward, 2013). Indeed, in researching the subjects for their stories, Ward (2013, p. 73) reports that the educators in her study 'dramatically increased their knowledge of plants, animals/insects and habitats'.

Where projects cross disciplines in holistic integrated ECECfS curricula, educators may lack the necessary knowledge and skills for teaching and facilitating expressive arts. Ward (2013) highlighted challenges faced by the educators in her study that could also apply to practitioners in other contexts: some people found difficulties in transforming factual information into story narratives and creative experiences, and they lacked confidence in their own artistic abilities, particularly in relation to musical skills and developing musical experiences. O'Gorman (2014, 2015) likewise points out that teachers may have low confidence in their ability to teach arts subjects to young children. This signals a need to extend initial training and professional development for early years educators in both arts education and education for sustainability and to research optimal ways of doing this. There is some evidence that input and inspiration from experts, combined with opportunities for educators to develop and trial ideas in their classrooms, is effective for supporting multi-modal, arts-based ECECfS work (Luff et al., 2015; Nikiforidou et al., 2015; O'Gorman, 2014; Tarr, 2008; Ward, 2013).

The arts and sustainability projects described above also raise questions about pedagogical approaches and ways and means of engaging with and extending children's interests to create rich knowledge and understandings of aspects of sustainability. There is some tension between a fully child-led approach, in which following the child's interests is paramount, and the delivery of adult-led, pre-planned content. In the EYFS there is an emphasis upon planning learning opportunities based upon the needs and interests of each individual child (Department for Education, 2017). When the bat project is presented to educators working in the EYFS, they sometimes question whether or not children's interests led to this particular topic. Whilst the project in itself was not initiated by a particular child or group of children, it was planned by educators who knew the children and their interests very well and who were able to design the project in ways that were appealing and meaningful. What is beyond doubt is that the children quickly became very interested and engaged in learning about bats. Many sustainability topics are outside children's immediate range of interests and yet skilled staff can link with children's current concerns to awaken their curiosity and broaden their knowledge of their local environment and the wider world. Ward (2013, p. 177) helpfully describes how, in her project, 'a nexus between intentional teaching and a child initiated curiosity and enquiry about the natural world formed interrelated and complementary pillars of the lived experience for both educators and children'. This is reinforced by O'Gorman (2015), who advocates for a 'hands-on' approach to arts and sustainability education in which a guided learning approach is adopted to scaffold children's learning and extend their thinking through co-construction of knowledge. Arts-based pedagogies provide a useful means for learning in this way, as outcomes are open-ended and can be negotiated.

Making and strengthening connections

Arts-based approaches to ECECfS can also be described as relational pedagogy, whereby children develop understandings in dialogue with practitioners and connect new experiences to their existing feelings, knowledge and interests. Children are encouraged and supported to relate in positive ways to one another and to the environment. This is seen in Tarr's (2008) study where children identified with the characters and action in the stories. Stories about groups of animals were seen to model social cooperation and to support the social dynamics of the group. Strengthening of positive relationships was also a feature of Barton and Baguley's (2014) project where collaborative teamwork was a feature of the arts practices. They expressed clear beliefs in the link between collaboration, communication and creativity and in the importance of work with others to consolidate individual understandings. In their study, the children worked together throughout the collaborative project, and the staged performance provided evidence of their awareness of one another, offering mutual support as members of a team.

Children in the arts and sustainability projects also showed empathy and learned to express care and nurture. For example, one two-year-old storyteller is cited as telling the small group who are listening, '… and you have to be careful because the egg is going to hatch soon and it needs looking after' (Tarr, 2008, p. 23). In Barton and Baguley's (2014) project, the multi-age group meant that older children were paired with younger children for the initial reading of the book and the older children also supported the younger children with learning to speak their lines for the production, gave help with dance steps and, on stage, gave reminders of what to do and when. In all the research projects above, the collaborations were within the immediate local group. In the bat project, in addition to care and cooperation amongst the children in the Sunbeams preschool group, friendship was extended to a partner: Nakuru West Preschool in the Rift Valley of Kenya. The children from Sunbeams sent a copy of the *Bat Loves the Night* book and a cuddly toy bat to their friends in Kenya, together with videos of themselves participating in some of the project activities (Luff et al., 2015; Nikiforidou, 2015).

In addition to building relationships with other people, through the arts projects educators and children developed a closer sense of connection to the natural world, specifically the flora and fauna in their environment (O'Gorman, 2015; Tarr, 2008; Ward, 2013). In the various projects, adults and children found different ways of seeing, knowing and understanding their locality. Through aesthetic experiences in interactions with nature children and adults began to notice further features of the world around them. Sensory impressions of the qualities of natural phenomena were appreciated and then further explored through the arts (Tarr, 2008). In O'Gorman's (2015) case study, Ava connected with the natural world through daily close observational drawings. As part of the bat project, Zoe took children and their families out for an evening of bat watching and they were thrilled to hear the bat calls, via the use of heterodyne detectors, and to observe Pipistrelle and Noctule bats (Luff et al., 2015; Nikiforidou 2015). O'Gorman (2015, p. 221) suggests that these kinds of early childhood experiences can have a lasting impact and 'form the foundation of children's advocacy for the natural world'.

The awe and excitement at seeing the bats can be described as engendering a 'sense of wonder', a phrase used by nature writer and pioneering environmentalist

Rachel Carson (1965) to describe the intense, uplifting and inspiring emotions that come from direct, close experiences in the natural world. Ruth Wilson (2010, 2012) also suggests that sensitivity to beauty in the natural environment can be developed in this way. She argues that children's ways of responding to the world are exuberant and directly engaged, at an age when perception leads thought. Joyful, aesthetic experiences and encouragement to represent beauty through the media of art, dance or music can enrich the lives of children and foster their well-being. Wilson (2010, p. 25) also expresses the aspiration that instilling a sense of wonder can enable children 'to see a future different from what currently exists, including the possibility of seeing beauty in places now filled with ugliness and seeing peace and harmony in places now filled with anger and discord' and to 'encourage further beauty into existence' (ibid). The arts can be valuable in this context as they provide means to connect deeply with aesthetic experiences and to express ideas and emotions that are beyond words.

Further potential of expressive arts for sustainability

Ward (2013) observed that educators' investigations and representations of local flora and fauna led to a stronger sense of place and feelings of responsibility towards the natural environment. Her project, and the others reported here, show that responses through various artistic means and modalities can be both emotional, connected to a sense of awe and wonder, and cognitive, as knowledge and understanding are gained and consolidated. O'Gorman (2014, 2015) goes further, suggesting that these emotional and intellectual connections reveal the potential of the arts to transform the ways in which people see the world. Arts education provides opportunities for critical thinking, problem solving, exploration of ideas and enacting change, all of which resonate with ECECfS (e.g. Davis, 2015; Davis et al., 2009; Siraj-Blatchford et al., 2012).

The transformative potential of arts-based ECECfS can be seen at different stages in the learning process. ECECfS involves questioning and challenging accepted mainstream values and behaviours and, as O'Gorman (2014, 2015) points out, many visual artists use their work to confront viewers and to raise awareness of social and political issues. O'Gorman (2014) showed student teachers photographs by artist Chris Jordan of dead albatross chicks, starved from being fed plastic marine debris. These images provoked discussions about pollution and unsustainable use of plastics as well as about what should or should not be shown to children. This shows how a piece of visual art can be used as a provocation to introduce a theme or topic. Children can be asked open questions about what they see to elicit responses, stimulate curiosity and generate further questions. A simple example of this is seen in the first OMEP World Project on Education for Sustainability, in 2009, in which a drawing of children washing a globe was shown to children aged two to eight years, in different countries, and they were asked to talk about the picture and say what they could see, what was happening in the picture and why. This provided an effective means of listening to young children's ideas and opinions and appreciating the breadth and depth of their knowledge (Engdahl, 2015).

Questions and questioning prompted by a visual stimulus or other form of art can be a one-off activity with a focus upon hearing and appreciating different viewpoints and perspectives. Alternatively, this can be a stimulus to open up enquiries in which children become curious, answer new questions and seek explanations. The place of expressive arts in these enquiries is manifold. As shown in the 'Hundred Languages of Children' that are at the heart of the Reggio Emilia approach to early childhood education (Malaguzzi, 2012), young children can explore their environment, experiment with ideas and make their understandings visible using many different means of symbolic representation (including oral storytelling, dance, drama, drawing, painting, sculpture, model making, puppet play and music). This ability is seen in the ways that children expressed themselves within the arts and sustainability projects, above, and there is great potential to explore and evaluate this further in new projects that are designed to integrate expressive arts with sustainability education in early childhood.

In addition to creating images to represent thoughts and emotions, and recognising the 'languages' through which different ideas and feelings can be expressed, gaining skills in expressive arts may increase feelings of self-efficacy. Arts educator and educational theorist Elliott Eisner (1978) identified that through mark making and creation of visual images children learn that their actions have consequences, that they can alter something in the world and bring something new into being. This can be intrinsically satisfying. It can also underpin children's active, agentic engagement in sustainability, via finding out about the positive and negative consequences of actions and enacting change to create good outcomes. Arts education can be linked with positive processes of creativity, care and repair. It can also be the basis from which children imagine possible futures and gain confidence to develop solutions and make a difference.

Finally, expressive arts are important not only for exploration of sustainability themes and issues but for the potential to communicate messages about these to others. Barton and Baguley (2014) report how the children performed their play based upon *The Sign of the Seahorse* story to an audience. The students in O'Gorman's (2014) study shared their self-portraits and short statements about their artwork in an online gallery. Expressive arts can also enable children to tell their stories and share their ideas and concerns. O'Gorman (2015) emphasises that arts can address complex issues and topics by connecting on an emotional and intellectual level, differently from but complementary to messages from science and other disciplines. Thus arts-based ECECfS may have power to engage young learners, to support their activities and investigations and to enable communication of findings and outcomes.

In conclusion, in this chapter I have looked at existing research linking arts and sustainability in early childhood education from Australia, and have linked themes from this work with an integrated curriculum project in England to show possibilities within the EYFS and other curricula. I would suggest that learning through story and imagination has great potential, especially when led by skilled and confident educators who are well supported in their roles. Expressive arts offer adults and children ways of experiencing and knowing the world and of creating meaningful connections, responses and actions. I am convinced that arts-based early childhood education has an important part to play in creating sustainable present-day lives for children and families and building towards sustainable, just and peaceful futures for humanity and Planet Earth. My enquiry will continue and I hope that readers of this chapter will join me to explore ways in which expressive arts can enrich and extend ECECfS.

Questions for you to consider

1. What types of arts experiences are important in early childhood?
2. What is the place and potential of expressive arts in ECECfS?
3. If you are an educator, how confident do you feel about integrating expressive arts with other subjects for learning and teaching about sustainability?
4. What can expressive arts contribute to the creation of a more equitable and sustainable world?

Further reading

Nikiforidou, Z., Miles, Z., & Luff, P. (2015). Bat conservation in the foundation stage: An early start to education for sustainability. In P. Bamber & A. Bullivant (Eds.), *From curriculum makers to world shapers: Building capacities of educators for a just and sustainable world* (pp. 68–76). Liverpool: Teacher Education for Equity and Sustainability Network (TEESNet) [Online resource]. ISBN: ISBN:9781898749158. Available at: https://hira.hope.ac.uk/1659/. Accessed 30 May 2017.

This article provides further information on a bat conservation project.

O'Gorman, L. (2015). Early learning for sustainability through the arts. In J. M. Davis (Ed.), *Young children and the environment: Early education for sustainability* (2nd ed., pp. 209–224). Port Melbourne: Cambridge University Press.

This chapter offers further insights into the deep learning that can occur when high-quality arts and ECECfS come together, leading to new understandings about sustainability.

References

Barton, G., & Baguley, M. (2014). Learning through story: A collaborative, multimodal arts approach. *English Teaching: Practice and Critique*, 13(2), 93–112.

Base, Graeme (1992). *The Sign of the Seahorse*. New York: Harry N. Abrams Inc.

Carson, R. (1965). *The sense of wonder*. New York: Open Road Integrated Media.

Davies, N., & Fox-Davies, S. (2015). *Bat loves the night*. London: Walker Books.

Davis, J. (Ed.) (2015). *Young children and the environment: Early education for sustainability* (2nd ed.). Port Melbourne: Cambridge University Press.

Davis, J., Engdahl, I., Otieno, L., Pramling Samuelsson, I., Siraj-Blatchford, J., & Vallabh, P. (2009). Early childhood education for sustainability: Recommendations for development. *International Journal of Early Childhood*, 41(2), 113–117.

Department for Education (2017). *Statutory framework for the early years foundation stage.* [Online resource]. Available at: www.foundationyears.org.uk/files/2017/03/EYFS_ STATUTORY_FRAMEWORK_2017.pdf. Accessed 3 March 2017.

Department of Education, Employment and Workplace Relations (2009). *Belonging, being and becoming: The early years learning framework for Australia.* Canberra: Commonwealth of Australia.

Egan, K. (1986). *Teaching as storytelling: An alternative approach to teaching and curriculum in the elementary school.* Chicago: University of Chicago Press.

Egan, K. (1988). *Primary understanding.* New York: Routledge.

Eisner, E. (1978). What do children learn when they paint? *Art Education,* 31(3), 6–11.

Engdahl, I. (2015). Early childhood education for sustainability: The OMEP World Project. *International Journal of Early Childhood,* 47(3), 347–366.

Luff, P., Miles, Z., & Wangui, C. (2015). A bat conservation project in the UK and Kenya. *Early Education Journal,* 76, 14–15.

Malaguzzi, L. (2012). No way—The hundred is there. In C. Edwards, L. Gandini, & G. Forman (Eds.), *The hundred languages of children: The Reggio Emilia experience in transformation* (3rd ed., pp. 2–3). Denver, CO: Praeger.

Nikiforidou, Z., Miles, Z., & Luff, P. (2015). Bat conservation in the foundation stage: An early start to education for sustainability. In P. Bamber & A. Bullivant (Eds.), *TEESNet 2015 conference proceedings: From curriculum makers to world shapers: Building capacities of educators for a just and sustainable world* [Online resource]. Liverpool: TEESNet. Available at: http://teesnet.liverpoolworldcentre.org/wp-content/uploads/2016/02/Teesnet_2015_ Conference_Proceedings_FINAL.pdf. Accessed 1 March 2016.

O'Gorman, L. (2014). The arts and education for sustainability: Shaping student teachers' identities towards sustainability. In J. M. Davis & S. Elliott (Eds.), *Research in early childhood education for sustainability: International perspectives and provocations* (pp. 266–279). Abingdon: Routledge.

O'Gorman, L. (2015). Early learning for sustainability through the arts. In J. M. Davis (Ed.), *Young children and the environment: Early education for sustainability* (2nd ed., pp. 209–224). Port Melbourne: Cambridge University Press.

Siraj-Blatchford, J., Smith, K. C., & Pramling Samuelsson, I. (2012). *Education for sustainable development in the early years.* Gothenberg: OMEP.

Tarr, K. (2008). Enhancing environmental awareness through the arts. *Australian Journal of Early Childhood,* 33(3), 19–26.

Ward, K. S. (2013). Creative arts-based pedagogies in early childhood education for sustainability (EfS): Challenges and possibilities. *Australian Journal of Environmental Education,* 29(2), 165–118.

Wilson, R. (2010). Aesthetics and a sense of wonder. *ChildCare Exchange,* May/June, 24–26.

Wilson, R. (2012). *Children and nature: Encouraging creative play and learning in natural environments* (2nd ed.). London: Routledge.

5

NESTLING INTO THE WORLD

The importance of place and mutuality in the early years

Alun Morgan and Sue Waite

Introduction

Small children can have meaningful encounters with wildlife—typical might be:

> Daisy looks up at her dad to see how he reacts as she watches the worm wriggle on the surface of the garden soil where they have just been digging up carrots for a snack later. She reaches out to touch it and cover it with the damp earth, showing no sign of disgust or fear; her hands already mucky from 'helping' in the garden. It's not her first encounter with other creatures sharing her space and already she has picked up on some the ecological needs of these creatures from observing her parents' behaviour.

However, as Huggins and Evans note in the Introduction to this book, for many children in the western developed world, wildlife encounters, even of this lowly worm variety, are increasingly rare. In this chapter we will consider what advantages reintroducing children to nature might have and what might be the role of place attachment in developing a sustainable approach towards the environment and its other inhabitants. We firstly look at concepts of place and sustainability in relation to young children's responses and understanding of their world. We then consider whether developmental ideas of the relationship of children to the natural environment are helpful in supporting sustainable attitudes to develop through childhood. To help theorise how place and children's attitudes and behaviours might intersect and support each other in coming to know their place in the world, we draw on concepts of bioregionality (McGinnis, 1999; Traina & Darley-Hill, 1995) and of cultural density (Waite, 2013, 2015), before suggesting how these might impact on appropriate pedagogical practices that take proper account of place. We conclude this chapter with some implications and suggestions for early childhood educators wishing to provide quality early childhood education and care for sustainability.

Nestling in early childhood

The period of early childhood (approximately 0–8 years) is a unique and foundational phase of individual and social development and of environmental awareness and concern (or lack thereof!). We use the term 'nestling' in a metaphorical sense to frame this chapter. A 'nest' is a specific 'place' associated with the very young, one providing shelter but also, crucially, a context for nurture and development, offering a safe base from which to explore and play. A 'nestling' (noun) is a creature transitioning from dependency to relative independence through maturation and learning. This is not to deny that there are various crucial developmental subphases within the 'nestling' period of life from newborn through to 'fledgling', which might mark a transition point from early to middle childhood at around eight or nine years in human terms; nor that nestlings are active in relationship to others in getting their needs met.

This developmental process, according to constructivist and social constructivist thinkers, is crucially supported externally by peers, parents, guardians, care workers, teachers, mentors and other concerned adults, but is also underpinned by an endogenous process (from within). A 'nestling' constructs a sense of the world (understanding, meaning, appropriate behaviour, how to manipulate) and their place in it through the transactional processes of interacting with the world. According to ecological-evolutionary perspectives on human development (Heerwagen & Orians, 2002), this process is largely characterised by play and exploration, whether in the animal or human world, and 'what is salient, what is ignored, and how a child responds is expected to vary with age, or more specifically, with developmental abilities' (Ibid., p. 35). This is something we will return to below.

Secondly, 'nestling' may be interpreted as a verb, akin to 'snuggling'. This conveys something of the pleasure and comfort of settling into one's existence as a participant in the world. We want our young people to feel safe and secure with a positive self-identity and sense of self-efficacy—in other words, 'to know their place in the world' (Waite, 2013). But more than this, we want them to enjoy the pleasure of simply 'being'—the joy of experiencing the present moment in a particular place. This can apply at any stage of life providing a person is suitably 'attuned'; indeed disruption to this capacity may account for a recent upsurge in interest in mindfulness. However, it is something that appears to come particularly naturally in this early phase of life. Some authors talk of the 'spirituality of childhood' (Hay & Nye, 1998; Selbie, 2015). This becomes particularly pertinent in the context of this chapter in terms of the spiritual significance of 'place' in childhood and the significance of early encounters with the natural world.

Thirdly, the notion of 'nestling' can convey a sense of cherishing that which one comes to hold dear through an intimate understanding and/or attachment (as metaphorically nestling something close to one's heart). This is a crucial aspect in terms of agency and stewardship in the context of sustainability. Finally, a 'nest' can also mean a set of things that fit together (e.g. a nest of tables or of Russian dolls). Here a 'nestling' can be thought of something—or someone—who is a *part-of-the-whole*, relatively autonomous, yet always connected and emplaced, whether we are talking of the wider social or of the ecological world. Fundamentally, we are all nested within the abiotic, biotic and cultural world—a complex nexus of dimensions that come together in a particular 'place'—and without the material and social we simply could not 'be', never mind 'become'. This is something we need to acknowledge and from the earliest age help our children to cherish and support.

Place: The first of all beings

> Place is the first of all beings, since everything that exists is in a place and cannot exist without a place.
>
> *(Archytas, cited in Basso, 1996, p. 3)*

This quote from a Classical Greek philosopher acknowledges place as foundational to everything. We contend that place can be understood as the primal context through which 'nestlings' construct a sense of self and the world through transactional processes of interacting with their immediate environment, but also that we are indivisible from the material and natural world. Disconnection from nature is only a cultural construct, although it may be experienced physically.

First, it is necessary to explore what we can mean by 'place'. An obvious starting point is to contrast it with the related notion of 'space'. Typically, space is thought of as a relatively homogenous 'nothingness', in the sense of outer space, extensive tracts of land or sea or an undesignated area. 'Place', in contrast, often represents a bounded portion of space that is distinct from the rest of space or other 'places', perhaps as a consequence of particular things in it or events that have happened there. Space is universal; 'place' is (and places are) particular. The boundaries may be 'objective' features that make the place obvious, such as the shoreline where sea delimits an island. However, a more sophisticated understanding that allows for a more subjective or human influence has been provided by Yi-Fu Tuan (1977), a Chinese-American geographer who came up with an often used formula: space + meaning = place. This suggests that 'places' are actually meaningfully constructed by humans as they 'live' in them. Importantly for the present discussion, the reverse can be seen to be true; places also construct the people in them. The particular attributes—things and events—of places can shape the identity and understanding of people who live there. This dialogue between ourselves and places operates throughout our lives (think of regional identifications) but it is particularly powerful for 'nestlings' since their immediate surroundings largely shape their emerging sense of self/non-self and of agency in the world as they interact with what is close at hand—that is, the place they find themselves, including significant people such as their parents, peers and carers. For example, babies' language acquisition is plastic and depends entirely on the context in which they are raised. We will develop this idea further below.

Another crucial question is 'how big can places be'? According to the account above, any identifiable (or constructed) portion of space can be thought of as a 'place'. So arguably, Planet Earth represents a 'place' in 'space', as does the solar system, our galaxy, and so on. Or we can flip to smaller units and think of a continent, a country, a biome (such as the rainforest) as places. Typically, though, people tend to think of places at a much smaller scale. This allies with different ways of thinking about meaning, and begins to point to the importance of an affective component in our usual use of the term 'place'. What does this place mean to you? What other meanings coexist within it?

According to Matthews, places can be considered 'macroenvironments encountered outdoors' (Matthews, 1992, p. 2). However, given our focus on Early Years, we contend that a definition of place should allow for microenvironments encountered both indoors and outdoors. Thus, 'places can be as small as a corner of a room or as large as the earth itself' (Tuan, 1974, p. 245), a highly relevant definition which includes the very small spaces and places that very young children typically engage with.

Another possible criterion we would take issue with is that the 'boundedness' of place is only ever relative! Their apparent boundaries are fluid and dynamic (think of how a beach shifts with the tides, changing the shape of an island); they are subjective (so one person's 'place' might not match another's); and they are inextricably linked to other places, both at the same scale and other scales (Allen & Massey, 1995). This reflects our earlier idea of 'nestling' as parts-in-whole; all places can be conceived as fitting within larger scale places (think of the fun that young people have writing out their postal address from their house to the planet, the solar system and beyond). Thus places are cross- and multi-scalar phenomena. This idea has been recognised in educational theorising in terms of the 'ecological systems theory of development' proposed by Bronfenbrenner (1979) which identifies various pertinent nested scales in a child's lifeworld: from the individual through micro-system (family); meso-system (neighbourhood); exo-system (national); and macro-system (international/world). Bronfenbrenner's model was based on sociocultural relations but these nested systems can represent the geographical scales of places too.

Finally, another vital characteristic of the concept of 'place' is that, unlike the homogeneity of 'space', places are complex, multidimensional phenomena, comprising a whole host and range of 'things' interacting in complex ways. One might define places as 'complex geobiocultural assemblages' since they involve non-living or abiotic elements (soil, rock, buildings), living elements (plants, animals, humans) and complex social and cultural relations. It is important to recognise the holistic nature of their complex make-up. This is one of the ideas behind the concept of the 'bioregion' which describes the following:

> ... an area without hard boundaries but which can be distinguished by its many natural features including the flora, fauna, soil, climate, geology, and drainage area. A critical component of each bioregion is the human culture which has developed within and is integral to that area.
>
> *(Traina & Darley-Hill, 1995, p. 1)*

This fact also underlines the powerful educational potential of place, particularly in the early years. The complexity and multidimensionality of place drives the process of exploration and discovery, including self/other boundaries and categorical aspects (living/non-living, hard/soft, friend/foe), which leads to learning within the lived world. Moore and Young (1978) propose a 'behaviour-environment ecological framework' to model how children simultaneously interact with three 'realms of experience' in geographical places (as the context for learning): physiological-psychological (body-mind, sensorimotor); sociological (interpersonal relations and cultural values); and physiographic landscape (material things including natural and manufactured). The innate tendency of nestlings towards inquisitive exploration drives this process of playful engagement and is not too 'high stakes' in terms of survival since they are in a protected and nurturing environment. The job of significant caregivers is to provide suitably rich learning contexts and opportunities for play and exploration to enable nestlings to develop as rich an understanding of the world as possible. It is our contention that learning outdoors and in natural settings can prove most efficacious in this respect (Huggins & Wickett, 2011). This is also supported by contemporary environmental psychology which posits a strong and innate natural affinity between people, especially children, and nature (Clayton & Myers, 2009) and deems this affinity as vital for physiological and psychological health and well-being.

Some consider this affinity in spiritual terms. According to Hay and Nye (1998), humans do have a phylogenetic tendency (sensitivity towards nature) and a propensity to relate on a spiritual dimension. They call this 'relational consciousness' (summarised in Table 5.1), and suggest that very young children are naturally attuned to this realm but that this harmony reduces as they mature.

TABLE 5.1 Relational consciousness

Awareness sensing	Here-and-now	Focusing on the present situation
	Tuning	Participating in shared stream of consciousness
	Flow	Action and awareness merged/self-transcendence
	Focusing	Using all senses/embodiment to focus on something in order to know it
Mystery sensing	Wonder and awe	Accepting the wonder and mystery of existence
	Imagination	Exploring situations through metaphors, symbols and narratives
Value sensing	Delight/despair	Using feelings as a way of knowing [emotional intelligence]
	Goodness	Trusting in one's being and others
	Meaning	Searching for meaning in a particular situation

Source: Adapted from Hay and Nye, 1998

Hay and Nye suggest that very young children are naturally attuned to this realm but that this harmony reduces as they mature. Chawla describes these as 'magic relationships' through which one experiences a 'unity with the world' (Chawla, 2002, p. 214). Unfortunately, the contemporary world seems to be closing down such opportunities; some commentators suggest this gives rise to modern maladies of 'nature deficit disorder' (Louv, 2005), 'generational amnesia' (Kahn Jr., 2002) and the 'extinction of experience' (Pyle, 2002).

Range

Moore and Young (1978) introduce the idea of environmental or territorial 'range' comprising the places (domestic, leisure, play, etc.) with which a child habitually interacts. Crucially, range is a dynamic concept, expanding in spatial extent through the process of maturation and development. This expansion occurs sporadically as new landscapes are discovered and added to the children's territory, and it is paralleled by the consolidation of a sense of place through 'the exploration, manipulation, and transformation of newly acquired territory *over time*' (Moore & Young, op cit., p. 93 [emphasis added]).

Matthews (1992) proposes age-related physical capability factors that influence child–environment interactions. She notes key developmental locomotor 'milestones' (see Table 5.2) in the early years with obvious implications for range extension and development. Some practitioners might take issue with such a predominately maturational perspective when the experience of children may well impact on these capacities. Nevertheless, there is a vast difference in terms of opportunities for environmental interactions and explorations between the 'pre- and post-independent locomotory' stages. In the earliest phases, children begin by manipulating the close-to-hand. The baby that puts everything to the mouth is exploring objects using her dominant sense. The crawler extends his curiosity range, whilst maintaining reassuring tactile contact over different terrains. The toddler tests her balance and confidence stepping on and off a rock before seeking increasingly sophisticated ways to explore the physical possibilities of bodies and environments. We need to remember that this developmental journey does not occur

TABLE 5.2 Locomotor milestones in the early years

Age	Locomotor Milestones
16 weeks	Moves from crib to cot
28 weeks	Sits; moves to chair; much time spent in active manipulation
44 weeks	Crawls on hands and knees
12 months	Stands momentarily alone; walks with one hand held
18 months	Runs stiffly; walks alone, seldom falls
2 years	Rides toy car; runs without falling
3 years	Rides tricycle
5 years	Climbs with assurance
5–6 years	First bicycle (two wheeler) ride
7 years	Rides bicycle some distance

Source: Matthews, 1992, p. 12

within the child in isolation but includes active material and social and cultural interplay. Once competence in walking is achieved, the world truly opens up for exploration and the 'range' can expand accordingly and mirrors developmental processes. Familiar places offer new opportunities for engagement. For example, a bookshelf that initially is a support to help the baby stand, a place where books may be initially explored by grasping and mouthing, can later become a source of wonder as the child encounters representations in pictures and print to extend their meaning making. Furthermore, as this process proceeds, newer places encountered as the range expands are literally and metaphorically 'at the edges'—they represent thrilling but also possibly scary places of adventure, creativity, increasing independence and challenge; whereas places encountered previously will likely remain relatively safe, familiar retreats (akin to 'nests') to return to for comfort and consolidation. Claire Warden (2015) recognises this expanding, and diversifying, geographical landscape and has presented a simple typology of places: 'inside', 'outside', and 'beyond', with the 'spaces' between representing 'transitional spaces'. As development proceeds, what constitutes these different types of place will also shift and expand (what was 'beyond' becomes integrated into 'outside', etc.).

'Natural places' for learning: The garden and the forest

Cultural influences are evident in two common 'natural place' metaphors (or literal inspirations) associated with early years education, namely the 'garden' and the 'forest' (Tovey, 2007). Fröbel, working in the early Victorian period in Germany, thought of the idea of the '*kindergarten*' (literally 'child-garden') as:

> [A] place where the child could develop in harmony with nature. Educators would provide a rich environment for growth, and would tend, nurture and cultivate each child, just as a good gardener would tend a young plant. Froebel believed in a divine unity and connectedness between all living things, and it was therefore important for children to be close to nature in the outdoor environment ... It was not a place for didactic lessons in nature study or for teaching skills of horticulture. Rather, children learnt through activity and experience. The garden then was educative, but only through the children's own activity.
>
> *(Tovey, op cit., pp. 40–41)*

Later theorist-practitioners in Early Years have also valued natural experiences, including Montessori, McMillan, Isaacs and Lady Allen. Tovey (op cit., pp. 50–51) notes the following commonalities in their approaches:

- The educative potential of the garden and the outdoor environment beyond.
- The value of time spent outdoors, and the importance of contact with nature and gardening.
- Respect for children and trust in their competence to do things for themselves.
- Risk taking and adventurousness.
- Children learning through active engagement and first-hand experience.

- Design of space that is underpinned by theoretical principles and close observation of children.
- Involving parents and the wider community in children's learning outdoors.

More recently the idea of a children's garden has been complemented by the idea of the forest as an inspiration—metaphorical and literal—for young children's learning, most notably in the Forest Schools movement. Here, '[t]he word Forest conjures up a different image, suggesting a wilder, riskier, scarier space, less confined and cultivated than the "garden"' (Ibid., p. 82). Such nuances in what counts as outdoor places for learning remind us that we need to think critically about what different places offer regarding learning opportunities (Malone & Waite, 2016). Forests may be viewed as less managed and culturally dense than cultivated gardens and therefore may be more open to co-creation of new ways of interacting and learning between children and adults or children and children (Waite, 2015).

Metaphorically, the garden can be seen to accord in part with current performativity discourses, in that teacher-gardeners nurture children by feeding them with the requisite knowledge; while hopefully also providing fertile soil as learning environments and watering with a range of refreshing pedagogical approaches that will satisfy children's innate desire to grow in understanding their world. However, to extend this analogy, gardeners may also root out plants as weeds if they do not conform to the accepted idea of beauty in a highly managed educational landscape. They may also prune, train or transplant to ensure greater conformity in the growth observed and monitored. We might even view the Office for Standards in Education, Children's Services and Skills (OFSTED) as the annual horticultural show in which the children are measured against standards by criteria that favour homogeneity. We wish to counter this passive view of children's development by suggesting that while nestling, attachment and security are important for children's well-being, uncertainty, exploration and riskiness are equally vital for children's learning to live well in the world (Waite, Huggins, & Wickett, 2014).

These themes of personal growth and expanding horizons through intimate contact with nature, and particularly gardening, can be discerned in a classic of children's literature, *The Secret Garden*, in which the chief protagonist, Mary, finds and nurtures a secret place through which she

> '... undertakes a journey of personal growth and development which is first precipitated by her appropriation of this particular "bit of earth" to which she becomes intimately attached, and within which she is able to develop a sense of self-efficacy, and meaningful relationships both with the natural world and with other people. And it is from this small bit of earth that Mary's horizons expand geographically, psychologically, and socially' (Morgan, 2011, p. 81).

Children's personal experience of special places, be they gardens, parks, or forests, definitely has a significant role to play in their own development and their care and understanding for the world.

Developmental attachment to nature

Where then does the child fit in these understandings of place? Kellert (2002) suggests that children's values related to nature change over time. He posits nine values/attitudes towards nature that emerge during children's development:

1.   Between the ages of 3–6 years

    a   *Dominionistic*   Related to mastery of nature and physical control of it.
    b   *Negativistic*   Experienced as fear and alienation from nature.
    c   *Utilitarian*   Involving practical and material exploitation of nature.

2.   Between the ages of 7–12 years

    a   *Humanistic*   Exhibiting a strong emotional attachment to nature.
    b   *Aesthetic*   Appreciating the beauty of nature.
    c   *Symbolic*   Using nature for language development.
    d   *Scientific*   Systematic study of structure and functions of nature.

3.   Between the ages of 13–17 years

    a   *Moralistic*   Inspiring spiritual reverence and ethical concern for nature.
    b   *Naturalistic*   Direct experience and exploration of nature.

However, in our view this sequence seems at odds with some research and observation of children's engagement with nature and seems to suggest that babies have no relationship with nature before the age of three. Yet very young children clearly engage in direct exploration of their surroundings; indeed this is their earliest form of learning. Consider also Daisy's actions towards the worm; she neither tried to exploit nor master it, exhibiting little fear of it. Davis, Rea and Waite (2006) suggest instead that children's relationship with(in) nature begins at birth as the newborn baby is a sensory being that reaches out to capture the smells, sounds, feel and tastes of its surroundings. Between three and six years of age, other innate values may emerge, such as humanistic and moralistic, expressed as the awe and wonder engendered by the wider world (Piff et al., 2015) and the child's attachment to familiar places. This mirrors their attachment to significant others (Bowlby, 1969) and is associated with well-being and the development of identity (Scannell & Gifford, 2016). Bowlby's attachment theory derives from animal behaviour known as 'imprinting' and so again this echoes our commonalities with the more than human world. While some of these values and attitudes may be innate, simply emerging as the child develops, some are most certainly influenced and learned from significant adults, so that the carer who reacts adversely to the wriggly worm may teach the child negativistic attitudes towards nature. Unfortunately current western modes of living in society also tend to reinforce a utilitarian attitude towards nature, so that exploitation of its resources can often become taken for granted as our human right to master and use nature for our own purposes. As this is predominately learnt behaviour, it leads us to consider how such commodification of natural resources might be counterbalanced by teaching in the Early Years that encourages sustainable attitudes and behaviour towards the more-than-human world.

Much of the current literature regarding children and nature focuses on the growing disconnect from nature over recent generations, so that children have less freedom to roam (Moss, 2012), are more likely to spend time indoors (Natural England, 2016) and to use screens, whether TV or tablets (Childwise, 2015). Yet Fletcher (2016) suggests that there is an inherent problem with this way of describing the problem, as it implies that humankind and nature are separate and the impetus for change in our environmental behaviours is so that we don't destroy 'our' planet, implying that we have dominion over it. If we think instead as ourselves being part of the wider ecosystems that make up our living earth, we begin to acknowledge that nature is not in service to humans but that we are part of the broader more-than-human world. This may shift our perception about what sorts of ways we should encourage children to relate within nature or train teachers to do so (Feriver, Teksöz, Olgan, & Reid, 2016). As we noted earlier, harmony with nature is something that very young children seem to possess but may lose as they grow older. Could it be that their original sense of unity with the more-than-human world is socialised out of our children by the way we model and teach relationship to nature? Somerville and Williams (2015) suggest that care for the environment in fact is part and parcel of more empathetic care for others. The blurring of boundaries between human and nature may help early years educators see their role as encompassing more than simply encouraging recycling. Instead it requires stimulating careful thinking about and empathy towards all others, human and more-than-human.

Knowing your place in the world in the Early Years

As Huggins and Evans suggest in the Introduction to this book, this means that early childhood education and care for sustainability (ECECfS) should aim to create 'a more equitable and sustainable environmental, economic and social world'. An overemphasis on 'green' issues may fail to encompass these wider aspirations, and our understandings of place, as discussed earlier, need to take on board the social and cultural aspects of place and their meanings for all community members. Waite (2013) suggests that a useful way to consider these multiple meanings and the dominance of different discourses is through the idea of 'cultural density'. This involves thinking which established ways of behaving and being may operate in different contexts, acknowledging that these may vary according to different players within them and considering the implications for appropriate teaching and learning opportunities. The dominance of certain discourses leads to a cultural density that makes it difficult to entertain other ways of being, so that action (even thinking) becomes limited within the behavioural norms. Schama (1995) proposes that cultural practices become sedimented within places; however, these practices may not always be recognised by all visitors—as we commented earlier, a 'place' may have several constructed identities. For example, Waite (2015) cites an example of schoolchildren being confused about a teacher's educational intentions in a park that was redolent with their personal memories of playing with parents and peers in the community and not associated with the practices of schooling. This resulted in a culture clash that obstructed the usefulness of that context for learning. Wickett and Huggins (2011) and Edwards et al. (2016) suggest that it is more productive to draw on children's 'funds of knowledge' (Moll, Amanti, Neff, & Gonzalez, 1992) to align community and educational interests. A partnership approach also has the advantage that learning about sustainability within an early childhood setting may also be adopted more widely rather than being seen as something which happens only within the context of the setting. It becomes more than a whole school approach but rather a whole community, or even, in the case of Edwards et al.'s (2016) use of children's popular media to promote healthy eating, a whole societal approach. Such cultural alignments are likely to embed positive sustainable practices to an even greater extent. Quay (2016) argues that place should rather be described as *cultureplace* to indicate its unified material and cultural import, but perhaps the singularity of this amalgam tends to privilege one particular perspective on a place. The complex interplay of cultural influences in place can also be understood through its affordances (Fjørtoft, 2001; Gibson, 1977; Heft & Chawla, 2006) for different purposes (Malone & Waite, 2016) and the diverse cultural densities that may meet, mingle or be missed within it (Waite, 2013). This complexity leads us to further discussion of how psychological and sociocultural theorisation help us to support ECECfS.

Children, place and sustainability

The ecological approach to psychology emphasises 'agency' and 'perceiving-acting', which are highly salient features in sustainability discourse—in particular, that which emphasises 'systems transformation participation' (Heft & Chawla, 2006). Heft and Chawla identify a range of environmental qualities that promote children's environmental competencies:

1. Affordances that promote discovery and responsive person–environment relationships.
2. Access and mobility to engage affordances.
3. Guided participation that supports perceptual learning and action.
4. Opportunities for meaningful participation in community settings.

From this perspective, 'people more fully realize their capabilities—more fully *flourish* in a human sense—when they have these opportunities [to act]'. Thus, sustainable behaviour is predicated on a capacity to act and an understanding of aspects or features in the environment that are pertinent (perception) and of appropriate behaviour (acting) within it. For very young children, the care for others and the environment is often embodied within their actions towards people and the more-than-human world. They may not easily explain how they feel about their world but their physical engagement with it and their actions, and those modelled by significant adults, will demonstrate and reinforce their propensity for empathy.

Pedagogies of place

The foregoing discussion has hopefully revealed the powerful and necessary relationship between children and places, particularly natural environments and outdoor settings. Increasingly educators have recognised this fact and have turned their attention to the kinds of place-based interactions, both in terms of the nature and design of the spaces and places themselves, and the type of activity that children should be allowed to engage in within them, with play and exploration being particularly powerful (Gruenewald, 2003; Sobel, 2008; Wattchow & Brown, 2014).

In considering suitable pedagogical approaches towards ECECfS, it is worth bearing in mind that Derr (2006) identifies four interrelated types of 'children–place' relations or 'over-arching ways that children interact with and learn from their environment':

1. Children's exploration.
2. Making forts and dens with 'place-making as a means of looking inward, of establishing something of their own and developing a sense of self'.
3. Learning care, when children 'develop a sense of responsibility, respect, and empathy toward other living things'.
4. Cultural web, 'where stories, histories, and places all converge' (pp. 108–119).

A useful checklist for a practitioner might therefore include asking yourself: Does your practice allow for free play that allows children to explore their environment in an unmediated way and to gain confidence in it? Do children have opportunities to create and build special places that have meaning for them and that represent their developing relationship with their environment and sense of place? Do the adults model care and empathy and sustainable practice in their work with children, other adults and the setting itself? Do sustainable practices and beliefs take account of, respect and have an influence beyond the setting through family and community involvement?

Implications for practice

In conclusion, what are the main messages we should take from this discussion for our practice in early years in order to foster ECECfS? First, we need to recognise the broader dimensions of what ECECfS entails and what learning methods and places might best support these outcomes (Malone & Waite, 2016). Learning to live well and fairly alongside others in our more-than-human world and to be thoughtful, critical and creative are fundamental dispositions that will equip young children to act in pro-environmental as well as pro-social ways (Ampuero et al., 2015). These are qualities that are frequently fostered by spending time in the less culturally dense contexts outside the classroom where increased freedom, flow and fairness offer opportunities to try out ways of being and behaving without recourse to unthinking conformity (Waite, Rogers, & Evans, 2013).

Second, we need to be acutely aware that not all outdoor spaces are equal and to be selective about where we choose to locate learning so that children can connect to their own funds of knowledge, become attached to places and value them and their more-than-human inhabitants as they would people (Moll et al., 2001; Taylor & Giugni, 2013).

Third, we should be conscious that young children learn through mimesis and that our behaviour and values influence them hugely in the early years. This means that we also need to be conscious of our own values and actions regarding the environment and others and the extent to which this can be construed as empathic and socially just (Ampuero et al., 2015; Feriver et al., 2016).

Finally, to acknowledge its broad base, we should perhaps think of good practice for ECECfS as symptomatic or indicative of good early years practice in general. As Wood and Hedges (2016) argue, in their critique of child developmental theories or academic outcomes as the basis for early years curricula, children's working theories offer a potentially promising coherence to weave together children's engagement with places and adult support for extending their thinking and doing. It positions children's agency and competence at the centre of policy, planning and practice. This theoretical approach has proved enormously successful in promoting the aims of education for sustainability in the Enviroschools movement in New Zealand in culturally relevant, responsive and flexible ways (see www.enviro schools.org.nz/).

The idea of 'nestling into the world' brings the mutuality of the human and more-than-human to the fore and may help us to realise a future where pro-environmental thinking is an integral part of being a well-educated person. We suggest that it is only through intra- and interpersonal embodiment of those values and attitudes that promote social and environmental justice that ECECfS can succeed.

Questions for you to consider

1. How does your Early Years setting provide opportunities for the children to develop a sense of place?
2. How does your own behaviour model sustainability thinking and action? Refer to the different strands in ECECfS. Remember you are a powerful role model!
3. What stories do you remember capturing your imagination and emotions as a child and inspiring you? Consider how 'narrating' engagement with the world might also help children to extend their own role within it.

Further reading

OMEP UK (n.d.) Education for sustainable development. London: OMEP UK. [Online resource.] Available at: www.omepuk.org.uk/index.php?option=com_content&view=a rticle&id=77.

This link has a useful diagram of how different elements of Education for Sustainability are linked together. It also has some resources for teachers.

Waite, S., Goodenough, A., Norris, V., & Puttick, N. (2016) From little acorns: Environmental action as a source of ecological wellbeing. *International Journal of Pastoral Care in Education*, 34(1), 43–61. [Online resource]. Available at: www.tandfonline.com/doi/full/10.1080/02643944.2015.1119879.

This article demonstrates how early experience perceived as 'fun' is repositioned through subsequent experience and valued in later life as a source of ecological well-being.

Care Inspectorate (2016). *My world outdoors: Sharing good practice in how early years services can provide play and learning wholly or partially outdoors.* Dundee: Care Inspectorate. [Online resource.] Available at: www.careinspectorate.com/images/documents/3091/My_world_outdoors_-_early_years_good_practice_2016.pdf.

This pdf details good practice for outdoor learning in early years in Scotland.

References

Allen, J., & Massey, D. (1995). *Geographical worlds.* Oxford: Oxford University Press.

Ampuero, D., Miranda, C. E., Delgado, L. E., Goyen, S., & Weaver, S. (2015). Empathy and critical thinking: Primary students solving local environmental problems through outdoor learning. *Journal of Adventure Education and Outdoor Learning*, 15(1), 64–78.

Basso, K. H. (1996). *Wisdom sits in places: Landscape and language among the Western Apache.* Albuquerque, NM: University of New Mexico Press.

Bowlby, J. (1969). *Attachment: Attachment and loss Vol. 1. Loss.* New York: Basic Books.

Bronfenbrenner, U. (1979). *The ecology of human development: Experiments by nature and design.* Cambridge, MA: Harvard University Press.

Chawla, L. (2002). Spots of time: Manifold ways of being in nature in childhood. In P. H. Kahn Jr. & S. R. Kellert (Eds.), *Children and nature: Psychological, sociocultural and evolutionary investigations* (pp. 199–225). Cambridge, MA: MIT Press.

Childwise (2015). New 2015 CHILDWISE report provides insight into children and teenagers' technology and media use. Norwich, UK: Childwise. [Online resource.] Available at: www.childwise.co.uk/uploads/3/1/6/5/31656353/childwise_press_release_-_technology.pdf

Clayton, S., & Myers, G. (2009). *Conservation psychology: Understanding and promoting human care for nature.* Oxford: Wiley-Blackwell.

Davis, B., Rea, T., & Waite, S. (2006). The special nature of the outdoors: Its contribution to the education of children aged 3–11. *Australian Journal of Outdoor Education*, 10(2), 3–12.

Derr, T. (2006). 'Sometimes birds sound like fish': Perspectives on children's place experiences. In C. Spencer & M. Blades (Eds.), *Children and their environments: Learning, using and designing spaces* (pp. 108–123). Cambridge: Cambridge University Press.

Edwards, S., Skouteris, H., Cutter-Mackenzie, A., Rutherford, L., O'Conner, M., Mantilla, A., Morris, H., & Elliot, S. (2016). Young children learning about well-being and environmental education in the early years: A funds of knowledge approach. *Early Years*, 36(1), 33–50.

Feriver, S., Teksöz, G., Olgan, R., & Reid, A. (2016). Training early childhood teachers for sustainability: Towards a 'learning experience of a different kind'. *Environmental Education Research*, 22(5), 717–746.

Fjørtoft, I. (2001). The natural environment as a playground for children: The impact of outdoor play activities in pre-primary school children. *Early Childhood Education Journal*, 29(2), 111–117.

Fletcher, R. (2016). Connection with nature is an oxymoron: A political ecology of 'nature-deficit disorder'. *The Journal of Environmental Education*. [Online resource.] doi:10.1080/00958964.2016.1139534

Gibson, J. J. (1977). The theory of affordances. In R. Shaw & J. Bransford (Eds.), *Perceiving, acting, and knowing: Toward an ecological psychology* (pp. 67–82). Hillsdale, NJ: Erlbaum.

Gruenewald, D. (2003). Foundations of place: A multidisciplinary framework for place-conscious education. *American Educational Research Journal*, 40(3), 619–654.

Hay, D., & Nye, R. (1998). *The spirit of the child*. London: Harper Collins.

Heerwagen, J. H., & Orians, G. H. (2002). The ecological world of children. In P. H.Kahn, Jr. & S. R. Kellert (Eds.), *Children and nature: Psychological, sociocultural and evolutionary investigations* (pp. 29–63). Cambridge, MA: MIT Press.

Heft, H., & Chawla, L. (2006). Children as agents in sustainable development: The ecology of competence. In C. Spencer & M. Blades (Eds.), *Children and their environments: Learning, using and designing spaces* (pp. 199–216). Cambridge: Cambridge University Press.

Huggins, V., & Wickett, K. (2011). Crawling and toddling in the outdoors: Very young children's learning. In S. Waite (Ed.), *Children learning outside the classroom: From birth to eleven* (pp. 20–34). London: SAGE.

Kahn Jr., P. H. (2002). Children's affiliations with nature: Structure, development, and the problem of environmental generational amnesia. In P. H. Kahn Jr. & S. R. Kellert (Eds.), *Children and nature: Psychological, sociocultural and evolutionary investigations* (pp. 93–116). Cambridge, MA: MIT Press.

Kellert, S. R. (2002). Experiencing nature: Affective, cognitive and evaluative development in children. In P. H. Kahn Jr. & S. R. Kellert (Eds.), *Children and nature: Psychological, sociocultural and evolutionary investigations* (pp. 117–151). Cambridge, MA: MIT Press.

Louv, R. (2005). *Last child in the woods: Saving our children from nature-deficit disorder*. Chapel Hill, NC: Algonquin Books.

Malone, K., & Waite, S. (2016). *Student outcomes and natural schooling: Pathways from evidence to impact report*. Plymouth: Plymouth University. [Online resource.] Available at: www.plymouth.ac.uk/uploads/production/document/path/6/6811/Student_outcomes_and__natural_schooling_pathways_to_impact_2016.pdf. doi:10.13140/RG.2.1.3327.7681

Matthews, M. H. (1992). *Making sense of place: Children's understanding of large-scale environments, Vol. 11*. Hemel Hempstead: Harvester Wheatsheaf/Barnes & Noble Books.

McGinnis, M. V. (Ed.) (1999). *Bioregionalism*. London: Routledge.

Moll, L., Amanti, C., Neff, D., & Gonzalez, N. (1992). Funds of knowledge for teaching: Using a qualitative approach to connect homes and classrooms. *Theory into Practice*, 31(2), 132–141.

Moore, R., & Young, D. (1978). Childhood outdoors: Toward a social ecology of the landscape. In I. Altman & J. F. Wohlwill (Eds.), *Children and the environment* (pp. 83–130). New York: Plenum Publishing.

Morgan, A. (2011). Places of transformation in *The Secret Garden*. In J. C. Horne & J. S. Sanders (Eds.), *Frances Hodgson Burnett's The Secret Garden: A children's classic at 100* (pp. 81–98). Lanham, MD: The Scarecrow Press.

Moss, S. (2012). *Natural childhood*. Corsham, UK: Park Lane Press. [Online resource.] Available at: www.nationaltrust.org.uk/documents/read-our-natural-childhood-report.pdf

Natural England (2016). *Monitor of engagement with the natural environment pilot study: Visits to the natural environment by children*. London: gov.uk. [Online resource.] Available at: www.gov.

uk/government/statistics/monitor-of-engagement-with-the-natural-environment-pilot-study-visits-to-the-natural-environment-by-children

Piff, P. K., Dietze, P., Feinberg, M., Stancato, D. M., & Keltner, D. (2015). Awe, the small self, and prosocial behavior. *Journal of Personality & Social Psychology*, 108, 883–899.

Pyle, R. M. (2002). Eden in a vacant lot: Special places, species and kids in the neighborhood of life. In P. H. Kahn Jr. & S. R. Kellert (Eds.), *Children and nature: Psychological, sociocultural and evolutionary investigations* (pp. 305–327). Cambridge, MA: MIT Press.

Quay, J. (2016). From human–nature to cultureplace in education via an exploration of unity and relation in the work of Peirce and Dewey. *Studies in the Philosophy of Education*, 36(4) 463–476. [Online resource.] doi:10.1007/s11217-016-9507-6

Scannell, L., & Gifford, R. (2016). Place attachment enhances psychological need satisfaction. *Environment and Behavior*, 49(4), 1–31.

Schama, S. (1995). *Landscape and memory*. London: Fontana.

Selbie, P. (2015). Spirituality and young children's wellbeing. In R. Parker-Rees & C. Leeson (Eds.), *Early childhood studies: An introduction to children's lives and worlds* (pp. 55–70). London: SAGE.

Sobel, D. (2008). *Childhood and nature: Design principles for educators*. Portland, ME: Stenhouse Publishers.

Somerville, M., & Williams, C. (2015). Sustainability education in early childhood: An updated review of research in the field. *Contemporary Issues in Early Childhood*, 16(2), 102–117.

Taylor, A., & Giugni, M. (2012). Common worlds: Reconceptualising inclusion in early childhood communities. *Contemporary Issues in Early Childhood*, 13(2), 108–119. [Online resource.] Available at: www.wwwords.co.uk/CIEC.

Tovey, H. (2007). *Playing outdoors: Spaces and places, risk and challenge*. Maidenhead: Open University Press/McGraw-Hill Education.

Traina, F., & Darley-Hill, S. (Eds.) (1995). *Perspectives in bioregional education*. Troy, OH: NAAEE.

Tuan, Y.-F. (1974). *Topophilia: A study in environmental perception, attitudes and values*. New York: Columbia University Press.

Tuan, Y.-F. (1977). *Space and place: The perspective of experience*. Minneapolis, MN: University of Minnesota Press.

Waite, S. (2013). Knowing your place in the world: How place and culture support and obstruct educational aims. *Cambridge Journal of Education*, 43(4), 413–434.

Waite, S. (2015). Culture clash and concord: Supporting early learning outdoors in the UK. In H. Prince, K. Henderson, & B. Humberstone (Eds.), *International Handbook of Outdoor Studies* (pp. 103–113). London: Routledge.

Waite, S., Huggins, V., & Wickett, K. (2014). Risky outdoor play: Embracing uncertainty in pursuit of learning. In T. Maynard & J. Waters (Eds.), *Outdoor play in the early years* (pp. 71–85). Milton Keynes: Open University Press.

Waite, S., Rogers, S., & Evans, J. (2013). Freedom, flow and fairness: Exploring how children develop socially at school through outdoor play. *Journal of Adventure Education and Outdoor Learning*, 13(3), 255–276.

Warden, C. (2015). *Learning with nature: Embedding outdoor practice*. London: SAGE.

Wattchow, B., & Brown, M. (2011). *A pedagogy of place: Outdoor education for a changing world*. Clayton, VIC: Monash University Press.

Wickett, K., & Huggins, V. (2011). Using the local community as part of the early years learning environment. In S. Waite (Ed.), *Children learning outside the classroom: From birth to eleven* (pp. 35–49). London: SAGE.

Wood, E., & Hedges, H. (2016). Curriculum in early childhood education: Critical questions about content, coherence, and control. *The Curriculum Journal*, 27(3), 387–405.

6

YES WE CAN!

Young children learning to contribute to an enabling society

Maria Assunção Folque

Introduction

In this chapter,[1] we will address the possibility and the relevance of young children learning to participate in society, going beyond a view of children as merely fragile, in need of receiving the society's attention, protection and fulfilment of needs, into a view of children as citizens, being active contributors to the common good of communities. A pivotal UNESCO paper (2015) takes up the ideas of earlier researchers (Cofield, 2002; Ranson, 2004) in critiquing the relatively narrow educational aim of 'engaging in lifelong learning' without encompassing another important aim of educational systems in democratic societies, namely the development of democratic citizens from an early age. In recent years many researchers, Early Childhood Education (ECE) experts and practitioners have been focusing on democratic approaches to ECE pedagogy (Lansdown, 2001; Linington, Excell, & Murris, 2011; Moss, 2007). This approach requires that we adopt the view, explicitly stated by Huggins and Evans in this book's Introduction, that children have:

> (...) potential for decision-making and problem-solving (...) linked to children's rights and responsibilities involving a democratic approach and collaborative work rather than to individual learning and development. It sees children as competent, to be empowered to act as agents of change within society.

Such a view is central to the movement supporting Early Childhood Education and Care for Sustainability (ECECfS) (Pramling Samuelsson & Kaga, 2008; Siraj-Blatchford, Smith, & Pramling Samuelsson, 2010), which requires that a specific focus be given to children's learning to participate in society, in order to strengthen the social and cultural fabric that sustains social networks as well as to support them in caring for the environmental and economical equilibrium that ensures our common future. If democratic societies are concerned not only with individual fulfilment but also with the cohesion and sustainability of our common good we ought to view education as a shared social endeavour, which encompasses shared responsibility and commitment to solidarity (UNESCO, 2014). Thus ECECfS should consider how young children become active participants in this process and should help them 'develop an effective sense of participating in an enabling society' (Bruner, 1996, p. 76). Indeed, recent educational publications assume the need to locate sustainable development at the core of a vision for education (UNESCO, 2015).

In the first section of this chapter we will focus our reflection on early dispositions that can contribute to young children's learning to participate in an enabling society. In the second section of the chapter – 'Yes we can!' – we will point out some practices that promote such ways of thinking and acting, and this will be clarified with two practical illustrations taken from research projects in which we have been involved: 1) 'The Council meeting' – children learning to solve problems together; and 2) children's engagement in intervention projects.

Dispositions to contribute to an enabling society

Dispositions have been defined as 'habits of mind' (Katz, 1993), or 'participatory repertoires' (Carr, 2001), or habits of thinking and doing (Da Ros-Voseles & Fowler-Haughey, 2007). Lilian Katz (1993) defined dispositions as 'relatively enduring habits of mind or characteristic ways of responding to experience across types of situations' (Katz, 1985, cited in Katz, 1993, p. 16). Without diminishing the importance of knowledge in Education for Sustainability, we choose to concentrate here on dispositions that young children must and can develop in order to actively participate and contribute to a sustainable world.

We can take a sociocultural view of education and learning, which understands learning as change in participation in cultural activities in which children have the opportunity to join (Rogoff, 1998). In this perspective, dispositions are not fixed traits children are born with, but rather, dispositions can be developed and strengthened in a particular sociocultural context. 'One does not "acquire a disposition", one "becomes more or less disposed"'(Carr & Claxton, 2002, p. 88), depending on one's experiences.

While it seemed at first that there was a need to identify the critical abilities and dispositions to an active citizenship, the complexity of the task soon became apparent and no attempt is made here to identify a comprehensive list that answers all educational needs. The following ideas come from the literature on citizenship and sustainability but also from our reflection about some research projects we have been involved in concerning Education for Sustainability (EfS). We consider/propose the following as critical abilities and dispositions to an active citizenship: 1) relational agency and active participation; 2) critical thinking and critical participation; and 3) moral development and responsibility.

Relational agency and active participation

Agency refers to the individual capacity to make choices by expressing preferences and constructing personal meanings and to actively participate in society, not only by conforming to it but also by acting to transform it (Ranson, 2004). Agency in ECE programmes is exercised with some degree of choice by the active child but within a bounded scope defined by adults. Furthermore, some researchers and teachers have been advocating and transforming their practices in order to give children not only choice but also voice (Fielding, 2004; Pollard et al., 2000). This view significantly expands children's possibilities to experience their agency and so to transform the communities they live in (Clark & Moss, 2005; Pramling Samuelsson, 2004).

It is also important to recognise that within a democratic framework individual agency – active, expressive, or interventive agency – expands to a group agency where individual actions and points of view are acknowledged and confronted and where, through negotiated consensus, shared values and creative changes are achieved. That means that agency is always relational to the material and social conditions of each culture, which condition children's opportunities to act in different contexts (Esser, 2016; Ratner, 2000). Ratner (2000) discusses the interplay of agency and culture and defends the view that agency is not something that can be enacted individually. Criticising some psychologists who put an emphasis on the individual's active role in making and remaking culture, Ratner (2000) states that agency can only be experienced within a culture where social relations facilitate such expression. This implies a democratic culture.

The above perspective calls for an ECEC culture grounded on a social organisation and on social relations that are democratic and which promote the relational agency of all its members (Edwards, 2004). Participation in decision-making, discussions, curriculum management and evaluation gives opportunities for children to be empowered and to contribute not only to their own learning process but also to the collective processes of knowledge generation, so ensuring the common good in the classroom (Folque & Siraj-Blatchford, 2011; Osterman, 2000; Rogoff, Turkanis, & Bartlett, 2001; Watkins, 2005) and also in the community.

Importantly, linked with this relational agency is the need for children to display reciprocity, which Carr and Claxton (2002) define as the ability and willingness to engage with others and to co-construct practical and theoretical knowledge. Central to this disposition are collaborative and communication skills, which children develop as they interact with others and are invited to talk, to act and to engage in collaborative activities and projects, co-constructing shared meanings and purposes.

Critical thinking and critical participation

Critical thinking is the ability to explore and appreciate different possibilities and viewpoints and to use criteria to formulate judgements (Cofield, 2002; Wilson, 2000). Such thinking is of major importance in modern democratic societies where active citizenship is required. Jane Davis-Seaver (2000) criticises viewing critical thinking as either a group of skills acquired separately through instructional programmes and then combined (reductionism) or as some form of formal thinking only acquired later in adolescence (developmental). The author advocates the constructivist viewpoint, where critical thinking abilities are built when children and teachers engage in discussions of problems that are relevant to their lives. This latter view sees critical thinking as including the abilities to ask questions, to wonder about the world, to discover and to criticise (involving negation, contradiction and refusal), where a child is not a passive receiver but an agent of change and political action (Apple & Beane, 1995; Giroux, 2001). Such critical thinking has been emphasised in programmes of personal, social and moral education, of education for citizenship (Davies, 1994; Dewey, 1966) and of inquiry and philosophy for children (Costello, 2000; Lipman, 1991).

For active citizenship, though, critical thinking is not sufficient if we are not also disposed to participate in addressing the problems we face. 'Critical participation' involves the disposition to think critically and the willingness to express individual views (Bronfenbrenner, 1979) but also to cooperate in transforming one's reality through active intervention. If children are to engage in intervention actions, they need to believe that transformation is possible and that they have the power to change the conditions of their current life. Crucially, they have to feel safe to take risks. For this to happen children need to experience an environment where disagreement is possible and criticism is taken positively as an opportunity to appreciate another's point of view and not interpreted as an act of aggression.

Moral reasoning and responsibility

Critical participation requires personal and social responsibility, and in this context it involves the socio-construction of moral thinking. Lillian Katz (2002) states wisely that not all dispositions are positive in themselves. For instance, being willing to persist despite frustration, to approach situations with imaginativeness and playfulness or to be sensitive to others' intentions and perspectives, and willing to engage in common goals, might also result in some unacceptable behaviour such as ganging up to shoplift, or to vandalise a public space. Critical participation requires the development of the ability and willingness to go beyond individual goals and values and to consider higher forms of moral reasoning. Deakin Crick (2005) places moral and social development at the core of citizenship education. From this perspective, reflection about shared values, human rights and issues of justice and equality can start to be addressed into ECEC classrooms, creating a Zone of Proximal Development (Vygotsky, 1978) where the children's need to consider others' views becomes increasingly relevant and starts to emerge, grounded in dialogues about meaningful issues.

Some researchers in the early years field (Paley, 1992; Siraj-Blatchford, 1994) have shown how young children can actively exclude others from their everyday activities, showing prejudice. Conflicts in preschool offer a great opportunity to discuss people's feelings, motivations, abilities and rights and to help young children acknowledge differences, begin to develop moral reasoning and progressively self-regulate their own behaviour in relation to the community to which they belong. One of the results of the Researching Effective Pedagogy in the Early Years (REPEY) research project (Siraj-Blatchford et al., 2002) shows the importance of conflict resolution and behaviour management strategies involving 'talking through conflicts' in moving towards positive social/behavioural outcomes in young children. Conflict resolution is an important part of some ECE pedagogical models such as the High-Scope Curriculum or the Modern School Movement (MEM) pedagogy (see the following section on Council Meetings).

Very young children show awareness of other people's feelings and states of mind, and also of issues of justice. The work of Judy Dunn (1998) shows how two- and three-year-olds, in the context of their families, display a 'grasp of the feelings of others, of their intended actions, and how social rules are applied to other people and to themselves' (Dunn, 1998, p. 103). With the acquisition of language, providing that they have the opportunity to interact with adults who themselves talk about feelings and intentions, children become progressively competent also to talk about and reflect upon others' states of minds and to consider different points of view (Bruner, 1996; Dunn, 1998).

To complement relational agency and critical participation, in democratic societies individuals are also accountable to the community and responsible for its good and progress (Morin, 1999). This social responsibility entails community involvement, such as being connected with the problems of the community and society and feeling responsible for contributing to the common good (Deakin Crick, 2005; UNESCO, 2015).

The involvement of young children in the city – Polis – challenges some views about what are appropriate experiences for young children and how far they should be protected from the problems humans face in the world. In 2015, in the context of an international summer course in Évora ('The crossroads of development: Our world, our dignity, our future') I had the opportunity to ask Sakiko Fukuda-Parr[2] what, in her view, should be the most important learning for a four-year-old child, if we want to build up sustainability. After one minute thinking about what she considered a tough question she answered: learning to collaborate and to live in the public space.

Encouraging young children to take responsibility for the common good requires some reflection about appropriate levels of responsibility for them to take as well as the meanings of such actions to them. The community can be the classroom, where they assume responsibilities in cleaning up; the school, where they take care of the garden; the local community, where they are involved in a recycling campaign; or the global community, where they start to adopt water-saving strategies despite having enough water supplies in their own country. Such actions can help children to feel they have the power to contribute to the common good.

The question we want to help answer is: how do we conceive ECE pedagogies that will promote young children's abilities and dispositions to engage with the world in a caring and responsible manner? How can we best help young children to be empowered and feel confident in contributing to a better world?

Pedagogies for participating in an enabling community

The idea of schools that empower children in engaging and participating in the world goes back to the ideas of Dewey (1966), who saw education as deeply linked with democracy. Central to his ideas was the need to involve children with real and meaningful problems that are part of their everyday lives. Many researchers, concerned with the way schools engage with the lives of citizens and the development of communities, follow Dewey's idea, advocating a curriculum based on life and inquiry which ensures that students use subject knowledge towards a better involvement with the community and the world they live in (Deakin Crick, 2005).

While considering what learning to live in a democratic society means, it is also important to reflect on the social organisation of the school communities, the interplay between the individual and the group, and the distribution of power between the teacher and children. The increasing interest in classrooms as learning communities (Watkins, 2005) provides a framework for discussing some of the classroom characteristics and the learning processes that enable participatory dispositions. Such classroom characteristics are: *inclusivity, an ethos of respect and support, shared responsibilities and shared power* and *control and dialogue.*

In democratic communities, differences are welcomed and diversity is valued for enriching experiences and viewpoints (Apple & Beane, 1995). The feeling of belonging, personal relatedness, trust in others and safety is fundamental to the functioning of any community (Osterman, 2000; Watkins, 2005). 'Members of a community feel that the group is important to them and that they are important to the group' (Osterman, 2000, p. 324). Democratic communities ensure the membership and participation of all; individual voices and views are respected and brought to discussion and decision-making (Ranson, 2004).

We want to stress the idea of multi-age classrooms in ECEC settings as a powerful organisational characteristic that promotes children's learning to care for each other, to acknowledge each other's needs, capabilities and feelings, and to develop social responsibility (Mendonça-Silva & Folque, 2016). In classrooms that operate as democratic learning communities there is a shared responsibility, and power is distributed between both children and adults (Folque, 2014; Folque & Siraj-Blatchford, 2011; Rogoff et al., 2001; Watkins, 2005) in conducting the curriculum and the everyday life of the group. This of course relates to things like leadership styles, how staff and parents talk to each other, about each other and about the children, as well as the extent to which they collaborate, or not!

I still encounter too many examples of practitioners and parents using a specially simplified artificial vocabulary and tone of voice with young children, and talking about them 'above their heads', which is both deeply disrespectful and weakens the children's sense of power and agency.

Dialogue is a paramount component of democratic learning communities. As stated before, dialogue is involved in negotiating, discussing, conflict resolution, building relationships, sharing knowledge and points of views and critical participation and collaboration. Alexander (2004) argues for the use of dialogic teaching in classrooms, not only as grounds of better learning but also for citizen education:

> Democracies need citizens who can argue, reason, challenge, question, present cases and evaluate them. Democracies decline when citizens listen rather than talk, and when they comply rather than debate; … talk builds relationships, confidence and sense of self; … talk creates and sustains individual and collective identities.
>
> *(Alexander, 2004, p. 33)*

We share Bruner's ideal view of the contexts schools provide for children in order to encourage them in participating in an enabling community:

> I conceive of schools and pre-schools as serving a renewed function within our changing societies. This entails building school cultures that operate as mutual communities of learners, involved jointly in solving problems with all contributing to the process of educating one another. Such groups provide not only a locus for instruction, but also a focus for identity and mutual work. Let these schools be a place for the praxis (rather than the proclamation) of cultural mutuality.
>
> *(Bruner, 1996, pp. 81–82)*

In the next section of this chapter we will offer practical examples of children learning that they can contribute to the common good, by drawing on some research projects that we have been involved in, including the work of the 'Building up sustainability from early childhood' project[3] (Folque, 2016; Folque & Oliveira, 2016).

Yes we can!

'The Council Meeting': Children learning to solve problems together

The Modern Education Movement (MEM) pedagogy is a well-disseminated Portuguese pedagogy, developed by teachers from all levels of education. Aiming to contribute to a democratic society, the exercise of cooperation and solidarity in the school community challenges both adults and children to construct themselves as democratic citizens. In their weekly schedule the teacher and the group of children[4] have regular Council Meetings (CMs) where they talk together about their lives, they plan and evaluate their learning and they jointly regulate the life of the group. They have a 'piloting tool' called the Diary, with four columns – 'We didn't like',

'We liked', 'We did' and 'We want' – where children and adults can write during the week (Folque, 2008, 2014; Folque & Siraj-Blatchford, 2011). In the 'We didn't like' and 'We liked' columns the children register individual or group complaints or appraisals of other children's behaviours or attitudes;[5] in the 'We did' column they register (during the end-of-the-day Council Meeting) the most significant activities; and in the 'We want' column they suggest ideas for new activities.

For the purpose of this chapter we will focus on the conversations the children and the teacher had, based on critical negative incidents. When children find difficulty in solving their conflicts they are encouraged to write in the 'We didn't like' column of the Diary and to postpone the discussion about the incident until the 'Friday Council Meeting'. In the meeting and with the support of the Diary, children talk through what has happened, they clarify their behaviour, and with the support of the group and the teacher, they try to find ways to prevent further conflicts.

> The sources of conflict are discreetly identified: what happened, where, and how it happened, what was recorded, without a judgmental atmosphere, but rather carefully seeking to understand the jolts of life, as someone who fraternally shares a cherished transformation project.
>
> *(Niza, 2007, p. 4)*

In these conversations, the children have the opportunity to become aware of, and to discuss, their feelings, motivations, capacities and rights. They also learn to consider different perspectives and to make judgements based not only on the morality of any behaviour but also on the situational conditions from which the problem developed. The main idea is that together they can go through and solve their problems, talking and negotiating ways that will prevent future problems from occurring. Children are supported to progressively regulate their behaviour in relation to the community where they belong. Social rules usually arise from these discussions and are displayed in the classroom. At other times, the children introduce changes in the classroom (e.g. space or materials) that prevent the problem from occurring; children take responsibility for helping each other in remembering some agreed rules; and in several conversations, just having the opportunity to talk to each other and to clarify what happened is enough for the problem to be solved. Through these discussions a regulative discourse and norms are constructed, building up the ethos of the community.

A deep analysis of the interactions (video-recorded) during Council Meetings and the children's interviews (Folque, 2008, 2014) indicates some differences in terms of the children's understanding of the regulative process co-constructed during the CMs and the use of the Diary in two different classrooms. Learning to solve problems, versus seeing who behaves and who misbehaves, were the two different perceptions that children held about the purpose of the Friday CM discussions. Some elements of the teacher's pedagogy were found to be critical for the progression children made in their personal and social development: 1) discussing each incident separately, avoiding judgmental generalisations (e.g. we are not respecting each other); 2) giving time to the children involved so that the event is clarified and the intentions and contextual features are fully understood by the group; 3) inviting the group to comment by clarifying and evaluating the behaviour without judging the person and by thinking about ways to solve the problem (without punishments) with the support of the group; and 4) giving the children involved the power to say whether the problem has been solved or not without the teacher's manipulation or judgment. During these processes the teacher's attitude was critical in holding a neutral, non-judgemental approach towards the children involved, supporting the child whose action was under criticism so that he/she did not feel accused as a person, encouraging a supportive but critical assessment of the event, respecting children's feelings and not imposing a quick resolution of the problem (Folque, 2008; Folque & Mello, 2015). Such factors led to a clear improvement in children's abilities to discuss behaviour without questioning the person's value, and to understand the role of the group as a supportive factor in solving their problems. Collaboration and cooperation episodes between the children increased and the disputes and competing attitudes decreased throughout the year. By contrast, in the classroom where children saw CMs as a place to establish who had behaved and who had not behaved, children showed a less sustained progressive pattern of positive interactions.

Therefore, we stress the need to have 'teachers able to understand the children through a deep understanding of human nature, able to talk with the children about complex problems and to accept the human being, teachers who understand and accept the children difficulties and who also believe in their capacities' (Folque & Mello, 2015, p. 101). When this happened, children spoke like this:

> Mr (5y 10m): And then, when it is meeting day, we ... eee ... the presidents go and get the 'Diary' ... and then, ... We're going to ... to solve everything!
>
> R: How do you solve things, Mr?
>
> Mr (5y 10m): It is like that: we have to find a way so that we will never hit children anymore
>
> ...
>
> R: ... and that meeting what is it called?
>
> Dg (5y 8m): The solving meeting!
>
> *(Folque, 2014)*

In the next example, the teacher asked the children what they do when they face a problem in the classroom

> I (5y): We speak about our problems.
>
> P (4y): We write what we agree and then we sign.
>
> M (5y): We write letters to the Mayor.[6]
>
> *(Melo, 2015)*

Children's engagement in intervention projects

Children's engagement in project work is widely recognised as an important learning strategy both in ECEC and at other levels of education (Delors et al., 1996). In Portugal, as well as in some other countries, there has now been a long tradition of project work (Sylva, Ereky-Stevens, & Aricescu, 2015; Vasconcelos, 2012) and this type of work that children do in preschool is associated with Quality ECE (Ministério Educação, 1998). Projects can be of different kinds: *investigations* in order to answer a question; *production* of some idealised cultural oeuvre (Bruner, 1996) such as a theatre or a wooden play house for the schoolyard, and *intervention* projects directed to solve (or contribute to) an identified problem in the community (classroom, school, local community or wider community), the last being least common in ECEC practice.

In the 'Building up sustainability from early childhood' project in Évora, we devoted particular attention to promoting such an ethos of intervention in the face of problems of a diverse nature: changing the school playground (Melo, 2015); fixing the classroom library; and cultivating vegetables for self-sufficient consumption in the ECE centre (Folque, 2016). All these projects emerged from the children's identification of a problem and they each involved small groups, with the classroom or the school, the adults and the community members (including politicians) working together.

As an example, in the project 'The Street is Mine!', children up to to six years old and their families and teachers organised a rally campaigning for traffic control and city mobility. The gradual removal of children from public spaces has its origin in the increasing concern of adults with children's security. Also, as cars have progressively occupied the public space of the cities, restrictions on pedestrian use have followed, reducing people's enjoyment of the facilities. Despite a considerable awareness of this problem in some countries or cities, in Portugal this is still a problem, which affects children's lives and their participation in public spaces.

The Centro de Atividade Infantil de Évora (CAIE) is a charity ECEC setting located in an old building in the historic city of Évora. With long-standing experience in working with children from birth to six years old, Education for Sustainable Development is at the core of its educational project. CAIE has been part of the ECO-schools project[7] since 2003, and a full partner in 'Building up sustainability from early childhood' project since 2012 (Folque & Oliveira, 2016; Godinho, 2016). One of the main aims of the staff is to promote children's integration into the community by using local resources in the city (gardens, public libraries, communal vegetable gardens, local swimming pools) instead of trying to have their own private resources inside the centre. This conscious practice contributes to the children's participation in the public spaces – social sustainability – as well as to environmental and economic sustainability through sharing resources of the community (OMEP, 2013).

This option implies those from the EY setting going out of the institution frequently, which raises a number of issues related to accessibility, mobility and safety. The narrow streets of Évora do not have sidewalks for pedestrians, and when CAIE children go out they often make comments such as 'Cars should not pass on our street!' The teachers and assistants have to adopt – and involve the children in – very strict security measures in their frequent outings.

During the European Mobility Week, the CAIE's staff encouraged children to develop various actions to promote the improvement of mobility and accessibility, and to explore issues such as pollution and excessive fuel consumption. In reflecting about the conditions for pedestrians inside the historic centre – of which children had extensive personal knowledge – they once again expressed the idea that 'Cars should not pass on our street!' From that, 'The street is mine' action was developed in partnership with the local authorities and the police. It involved the temporary closure to car traffic of the street of the setting, and aroused the interest of the community and the media. Tricycles, bicycles, scooters, walkers and baby strollers filled the street that morning. The children showed up shouting 'The street is mine!' and holding campaign banners. The municipality collaborated, promoting a hip-hop class on the street that managed to capture the attention of passers-by who were sensitive to the problems concerning mobility. The initiative was published on the local newspaper *Diário do Sul*'s first page: 'Children Marked the European Day Without Cars'. In the preschool classrooms, the teachers showed the newspaper to the children and they revisited and commented on what happened. They discussed further the meanings of their own actions and the importance of this initiative, and talked of the potential environmental and social implications for the future. After this event, parents got more involved and motivated to collaborate in solving the CAIE accessibility problems. There was a meeting with the local authority, where various parties made wider 'commitments'! For example, the municipality is considering a change of traffic rules and defining areas where cars have to slow down their speed and give priority to pedestrians. The CAIE parents have started a pool system in order to reduce car traffic in taking their children to school.

Intervention projects are not so common in ECE, perhaps due to the difficulty in adopting what is a relatively recent view of children as citizens (already discussed in this book). Nevertheless, we want to emphasise its relevance in helping children build up a sense of responsibility and also in empowering children in their lives. Through intervention projects children learn that in face of a problem they can do something about it, instead of either feeling helpless or dependent on adults.

Yes – children can contribute to changing some of the problems that affect our daily lives! These are the lessons learned by the children in Évora.

Conclusion

In this chapter, we hope to have contributed mainly to understanding some social and political dimensions of sustainability, debating how to promote young children's dispositions to act for change as they get involved in decision making and problem solving. We started by identifying critical dispositions, which children can develop from a very young age and which will allow them to face problems with confidence and to find ways to solve them in cooperation with others. We saw how young children did this in relation to their everyday, common problems (i.e. conflicts, disputes) in and out of the classroom, and also to more complex problems which they identified in their communities. By doing this we claim that they learned to consider other people's points of view, to recognise material and economic constraints, and to critically appreciate ideas and values in order to find ways to contribute to an enabling society. Most importantly, they learned that '*Yes they can*'. They can face these problems not by themselves but by collaborating with others (peers, teachers, families and members of the community), through dialogue and mutual work.

Questions for you to consider

1. From reading this chapter, what approaches and activities do you think are relevant to your practice? Which ones do you think may be more difficult to take on board?
2. In the face of a problem, do you involve children in thinking and finding ways to solve it? If so, in what kind of problems does this happen? If not, why not?
3. How do you think young children can contribute to the common good of their own community?

Notes

1 This paper is financed with National Funds through Foundation for Science and Technology (FCT), within the scope of the project CIEP-UID/CED/04312/2016.
2 Sakiko Fukuda-Parr is Professor of International Affairs at the New School. She is a development economist who has published widely on a broad range of development policy related issues including poverty, gender, technology, capacity development and agriculture. She is best known for her work as director and lead author of the Human Development Reports 1995–2004 of the United Nations Development Programme (UNDP). http://sakikofukudaparr.net/c-v/
3 The project 'Construir a Sustentabilidade a partir da Infância' is a comprehensive action-research project, which started in 2012 with an invitation to participate in the OMEP International Education for Sustainable Development Rating Scale (OMEP, 2013). The project in Évora has a specific focus in teachers' training and in improving quality Education for Sustainable Development practices in ECE through action-research projects. The partners of this project are as follows: University of Évora, Centro de Atividade Infantil de Évora (CAIE), Centro Infantil Irene Lisboa (CIIL) and Escola Básica Manuel Ferreira Patrício.
4 MEM classrooms have multi-age groups with children from three to six years old. The groups can go up to 25 children. Every year the group has new children as well as children who are already socialised into this organisational structure. The older ones help the new children to assimilate such practices as they come to understand their functions and processes.
5 Usually an adult writes down what the children want to register. Although often children start to independently register by writing the names of the children involved.
6 The children wanted to make some changes in their playground, as it had some problems: no shade, and they hurt themselves when falling on in the ground.
7 Foundation for Environmental Education. Eco-schools programme. http://www.eco-schools.org/

Further reading

Siraj-Blatchford, J., Mogharreban, C., & Park, E. (Eds.) (2016). *International research on education for sustainable development in early childhood*. New York: Springer. doi:10.1007/978-3-319-42208-4

This text collates the outcomes of an OMEP world-wide research project into EfS.

Education for Sustainable Development OMEP web-page: http://worldomep.org/en/education-for-sustainable-development/.

An invaluable source for ongoing research in EFS.

References

Alexander, R. (2004). *Towards dialogic teaching: Rethinking classroom talk*. York, UK: Dialogos.
Apple, M. W., & Beane, J. A. (Eds.) (1995). *Democratic schools*. Alexandria, VA: Association for Supervision and Curriculum Development.
Bronfenbrenner, U. (1979). *The ecology of human development*. Cambridge, MA: Harvard University Press.
Bruner, J. (1996). *The culture of education*. Cambridge, MA: Harvard University Press.
Carr, M. (2001). *Assessment in early childhood settings: Learning stories*. London: Paul Chapman Publishing.
Carr, M., & Claxton, G. (2002). Tracking the development of learning dispositions. *Assessment in Education*, 9(1), 9–37.
Clark, A., & Moss, P. (2005). *Spaces to play: More listening to young children using the Mosaic approach*. London: National Children's Bureau.
Cofield, F. (2002). Skills for the future: I've got a little list. *Assessment in Education*, 9(1), 39–43. doi:10.1080/09695940220119157
Costello, P. J. M. (2000). *Thinking skills and Early Childhood Education*. London: David Fulton Publishers.
Da Ros-Voseles, D., & Fowler-Haughey, S. (2007). Why children's dispositions should matter to all teachers. *Beyond the Journal: Young Children on the Web*. Washington, DC: National Association for the Education of Young Children. Available at: www.naeyc.org/files/yc/file/200709/DaRos-Voseles.pdf
Davis-Seaver, J. (2000). *Critical thinking in young children*. New York: The Edwin Mellen Press.
Davies, I. (1994). Education for citizenship. *Curriculum*, 15(2), 67–76.
Deakin Crick, R. (2005). Citizenship education and the provision of schooling: A systematic review of evidence. *International Journal of Citizenship and Teacher Education*, 1(2), 56–75.
Delors, J., Al Mufti, I., Amagi, I., Carneiro, R., Chung, F., … & Nanzhao, Z. (1996). *Learning: The treasure within*. Paris: UNESCO.
Dewey, J. (1966). *Democracy and education*. New York: Free Press.
Dunn, J. (1998). Young children's understanding of other people: Evidence from observations within the family. In M. Woodhead, D. Faulkner, & K. Littleton (Eds.), *Cultural worlds of early childhood* (pp. 101–116). London: Routledge.
Edwards, A. (2004). Relational agency and disposition in sociocultural accounts of learning to teach. *Educational Review*, 56(2), 147–155.
Esser, F. (2016). Neither "thick" nor "thin": Reconceptualising agency and childhood relationally. In F. Esser, M. S. Baader, T. Betz, & B. Hungerland (Eds.), *Reconceptualising agency and childhood: New perspectives in childhood studies* (pp. 48–60). New York: Routledge.

Fielding, M. (2004). 'New Wave' Student Voice and the Renewal of Civic Society. *London Review of Education*, 2(3), 197–217.

Folque, M. A. (2008). *An investigation of the Movimento da Escola Moderna (MEM) pedagogy and its contribution to learning to learn in Portuguese pre-schools*. PhD Thesis, Institute of Education, University of London.

Folque, M. A. (2014). *O aprender a aprender no Pré-escolar: O modelo pedagógico do Movimento da Escola Moderna* (2nd ed.). Lisboa: Fundação Calouste Gulbenkian.

Folque, M. A. (2016). Construir a sustentabilidade a partir da infância. Poster presented at the conference A Formação de Educador@s e Professor@s na UniverCidade de Évora, Universidade de Évora, 19 February 2016.

Folque, M. A., & Mello, S. (2015). Criar uma comunidade com crianças dos três aos seis anos: O desenvolvimento pessoal e social na infância. In C. dos Anjos (Org.), *Infância e Educação: Olhares sobre contextos e cotidianos* (pp. 89–104). Maceió: Universidade Federal de Alagoas.

Folque, M. A., & Oliveira, V. (2016). Early childhood education for sustainable development in Portugal. In J. Siraj-Blatchford, C. Mogharreban, & E. Park (Eds.), *International research on education for sustainable development in early childhood* (pp. 103–122). New York: Springer. doi:10.1007/978-3-319-42208-4

Folque, M. A., & Siraj-Blatchford, I. (2011). Fostering communities of learning in two Portuguese pre-school classrooms applying the Movimento da Escola Moderna (MEM) pedagogy. *International Journal of Early Childhood*, 43(3), 227–244.

Giroux, H. A. (2001). *Theory and resistance in education: A pedagogy for the opposition*. London: Bergin & Garvey.

Godinho, F. A. (2016). A rua é minha! *Cadernos de Educação de Infância*, 106, 16–19.

Katz, L. (1985). Dispositions in early childhood education. *ERIC/EECE Bulletin*, 18(2), 1–3.

Katz, L. (1993). *Dispositions: Definitions and implications for early childhood practices*. Catalog No. 211. Perspectives from ERIC/EECE: Monograph series no. 4. [Online resource.] Available at: http://ceep.crc.uiuc.edu/eecearchive/books/disposit.html

Katz, L. (2002). Not all dispositions are desirable: Implications for assessment. *Assessment in Education*, 9(1), 53.

Lansdown, G. (2001). *Promoting children's participation in democratic decision-making*. Florence: Innocenti UNICEF.

Linington, V., Excell, L., & Murris, K. (2011). Education for participatory democracy. *Perspectives in Education*, 29(1), 36–45.

Lipman, M. (1991). *Thinking in education*. Cambridge: Cambridge University Press.

Melo, I. (2015). *Aprender a resolver problemas em conjunto*. Paper presented at Seminário internacional Construir a Sustentabilidade a partir da Infância, Universidade de Évora, 11 April 2015.

Mendonça-Silva, A., & Folque, M. A. (2016). *Processo de aprendizagem em grupos heterogeneous*. Paper presented at II Seminário Luso-Brasileiro de Educação de Infância, Braga.

Ministério da Educação (1998). *Qualidade e projeto na educação pré-escolar* [*Quality and project in pre-school education*]. Lisboa: DEB-GEDEPE.

Morin, E. (1999). *Seven complex lessons in education for the future*. Paris: UNESCO.

Moss, P. (2007). Bringing politics into the nursery: Early childhood education as a democratic practice. *European Early Childhood Education Research Journal*, 15(1), 5–20.

Niza, S. (2007). Editorial. *Escola Moderna*, 30(5ª série), 3–4.

OMEP (2013). *OMEP Environmental Rating Scale for Sustainable Development in Early Childhood (ERS-SDEC)*. [Online resource.] Available at: www.worldomep.org/en/esd-scale-for-teachers/

Osterman, K. F. (2000). Students' need for belonging in the school community. *Review of Educational Research*, 70(3), 323–367.

Paley, V. G. (1992). *You can't say you can't play*. Cambridge, MA: Harvard University Press.

Pollard, A., Triggs, P., Broadfoot, P., Osborn, M., & McNess, E. (2000). *What pupils say: Changing policy and practice in primary education*. London & New York: Continuum.

Pramling Samuelsson, I. (2004). How do children tell us about their childhoods? *Early Childhood Research & Practice*, 6(1). [Online resource.] Available at: http://ecrp.uiuc.edu/v6n1/pramling.html

Pramling Samuelsson, I., & Kaga, Y. (Eds.) (2008). The contribution of Early Childhood Education to a sustainable society. Paris: UNESCO.

Ranson, S. (2004). Configuring school and community for learning: The role of governance. *London Review of Education*, 2(1), 3–15. doi:10.1080/1474846042000177447

Ratner, C. (2000). Agency and culture. *Journal of the Theory of Social Behaviour*, 30(4), 413–434.

Rogoff, B. (1998). Cognition as a collaborative process. In D. Kuhn & R. S. Siegler (Eds.), *Handbook of child psychology: Cognition, perception, and language* (Vol. 2, pp. 679–744). New York: John Wiley & Sons.

Rogoff, B., Turkanis, C. G., & Bartlett, L. (2001). *Learning together: Children and adults in a school community*. New York: Oxford University Press.

Siraj-Blatchford, I. (1994). *The Early Years: Laying the foundations for racial equality*. Stoke-on-Trent, UK: Trentham Books.

Siraj-Blatchford, J., Smith, K. C., & Pramling Samuelsson, I. P. (2010). *Education for sustainable development in the early years*. Sweden: OMEP.

Siraj-Blatchford, I., Sylva, K., Muttock, S., Gilden, R., & Bell, D. (2002). *Researching effective pedagogy in the early years* (Research Report No. 356). Norwich, UK: Department for Education and Skills.

Sylva, K., Ereky-Stevens, K., & Aricescu, A. M. (2015). *Overview of European ECEC curricula and curriculum template* (Report D2.1). Oxford: CARE (Curriculum and quality analysis and impact review of European early childhood education and care). [Online resource.] Available at: http://ecec-care.org/fileadmin/careproject/Publications/reports/CARE_WP2_D2_1_European_ECEC_Curricula_and_Curriculum_Template.pdf

UNESCO (2014). *Sustainable development post-2015 begins with education*. Paris: UNESCO.

UNESCO (2015). *Rethinking education: Towards a global common good?*Paris: UNESCO.

United Nations (2015). *Transforming our world: The 2030 agenda for sustainable development*. New York: United Nations Department of Economic and Social Affairs. [Online resource.] Available at: https://sustainabledevelopment.un.org/post2015/transformingourworld

Vasconcelos, T. (Ed.). (2012). *Trabalho por projetos na educação de infância: Mapear aprendizagens, integrar metodologias*. Lisboa: Ministério da Educação, DGIDC.

Watkins, C. (2005). Classrooms as learning communities: A review of research. *London Review of Education*, 3(1), 47–64.

Wilson, V. (2000). Can thinking skills be taught? In V. Wilson (Ed.), *Education forum on teaching thinking skills: Report* (pp. 17–18). Edinburgh: Scottish Council for Research in Education.

Vygotsky, L. (1978). *Mind in society*. Cambridge, MA: Harvard University Press.

7

EDUCATION FOR SUSTAINABILITY IN HUNGARIAN KINDERGARTENS

Anikó Nagy Varga, Balázs Molnár, Sándor Pálfi and Sándor Szerepi

Introduction

Love the tree as it also has feelings,
Touch its leaves with much ease,
Do not crush its branch do not tear its shroud
Leave it as it is – nice and proud –
Do not hurt the tree!

('Love the Tree', Elek Benedek)

The first kindergarten in Hungary was opened on 1 June 1828 in Buda by Teréz Brunszvik. It was the first institution of this kind in Europe and was followed by many in the whole of Hungary. We believe that the Hungarian kindergarten has a long tradition in pedagogical methodology, and its use of children's literature, children's songs, folk music, art, movement/motorial activity and handicrafts has placed it among one of the most successful kindergarten models in Europe. The Hungarian professional pedagogical approach is play-based and child-centred in an unconditional loving atmosphere, the main principles of Hungarian Early Childhood Education and Care (ECEC). Different theories and philosophies from across Europe have influenced it, but the highly important, unique and main pillar of Hungarian ECEC is its folk tradition (Nagy Varga et al., 2015).

We believe that quality early childhood education remains the focus of education strategies in Europe. To become more professional, one must have a higher education qualification. ECEC pedagogues in Hungary need to have a university-level degree and it is a requirement for those undertaking training to become a kindergarten pedagogue to also have skills in music and singing. The mission of their programme is to be more professional in the science of ECEC. Hungarian kindergarten provisions focuses on shaping children's habits through encouraging their free play in accordance with Hungarian approaches. According to the Hungarian approach to the kindergarten, using the phrases 'nursery school' or 'preschool' are not accurate as they do not mirror the local specialities of this field of science, and those who work in a kindergarten are 'kindergarten pedagogues', not 'preschool teachers' (Nagy Varga, 2016).

The impacts of an increasingly globalised world are bringing the future of the coming generation into an unprecedented situation. That is why early childhood education, with its key roles of sensitising, attitude forming and talent development, is vital to preserve important natural values and attitudes. It is also crucial in encouraging and supporting the ability of children to find open and creative solutions in a yet unknown situation.

The Hungarian Core Programme for Kindergarten Education was issued twenty years ago and takes a stand on this question. It says in its newest amendment: 'It is to help the child in the development of his self-contained opinion making and decision making skills in connection with contemporary relationships and shaping the environment and also to put an emphasis on the groundwork and formation of environmental conscious behaviours' (Óvodai Nevelés Országos Alapprogramja, 2012).

Children of kindergarten age have a stimulus hunger that targets every aspect of their environment. Therefore we consider that such characteristics as the digital environment and its tools thriving today have a comparable effect on the children as does the natural environment. Children cannot choose where they live and what objects they are surrounded by, so the responsibility of adults (particularly parents/ educators) is unredeemably significant and unquestionable. Do not forget that the early years period has a strong impact on maturation, which keeps the nervous system excited and alert. The programming of the children's nervous system drives them into contact with their environment, once their need for safety and other primary needs are met. 'Kindergarten education ensures various activities for the child based on his individual interest and curiosity – as an age peculiarity and also on his existent experiences and knowledge; through which the child can attain further experiences about the natural and social environment surrounding him' (Óvodai Nevelés Országos Alapprogramja, 2012, p. 7). That is why the kindergarten's pedagogical thinking and even planning cannot be independent from such experiences and emotions.

The Hungarian kindergarten builds upon this openness of children, helping them to get to know their immediate and then wider environment as the basis for patriotism and bonding with their native land, so that they can admire and appreciate the good and the beautiful found both in the natural and in the human environment. The Core Programme emphasises key notions in this process: bonding, nature and motherland. Children start to interpret the world through their bonding to their mother in their first sensitive years; then, after getting into the kindergarten, other objects and other adults substitute for the mother and home safety since the need for bonding is still really strong in them. Within the Hungarian ECEC context candidates for becoming kindergarten pedagogues must accept a 'mother role' in the creche or kindergarten whilst the parents are away, since the need for bonding and a sense of home safety is still really strong in the children, guaranteeing the stability of their existence. Events missed or skipped cannot be repeated in this procedure and there is an irreplaceable role for the natural environment that welcomes children in the kindergarten day after day. So, children can make bonds not only with people but with nature as well, if it is made available as part of the activities initiated by the kindergarten pedagogues. That is how, unperceived and unintentionally, children begin to bond to their motherland on the basis of their emotional memories and experiences. Actions done by the child are stored among early codes in the personality as positive experiences during the early years. We believe that sustainability, attainment of the balance between man and nature and the protection and maintenance of the environment can be most effectively done not by direct instruction and verbal transmissions of adult knowledge but by forming habits through the activities which are done regularly in connection with the weather and seasons – the forming of the environmentally conscious approach.

In the pedagogical practice of sustainability it is important to have the pedagogical devotion prevail as those who work with the forming of the future environmental citizen have to make their students feel an intensified environmental consciousness. That is when students' personal responsibility and devotion are strengthened and elaborated. The principle 'to think globally but act locally' is too idealistic and not enough in today's environmental protection and environmental education (Havas & Varga, 2009). Nowadays protecting the environment depends on the pedagogues' attitude mainly in the local society. We do think it is time to support any educational provision by the local municipality which emphasises and supports ecological and environmental functions.

The indoor-outdoor natural possibilities of the kindergarten with regards to sustainability

One of the key features of sustainability lies in making the human–nature relationship harmonious – in other words, the restriction and curtailment of 'overuse' of nature. This long process has a first and not omissible step – that is, the more complete recognition of the reality of nature. This recognition can be regarded as coming too late if we only build it into the studies of school-aged children. Even babies meet nature and so collect their first authentic experiences and pieces of information about it, but it is in the informal world of the crèches and kindergarten that children from age 0 to six/seven years old can gain such positive and life-defining experiences about nature, making them more deeply sensitive to protecting and maintaining nature and their immediate environment. In this respect, we believe, there can be a defining role of the early childhood education period in the institutional education of the kindergarten that has a rich range of traditions and possibilities.

Hungarian kindergarten life is rooted in decades of integration of the natural environment. One approach has been the representation of the natural environment in the small world of the kindergarten; namely, setting up an environment that reflects the reality of natural elements (use of natural materials, including an element of the natural plant life). Another approach involves the 'invasion' of the natural environment: observation of nature in itself, in reality. These two aspects can be found in the Hungarian kindergartens, supported by an intense professional and infrastructural helping background, and the approaches are defined in the third chapter of the Core Programme among the tasks of the kindergarten education: 'the formation of habits to the protection and preservation of nature and the foundation of environmental conscience'. Thus, on the ground of environmental protection and environmental conscience, kindergarten education must be realised in a way that all of this is included in a harmonious coexistence, respecting the natural environment as well as the built human environment. Possibilities of representing nature in the kindergarten practice are summarised in Table 7.1.

TABLE 7.1 Nature in the kindergarten practice

According to location	Continual, regular	Occasional
Inside the building; indoors	Care for ornamental plants and flowers	Germination and planting of seeds
	Animals in aquarium and terrarium	Care for seedlings before setting out
	Tools and toys made of natural materials	
	Tables for exploration, including sand, soil, stone, wood, water, etc.	
Outside the building; outdoors	Plants and animals in the courtyard and garden of the kindergarten (primarily birds)	Kitchen garden
		Planting trees, bushes and flowers
	Non-governmental organisations (NGOs) specialising in environment/ nature protection give presentations regularly involving the children (e.g. bird-ringing, selective waste collection, etc.)	Spice garden
		Rock garden
		Garden lake (with plants and animals)
Outside the site of the institution	Regular trips to the same forest, meadow	Exploring walks around the kindergarten
		Occasional trips (forest, botanical garden, national parks, town parks, zoos, safari parks, etc.)
		Visiting families who keep livestock
		Harvesting work in autumn with the children and parents (vintage, potato harvest, etc.)
		Open-air kindergarten (at the end of term, in summer)

Naturally, with the opportunities mentioned in Table 7.1, there may well be major differences between the kindergartens, as all of this depends on the geographical setting of the institution, the financial background, the active role of the kindergarten pedagogues, their intentions for innovation and also the extent of including parents. A small village kindergarten has situations where it carries out the environmental education through practical work in a 'state' of closeness to nature. There has to be a way to do the same in an institution situated in the downtown of the capital.

Supplying and maintaining the aquariums and terrariums in the kindergarten is usually not hard but children can collect really important pieces of information by observing and caring for the animals' lives. The latter process also helps the evolution of respect for wildlife. Seeing the growth of ornamentals and other kinds of plants is just as important because the presence of plants becomes more and more natural for the kindergarten children and hopefully this will become an expected part of their later life. The care for plants, planting seeds and looking after seedlings is an activity historically present in kindergarten life. Participation is offered to all children quite independent of their age, gender and other factors. The product of the activity can be closely observed, and all this explains why it is always a popular activity.

After the plastic-centred 1970s and 1980s of the last century – at the same time as the rebirth of alternative programmes along with the renaissance of alternative initiations – it was following the change of regime and democratic change (1990) that the use of tools and toys made of natural materials began again. Today most kindergartens try to make and develop their physical environment according to this principle – of course restricted by their financial possibilities.

Activities outside the kindergarten that are close to nature often include walks when children visit nearby parks or forests with the pedagogues. Over and above the simple observation of natural phenomena (such as the change of seasons through observation and collection of tree leaves) we can organise trips with a theme (e.g. the blooming of water lilies on the botanical lake) that might well be a starting point for project work.

The open-air kindergarten movement

A special Hungarian way of relating children to nature is the 'institution' of the open-air kindergarten. In 2015, more than 100 qualified open-air kindergartens and schools throughout Hungary welcomed children who wanted to explore nature more deeply in summer. Open-air kindergartens are a great opportunity to have activities planned and realised in a natural environment, demonstrating the relation of humans and nature to the children in an authentic way. As an example, here is a list of goals of the Játékvár Óvoda, a kindergarten in Budapest's urban 6th District:

- Immediate experience in a village setting
- An understanding of environmental protection
- Helping the process of independence of children

The goals, as we can see, cover three areas: direct (meaning mainly the sensory) experience, independence in children's activities and the basic issue of environmental protection. This downtown kindergarten is a classic example of an institution which is far from the natural environment and so is trying to organise its open-air kindergarten to get children closer to the world of the village and forests. However open-air kindergartens are popular not only among the kindergartens of the capital and towns but also among some families in the country whose children, socialised in a digital-virtual world, can also become separated from natural reality.

In the past decades there has been the initiation and then development of a movement of 'Green Kindergartens' that try to help develop the natural and environmental consciousness of the kindergartens that join the movement.

As Könczey et al. (2014) note, in 2006 the departments for environmental protection and education were made responsible and by 2014 the number of Green Kindergartens had reached 700 nationally. Kindergartens with the title of "Green Kindergarten" automatically become a member of the Network of Hungarian Green Kindergartens. The Network is supported by professional journals and publications and a network homepage (www.zoldovoda.hu), and for the development of the Network seven basic institutions were set up in 2009 that have a high priority in helping non-Green Kindergartens join the network successfully (Könczey et al., 2014). Being a Green Kindergarten means not only organising activities close to nature and raising environmental awareness but also indicates a 'green thinking' – namely, a positive attitude to nature that is realised daily in the life of the kindergarten.

The concept of the Green Kindergarten, on the whole, is able to unite the elements of environmental and natural education mentioned above. The cited methodological material (Könczey et al., 2014, p. 9) contains examples of good practice for the to-be Green Kindergartens that have been successful in the past years; the following examples include some elements discussed above:

- The role of folk customs in education for sustainability.
- The 'perceptivity cave' as a place for environmental education. 'The child navigates the world around him through his emotions. With this in mind we have a perceptivity cave where he can use more of his senses and can see the objects collected in one place that he has seen in his immediate surroundings; in the courtyard of the Kindergarten, during walks and trips or experiences in a Green Kindergarten. Firstly he meets the crops, seeds, leaves, other parts of plant and insects etc. in nature. Later he can recall the experiences and information about them in the cave' (Könczey et al., 2014, p. 43).
- Making the kindergarten garden and the role of work in the garden.
- Activities onsite (walks in terrains, making fire and the project of fruit picking).
- 'Birdman' kindergarten programme: 'Spontaneous and directed observation: letting the beauty of natural values be seen, for example: old, rugged alders, their branches, leaves and nests, nesting birds. When bird-ringing they get to know the name, gender of the caught bird; its feathers' form, shape and size,

also naming its body parts. We use magnifiers and binoculars' (Könczey et al., 2014, p. 54).

- Kindergarten study tours, Green Kindergartens and trips.
- Family field trips.
- Celebration of world days of wetlands, water and Earth.

The practice of recycling in the kindergarten

Hungary was basically regarded as an agrarian country until the Soviet-patterned industrialisation programme of the 1950s. Society was largely made up of people with low socio-economic status, who represented traditional values and lived off agriculture (peasant, shepherds, day-labourers, etc.). For them, not only economising but the recycling made necessary by economising was part of their everyday lives. Thus forms of recycling have deep roots in Hungarian society. However, this kind of recycling was from constraint and not inspired by sustainability, a deliberate action.

Recycling serving social and political purposes appeared – not counting the war periods – during the era of the communist age. In 1950, the Company for Utilisation of By-products and Waste (MÉH) was established that primarily collected paper and metal waste (for the story of MÉH before the change of regime, see Lászlófi, 1988). This collected waste became an important basic commodity for the fast-improving Hungarian industrial corporations. The collectors of waste did not only receive money but they could feel that they were part of a higher call – this is well-put in a propaganda rhyme of the 1950s: 'Collect iron and metal – that's how you serve the peace of all.' From the 1960s Hungarian schools organised paper and iron waste collecting competitions (the collected material was bought by the MÉH) that continue even today at the Hungarian schools.

The idea of recycling for sustainability started to spread in both the Hungarian common talk and professional discourses after the democratic change from communism to civilian democracy, linking the previous practice of recycling for economising to the idea of sustainability from 1991 onwards and giving it a modern frame of reference.

We can see the two categories linking more and more organically in the pedagogical professional literature, but as we have seen, sustainability and recycling are not inseparable concepts. Recycling has a longer history and this can be seen in everyday practice: in everyday life we can meet pedagogical activities aiming at recycling that do not tie to sustainability. In these cases, the goal of recycling is more about personal or institutional economising, teaching economising to save money, doing craft work, developing creativity, preserving traditions, making an income and so on. However, independent of the goals, these activities include recycling serving sustainability, although not intentionally.

In Hungarian kindergarten pedagogy, the techniques of recycling are part of everyday life and are organically part of the pedagogical practice. This has three pedagogical reasons:

1.   Hungarian kindergartens have long-standing traditions of making toys and of the active use of ready tools and toys (for a classic example from professional literature for toy-making in kindergarten, see Kardos & Nagy, 1985). Often it is the kindergarten pedagogue who makes toys, puppets, costumes for role play, and so on for the group, but it is also very common for children to make gifts for parents and decorate tools together. It is not surprising then to see that in some cases children make toys on their own or the parents make something at home that they offer to the kindergarten group. Of course, during such creating it happens a lot that the new tool or toy is made of recycled materials (such as a puppet made of a sock or old shirt, a small robot made of a milk carton, a rocket or car made of a PET bottle). As Hungarian kindergartens often use equipment from everyday life in play activities, old and out-of-use equipment can get a new life as part of role play: the old wooden spoon gets to the play kitchen or the old computer keyboard is great to 'imitate mummy or daddy' in the kindergarten.

2.   The Core Programme of Hungarian kindergartens puts special emphasis on free play with a substantive element saying that any object can become another object, natural phenomenon or living creature (Óvodai Nevelés Országos Alapprogramja, 2012). Early free play containing such transformations pre-pares children really well to have them see newer and newer possibilities in objects and materials, using them again and again in different situations and adding different functions to them. All of this – through age and devel-opmentally appropriate situations – tunes them intellectually and emotionally to the thinking and practical realisation of recycling.

3.   The third feature that makes recycling natural in the Hungarian kindergarten practice is that kindergartens are activity-centred. In kindergartens there is no such thing as teaching or training in a school sense, but pedagogues try to have children learn through activities. This stimulation and encouragement helps children think positively about the alteration and recycling of present objects and materials, and also to carry out their ideas.

In educational recycling, easy formability and aspects of safety play important roles, so it is mainly materials and tools made of appropriate materials that can be part of the above-mentioned activities. Therefore, in the process of recycling the most common material is paper. Paper is easily formable by cutting, tearing, folding, gluing and colouring, and it is accessible in great amounts as waste, too. Big cardboard boxes offer many possibilities (a doll's bed made from a shoe box, a stove or washing machine made from bigger boxes, or vehicles, space shuttles, houses and fortresses made of even bigger boxes), as do cardboard tubes (binoculars, a small car or toy figures made of toilet roll centres or aluminium foil tubes) and newspapers (e.g. new and various objects can be made by cutting pictures, folding, mounting and millboard making). All these activities are especially popular.

Other popular and often recycled materials are textiles. Textile waste can be found in every household and can be variously recycled, even at the kindergarten stage. An old piece of clothing and parts of textiles can be directly used in role play, but dyeing or cutting can make them useable for children as well. Pieces of textile can be cut into strips (e.g. turning a tablecloth into macramé carpet) and old pieces of thread and yarn can be recycled, usually by tying and gluing because it is a disadvantage when there is sewing involved in recycling. Sewing requires a parent's or a kindergarten pedagogue's help and so takes away some of the child's own agency.

We sometimes find a deliberate avoidance of artificial or synthetic materials in the kindergarten (for example, in Waldorf pedagogy), but most local kindergarten programmes do not differentiate natural and synthetic materials, so plastic equipment and materials are everyday objects in most kindergartens. In recycling in kindergarten, the most popular objects are PET bottles and caps, plastic boxes (yogurt cartons), disposable plastic cups, all altered by cutting, gluing, decorating and filling to make various things, from flower pots to ninepins and figures.

As there is strong respect for 19th century peasant traditions and an intention to preserve them, recycling of natural materials and organic waste is really regular in the kindergartens. There is a great tradition of making toys and objects from cornhusk: dolls, angels, baskets. We can also find creative ways of recycling branches, rods, leaves, flower petals, harvests and pebbles, as in creations of land art, playing in the courtyard or making figures from harvest. These all help children in Hungarian kindergartens to see the potential of recycling and ways to creatively use not only manufactured objects but also elements of nature that seem to be 'redundant'. Ready-made objects made with processed organic materials (like corks and wooden tools) are often subject to recycling – a wooden spoon becomes a puppet or corks and chestnuts are used to make necklaces and nutshells make different animals or instruments.

Recycling of metal (like wires) and glass waste (bottles or perfume decanters can make story figures) are also present in kindergarten life but they are restricted due to their more difficult shaping and because they carry more dangers for children's use. We also see recycling of fluid or melted materials in the kindergartens (e.g. new candles made of old ones, new soap from soap pieces, paint or dye strained from plants), but these are not frequently part of the everyday practice – on the one hand, these processes require greater attention from the kindergarten pedagogue, and on the other hand, further possibilities of creative use are less known (for further ideas about materials for recycling in the kindergarten, see Kanczler, 2003).

On the basis of the foregoing we can state that in early childhood education almost all kinds of waste can be recycled except for dangerous waste. A new function can be given to an object (e.g. an old wooden spoon becomes a toy spoon in the play kitchen) or the given object or material can be altered (e.g. making figures from pine cones). The new object can be made completely from recycled elements (e.g. button football team from bottle caps) or can be expanded with non-recycled elements (e.g. the house made of cardboard paper is glued with colourful paper that we have bought).

Recycling of any kind of material is originally an integral part of Hungarian ECEC. It originally derived from the approach that 'any left over and unused goods can be good for something useful' in a kindergarten. This is part of the thrift and economy approach of the society. From this point of view, paper from offices, leftover textiles from factories, any size of box from a shop and so on can be valuable and suitable for making equipment in the kindergarten. There is a deliberate approach behind it – pedagogues and kindergarten pedagogue candidates are very creative in deciding what to do with leftover treasures that will not ever be used in their original manner. This is part of sustainability education in the Hungarian context.

However, we need to pay attention to not relaying the 'culture of poverty' through recycling and economising lest the children should feel that they need to insist on keeping objects and materials as they have so little. This fear can easily lead to them not sharing their resources with anyone and not giving selflessly as they do not have much themselves. Instead, as adults we have to emphasise the protection of our planet and mutual solidarity in the process of environmentally conscious recycling.

Solutions and methods deriving from the Hungarian traditions in the framework of kindergarten education

As part of the activities of kindergarten life, pedagogues ensure rich opportunities for children to experience the world around them. Their task is to guarantee a wide range of opportunities for children so that they gain experience and knowledge in an active way. They offer the place, time, occasions and tools needed for children to benefit fully from the experiences. Above all this, the Core Programme identifies the tasks of kindergarten pedagogues by saying that they have to 'put an emphasis on the foundation and formation of environmental conscience for the sake of sustainability' (Óvodai Nevelés Országos Alapprogramja, 2012, p. 17).

This document declares that the development of the child is served best by the family and kindergarten education working together, assuming a close cooperation between the kindergarten and the family. Cooperation can be realised in various ways, and its opportunities can be carried out adjusted to the local facilities in the family and the kindergarten. Cooperation between civil organisations and institutions of the local environment has become closer as well, as the organisation of experiences is increasingly done by the kindergarten outside the institution itself. We think these public organisations must have a significant role in the life of the society. At present, there is no separate measure, making it hard to do this form of activity in Hungary. Kindergartens show children different traditions connected to the local environment, local environmental specialities, traditional clothing culture and specialities appearing in the treasures of folk music, dances and songs and different harvest festivities. Kindergarten pedagogues believe that with these customs and celebrations, life becomes more interesting and colourful for children.

The Core Programme regards the family as a high priority, where children must have the same quality of upbringing no matter what kind of family background they come from. Kindergarten education regards cooperation with the family as a basic condition. The kindergarten has to take the features and traditions of the family into consideration in their cooperation. From the age of three until the child reaches school age, kindergarten is an extension to the family upbringing (Magyar Kormány, 2011, p. 8).

It needs rethinking how folk tradition and sustainability may meet and be preserved in the modern Hungarian context. Traditionally, it was the basic and most ancient task of the grandparents and parents to pass on previously gained experiences to the next generation, thereby guaranteeing their continued existence. Such transmission includes a lot of things – above all, the folk traditions and folk-lore that are embedded organically from ancient times in the Hungarian society and that still define our present-day patterns of work and lifestyle. In the history of the Hungarian kindergarten pedagogy, folk traditions are more or less part of everyday life in kindergartens. Although folk traditions have been overshadowed at times in our socio-political history, they are now an important part of our kindergarten education (Nagy Varga et al., 2015). The folk feasts, folk dances, folk musical instruments and folk costumes are now integral elements of everyday life in the kindergartens.

We believe that the child's everyday life spent within institutional boundaries should reflect the life of the family, with its atmosphere and family patterns. These can be assured with groups of mixed ages and by undertaking activities that are done together at home, or used to be done together in the past. For instance, canning is useful and also great work for the family, as all members take part and children learn the division of roles, the joy of work done together and the satisfaction of shared labour.

Kindergarten life that follows the cycle of nature organically includes the production and processing of goods found in nature. Each term of kindergarten can be an active process of becoming acquainted with the outer world and the progression of the treasures of nature. The term starting in September is about autumn harvests, preparation for the winter and processing of crops that have really rich potential. Hungarian kindergartens have numerous ways of presenting the world to the children by using their local opportunities and the special country atmosphere. Meanwhile, children do get direct experiences of their immediate environment. Amongst other activities we can list the grape vintage in autumn, potato harvest, corn harvest, fruit picking and other harvest pickings. These harvested goods provide colourful possibilities for processing by the children in the kindergarten.

The education programmes of the Hungarian kindergartens draw another valuable aspect from the Hungarian traditions – namely, the home preservation of food. In Hungarian society, and here we mean not only in the country, the conservation of purchased or harvested goods (e.g. canning and drying of fruits, pickling of vege-tables, making pasta) is more than a hobby – it is an important part of Hungarian households and of the national identity. Besides its many other functions, a main task of the family is the transmission of traditions and customs. Sharing recipes and implementing the tradition of canning into the lifestyle is the task of the grandparents' and parents' generations, who by conserving the goods and storing them for the winter period also conserve the accumulated traditional knowledge and so prepare and train the next generation for future profitable work. Foods made this way keep their content of vitamins and, as opposed to the food industry with its artificial additives, we know what they contain. They also have a health-preserving function as whatever we make is free of preservatives. There is a greater need for foods preserved by traditional methods. The food made together is consumed together by the children according to their own taste and needs.

Other activities done together with children model the family farm along with its traditional nature and support sustainability; these are part of the educational and pedagogical methods of the kindergartens in terms of sustainability. Nutrition is vital for personal and community welfare. The task of the kindergarten is to provide the time and regular routine for collective cooking by adults and children. In terms of sustainability, canning and preservation offers the following excellent opportunities:

- Conservation of fruits
- Drying fruits
- Making jam
- Pickling of vegetables
- Making fruit and vegetable drinks
- Making syrup
- Collective cooking and baking with children (raw salads, making sweets, baking bread, etc.)
- Making of traditional and local specialities

Parent and family involvement and their active participation in the kindergarten can create new and innovative ways of collaboration, as opposed to the time when the parent was seen as a passive and outside observer of the happenings in the kindergarten, and it makes possible more complete provision for the welfare of the children. It is worth thinking about the organised and regular ways of parents' involvement so that the life competencies of the parents can serve as a pattern for the children to follow. Beside the former formal cooperation frameworks, there are innovative occasions for meetings that strengthen the parent community, as opposed to the older passive parental participation where the parent was an inactive and outside observer of the activities in the institution. With this progress, there has been a spectacular movement towards cooperation with underprivileged families living in poverty and towards setting up new types of connection: family afternoons, family clubs, creative activities, cooking together with the families, and so on. The new and innovative way of keeping in contact with families, which is outlined in the basic programme, is present in kindergartens precisely because of Romani and other disadvantaged families. This new type of parental presence strengthens early education.

These occasions also provide great opportunities for parents to share traditions that exist in every family. Therefore, kindergartens use all the opportunities to visit family farms, where children can get acquainted with the natural environment offered by the farm. Kindergarten pedagogues also invite parents and grandparents to show them specialties that can be cooked in the courtyard of the kindergarten, on open-air stoves, in a cauldron or in an oven. In this way, parents and grandparents can be an active part of the everyday lives of their children and grandchildren. On these occasions, families get to share carefully treasured family traditions of recipes with other families.

When we discuss sustainability, we must not forget the fact that the preservation of food and recycling not only serves sustainability but it also provides great help for families who have low income and live in poverty by ensuring food for the winter period. The government's National Reform Programme (NRF) discusses social exclusion and poverty, and says that the deterioration of the standard of living affects children the most, other than people living in disadvantaged regions and the Romas (Albert, 2014). We believe that kindergartens have a significant role in helping parents who do not use canning or preservation in their everyday practice to relearn and gain experience in home preservation as it can be more efficient and economical for them, too. Involving parents is greatly significant for families living in poverty, as kindergarten pedagogues help uneducated and poor parents in their parental role with professional knowledge. In this way they can incorporate parts of the household economy model and increase the use of their environment in a natural way.

Conclusion

Hungarian kindergarten provision focuses on shaping children's habits in relation to the protection of the environment by providing a foundation for the development of environmentally aware behaviour. The National Hungarian Core Programme prescribes expectations for all Hungarian kindergartens to contribute to forming attitudes and skills for sustainable development for future generations. Included in the Core Programme is a separate chapter on the importance of activities that shape children's active exploration of the outside environment, so that they may gain experience of the natural and social environments surrounding them. The main goals are to strengthen the environmental consciousness of children and to improve their eco-friendly educational activities. Kindergarten pedagogues develop the child's needs for sustainable development through creating environmentally aware education, but in accordance with Hungarian approaches and principles. The growing and preserving of fruits, the use of folk traditions and making toys out of recycled objects whilst collaborating with families are all areas where these principles in the Hungarian context can be illustrated.

Questions for you to consider

1.   Do you use intergenerational learning in your setting to make use of local traditions and activities? Might you do more?

2. Do you think there may be a danger in the Hungarian approach in being backward-looking rather than responding to contemporary sustainability issues?

Further reading

For further information about the Hungarian context, the following resources are useful:

Nagy Varga, A., Molnár, B., Pálfi, S., & Szerepi, S. (2015). Hungarian perspectives on early years workforce development from the beginning till today. In V. Campbell-Barr & J. Georgeson (Eds.), *International perspectives on workforce development in early childhood education and care: History, philosophy and politics* (pp. 109–121). St. Albans, UK: Critical Publishing.
Hungarian Institute for Educational Research and Development (2012). Early childhood education and care: Specificities of the Hungarian system. [Online resource.] Available at: http://ec.europa.eu/dgs/education_culture/repository/education/policy/strategic-fram ework/doc/hungarian-ecec-specificities_en.pdf. Accessed 22 May 2017.

References

Albert, F. (2014). *Beruházás a gyerekekbe – a hátrányos helyzet továbbörökítésének megszakítása. A nemzeti szakpolitikák vizsgálata Magyarország.* Luxembourg: CEPS Instead. [Online resource.] Available at: http://ec.europa.eu/social/BlobServlet?docId=11650&langId=hu. Accessed 28 November 2016.
Havas, P., & Varga, A. (2009). A környezeti neveléstől a fenntarthatóság pedagógiai gya-korlata felé. Budapest: Hungarian Institute for Educational Research and Development. [Online resource.] Available at: http://ofi.hu/havas-peter-varga-attila-kornyezeti-neveles tol-fenntarthatosag-pedagogiai-gyakorlata-fele. Accessed 28 November 2016.
Kanczler, G. (2003). *Hulladékgazdálkodásról óvodapedagógusoknak.* Budapest: KVVM ELTE TÓFK.
Kardos, M., & Nagy, M. (1985). *Játékkészítés és kézmüvesség óvodásokkal.* Kecskemét: Szórakaténusz.
Könczey, R., Kovács, E., Kovács, L., & Varga, A. (2014). *Zöld Óvoda leszünk! Módszertani segédanyag és útmutató.* Budapest: OKI.
Lászlófi, P. (1988). *A Kelet-magyarországi MÉH Nyersanyaghasznosító Vállalat története, 1951–1987.* Debrecen: Kelet Mo. MÉH Nyersanyaghasznosító Vállalat.
Magyar Kormány (2011). Köznevelési törvény CXC. 2011: Törvény a nemzeti köznevelésről [Public Law CXC 2011: On Public Education]. [Online resource.] Available at: https://net.jogtar.hu/jr/gen/hjegy_doc.cgi?docid=A1100190.TV.
Nagy Varga, A. (2016). Aspects of ECEC in Hungary: A Hungarian–English wordlist for students. In R. Jukic (Ed.), *Global and local perspectives of pedagogy conference proceeding book* (pp. 179–190). Osijek: Faculty of Humanities and Social Sciences.
Nagy Varga, A., Molnár, B., Pálfi, S., & Szerepi, S. (2015). Hungarian perspectives on early years workforce development from the beginning till today. In V. Campbell-Barr & J. Georgeson (Eds.), *International perspectives on workforce development in early childhood education and care: History, philosophy and politics* (pp. 109–121). St. Albans, UK: Critical Publishing.
Óvodai Nevelés Országos Alapprogramja (2012). Kormányrendelet (363/2012 XII.07.) [The Hungarian National Core Programme for Kindergarten Education]. Budapest: Ministry of Human Resources.

8

COMPLEXITIES IN IMPLEMENTING EARLY CHILDHOOD EDUCATION FOR SUSTAINABILITY IN A MAJORITY WORLD CONTEXT

Valerie Huggins

Introduction

With the United Nations' introduction of the Sustainable Development Goals (SDGs) in 2015 (UN, 2017) has come a welcome and very necessary emphasis on Early Childhood Education (ECE) in the Majority World. ECE is well established in most Minority World countries – in the UK over 90 per cent of all children have at least a year of ECE before formal schooling starts at five. However, the provision in many Majority World countries is still minimal. On average, only 20 per cent of children in Africa are enrolled in pre-primary education (AAI, 2015). This is despite the evidence that such investment in the Early Years can bring a multitude of social and economic benefits: less dropout from primary school; higher motivation to learn; earlier identification of special educational needs and disabilities (SEND); the freeing of parents to work; a reduction in child labour; less child marriage; and a growing perception in society (OECD, 2016) that children in education are not a burden but an investment leading to later economic benefits (Nega & Merry, 2012). Moreover, research by Woldehanna (2016) in Ethiopia reports that although only a quarter of children have so far attended preschool, tests of maths and receptive vocabulary demonstrate statistically positive effects of this upon their early learning. It would seem from this that the arguments for a very considerable expansion of ECE in the Majority World are incontrovertible (OECD, 2015; UNICEF, 2014).

In many low-income Majority World countries such an expansion of ECE provision is possible because of a rapid improvement in terms of both wealth and infrastructure. For example, although Ethiopia remains one of the poorest African countries, with a per capita income of $590 that is substantially lower than the regional average, it has experienced strong growth over the past decade, averaging 10.8 per cent per year (World Bank, 2017). This has helped to support its government's introduction of ECE in 2011, based largely upon the presumption that this will in itself make a long-term contribution to economic growth. The hope is that ECE will have a considerable positive impact upon children's education, on their health and lifestyles and upon the national economy. However, there are proving to be a number of factors which complicate or even inhibit its introduction, and if one factors in the suggestion that they need to take advantage of this opportunity to embed Education for Sustainability (EfS) into ECE at this early stage of its development, one encounters a further range of constraints.

Contextual factors which may inhibit Early Childhood Education for Sustainability (ECEfS)

One major inhibiting factor has derived from the earlier successful implementation of the Millennium Development Goal (MDG) to bring a higher percentage of the world's children into formal schooling. A very large proportion of the population in many Sub-Saharan Africa (SSA) countries are of school age, and ±90 per cent are now in elementary schools (UN, 2015). But this increase has had the knock-on effect that very many more children are now progressing through the education system into secondary schools and beyond (UNESCO, 2016). Thus they are absorbing an increasing proportion of available funding and of qualified teachers, leaving little scope for the provision of ECE.

This has not deterred some African countries from trying to expand their previous patterns of preschool provision, which catered for only for a small minority of children, and to aim for universal ECE. There is often a limited and uncoordinated mix of private and public providers of ECE which include parenting programmes, community-led childcare and formal pre-primary settings linked to schools (Awopegba et al., 2013). Many of these are not available to children in more rural areas. For example, in Ethiopia the 2015 Fifth Education Sector Development Programme (or ESDP V) sets ambitious targets for early learning in Ethiopia through the introduction of O-grade classes for children aged four to six years of age within all government primary schools (Woodhead et al., 2017). The aim is to increase enrolment from 35 per cent in 2015 to 80 per cent in 2020. But the earlier successful widening of access to primary education has meant that the 2011 government requirement for O-grade provision has in most cases not been able to be accompanied by additional resourcing for the schools. There is also a realisation that although more children are now in primary school, as many as 40 per cent in Eastern and Southern Africa (SSA) do not reach the expected levels in literacy and numeracy (Friedman et al., 2016), a finding which confirms that increased enrolment does not in itself improve quality.

Another factor is that there is an acute shortage of trained ECE teachers (Tigistu, 2013). Woodhead et al. (2017) note that the proposed level of expansion in Ethiopia will require the training of 100,000 extra teachers in colleges and universities, who themselves currently have very few teacher educators with ECE expertise due to the focus on the expansion of the elementary sector. If ECE is to achieve the anticipated results it will not be enough to place 50 four- to six-year-olds in an unresourced room with an inexperienced and/or untrained adult.

A further complication is that in many SSA countries there is an ongoing debate about the purposes and aims of ECE, with tensions emerging over potential contradictions in the Western-based approaches embedded in many privately run settings and the desire for 'African-centred' approaches that emphasise indigenous social-cultural values and norms (Serpell & Nsamenang, 2014). In many countries such as Ethiopia there is also powerful parental pressure that the priorities for ECE should be earlier formal teaching of literacy and numeracy, in English, as 'readiness' for subsequent schooling. If one is to add to this an expectation that ECE will also make a significant contribution to EfS, it is difficult to envisage how the schooling systems of low-resource, low-income countries can cope with such demands.

Such countries will require considerable amounts of support. Previously, Sub-Saharan African countries lacking expertise for introducing major educational initiatives have usually looked to the Minority World agencies for direct support in terms of curriculum organisation, the training of teachers and the provision of resources, often through international non-governmental organisations (INGOs) such as UNICEF and Save the Children. However, the limitations and dangers of this are being increasingly recognised. One is that educational advisers from Minority World backgrounds may be unaware of (or ignore) the nuances of the local context and so offer inappropriate advice; the needs and interests of many children in Sub-Saharan Africa, for example, are unlikely to be the same as children in the UK or USA. Another danger is that such support encourages the perpetuation of long-term dependency and a passive reliance upon Minority World expertise and resources (Huggins et al., 2015). In order to be sustainable and relevant in the long term, the new provision needs to draw on and be shaped by the resources and ideas of people in the local communities involved as well as being informed by Minority World inputs. As Ball (2010) suggests, any approach to Early Years provision should include the following:

> [T]raditional and modern, indigenous and transcultural approaches to create new preschool practices that are fitting to the particular children, parents and schools in a particular community.
>
> *(cited in Penn, 2010, p. 4)*

But both the Ethiopian schooling system itself and the expectations of families and local communities do not currently take into account fully what ECEfS may require.

At the end of the Decade of Sustainable Development UNESCO (2012) urged that from preschool to university education globally must be rethought and re-formed to be a vehicle of the knowledge, thought patterns and values needed to build a sustainable world. As Warwick et al. argue in Chapter 3 of this text, an imposition of a narrow model of education in the Early Years, such as one focused upon compliance in terms of a national curriculum, assessment and testing, as in the UK, may leave little room for the critical thinking required by EfS. To improve the quality of schooling in ESA, Friedman et al. (2016) recommend providing rich playful environments involving early literacy and numeracy skills development. However, such an overwhelming focus on literacy and numeracy when children only have a few hours in the classroom raises questions of how to incorporate a wider EfS curriculum, as well as how to make use of the children's wider learning in the community. The UNESCO (2012) report argued that interactive, integrative and critical forms of learning are needed but also that routines need reorienting. It suggested that such changes are possible within the remit of ECEfS:

> [E]ducation and learning are part of the iterative dynamic of social change: in order to change society we need to change the way we learn and educate and in order to change the way we learn and educate, we need to change society.
> *(UNESCO, 2012, p. 12)*

But such change can be a huge challenge in many low-income countries with very limited resources, few qualified ECE staff and few appropriate models of quality provision to draw upon.

Indigenous Early Childhood Care and Education (IECCE) and EfS

One powerful driver for change within the expansion of ECE in African contexts is the debate about the notion of Indigenous Education. This recognises that most of the established discourses in ECE literature and research are deeply rooted in Western/Minority World ideas (Dahlberg et al., 2007) and so may not be culturally relevant elsewhere. Advocates for indigenous education argue that schooling systems should be substantially based in the social and cultural context of the Majority World country in which they operate. In support of this, Awopegba et al. (2013, 2016) illustrate and discuss an IECCE Curriculum Framework that recognises the importance of making ECE relevant to the needs of indigenous children by putting in place:

> ... culturally acceptable best-practices that are available in the cultural background of the child ... pay attention to cultural processes that are underlying the differences in patterns of behaviour of indigenous and non-indigenous children ... developmental programmes and services should be contextually relevant to the African child.
> *(Awopegba et al., 2013, p. 10)*

But there is a danger in an uncritical acceptance of the idea that quality educational provision should be largely or entirely determined and shaped by local beliefs, traditions and cultural processes, since this might well devalue or even ignore the well-established findings from Minority World and global research such as the role of Play, the developmental and educational needs of young children and the patterns of provision which effectively meet such needs. This would suggest that these findings should be well represented in the planning and implementation for Majority World ECE, but that all Minority World definitions, ideas and approaches should be critically assessed within the local context and adapted where necessary before being adopted as part of ECE provision.

A further consideration about the IECCE agenda is that as yet it places limited emphasis upon EfS. For instance, the IECCE Curriculum Framework (Awopegba et al., 2013) clearly has the potential to reflect and support the cultural and social aspects of sustainability, especially through its valuing and preserving of diversity (Bollier, 2017). However, the document contains only one direct mention of sustainability, referring to resources in Senegal, and only one use of 'sustainable', in a quote from the Director General of UNESCO emphasising that young children in Sub-Saharan Africa must not have to wait to enjoy ECE, which she characterised as a 'force for human dignity with lifelong benefits' and 'a powerful motor for the sustainable development of societies over the longer term' (Awopegba et al., 2013, p. 7). Moreover, the document makes no specific mention of the EfS movement. Arguably, IECCE needs to take greater account of the arguments for EfS as a central aspect of ECE. For instance, the Gothenburg Guidance (SWEDESD, 2008, p. 3) recommends building upon the everyday experience of children in accordance with these broad strands to embed EfS:

- Curriculum integration and creativity
- Intergenerational problem solving
- Promotion of intercultural understanding and recognition of interdependency
- Involvement of the wider community
- Active citizenship in the Early Years
- The creation of cultures for sustainability

To translate these broad ideas of EfS into specific objectives and activities directly related to the local context, a starting point could be community-based participatory research exploring local knowledges and identifying local concerns, needs and ambitions for young children in a community, all informed by the wider, research-based perspectives upon learning and development. This would enable the identification of relevant aspects of Indigenous Education to support teachers' practice, such as the following:

- Use of mother tongue. For example, Rwanda's Competence-Based Curriculum (REB, 2015) gives priority to the national language Kimyarwanda over English in the Early Years.
- Use of locally sourced materials.
- Culturally relevant topics and starters for learning.
- Dual language posters and learning aids, with culturally appropriate pictures and vocabulary.
- Integration of health education, such as WASH (water, sanitation and hygiene), into daily routines (UNICEF, 2017).

- Celebration and appreciation of care for the environment and the sparing use of finite resources.
- Projects emerging from local contexts that consider the sustainability of familiar systems, such as collecting water and firewood.

More controversially, this might lead to the systematic envisioning with families and the community of alternative futures, potentially leading to realistic changes in patterns of everyday actions, and even to a critique of global trends such as consumerism. One of the key tensions, though, is that many parents are seeking an education for their children that will give them access to a Minority World consumerist lifestyle. They may dismiss the arguments for aspects of an indigenous education, such as learning in mother tongue, in favour of a narrowly focused curriculum based on Minority World models and taught in English. But advocates of IECCE, and indeed of EfS, must avoid the equally narrow assertion of the preeminence of traditional patterns of education and of local knowledge. Negotiating in order to arrive at an acceptable balance must be the way forward. But Majority World countries do have a small advantage, in that most do not have a history of EfS, and so have the space to move forward in a fresh, integrated, holistic way, if given political support. The SDG agenda does provide powerful encouragement for this educational ambition.

What might ECEfS look like in a Majority World context?

Advocates of IECCE suggest that ECEfS in Majority World contexts will differ from Minority World patterns as the result of finding answers to three broad questions:

- How can ECEfS be delivered within the local constraints, and how may the resulting teaching and learning shape young people's responses to sustainability issues?
- What are the important messages and areas of content in the local context, and how may the resulting emphases differ from Minority World approaches?
- Can ECEfS and IECCE approaches be integrated to match the ambitions and expectations of families and the local community?

We have already noted how ECE in Ethiopia has been constrained and inhibited by inadequate resourcing. The common situation of 50+ children meeting with a single adult with minimal ECE experience (and possibly with no teaching qualifications) hugely restricts what can be taught and learned. Even more significantly for ECEfS may be restrictions upon how it is taught, since the patterns of schooling children experience will influence their values, attitudes and behaviour, and so, as UNESCO (2010) argues, will shape their subsequent choices and actions contributing to the promotion or inhibition of a sustainable future. For instance, in much of the writing and research about ECEfS (e.g. Davis, 2015; Davis & Elliott,

2014; Siraj-Blatchford & Huggins, 2015), there is a powerful emphasis upon young children becoming active, confident and independent decision-makers. If we acknowledge that children can learn to be active agents in their own lives (as we are encouraged to do by Ärlemalm-Hagsér and Pramling Samuelsson in Chapter 2 of this text) and that they have the right to be heard in matters that are affecting them, as stated in the United Nations Convention on the Rights of the Child (UNICEF, n.d.), we have to take into account the contexts in which this may be helped to happen, or may be inhibited and repressed.

As an exemplar, my extensive observations in Ethiopian O-grade and primary classrooms indicate that the schooling approach there has historically been authoritarian and didactic, especially where girls are concerned. Children are given very few opportunities to ask questions or to express opinions or ideas (except in response to direct and often closed teacher questions). They rarely work on projects in small groups or engage in self-organised and self-directed play activities, and this inhibits their willingness and ability to respond individually and independently. They certainly have no say in what they are being taught or in negotiating how best they might learn (Westbrook et al., 2013). This pattern largely continues throughout the schooling system, with the result that many intelligent young people arrive in Ethiopian degree courses unwilling if not unable to question, challenge, or even to contribute to discussions. It is arguable that changing this may be a necessity in fostering sustainability, and as with many 'remedial' approaches the earlier this begins, the better.

Yet viewed in the wider social and cultural context, the reality is less simple. Most children in Ethiopia, and in many Majority World contexts, get far more opportunities than do many Minority World children to be independent outside school, in their local community. I have observed that much of their play and social activity takes place outside the home and away from adult organisation and supervision. From a young age, many children take responsibility for chores, childcare and animal care, earn money for the family, independently get to and from school and the markets, and in the process strengthen their ability to take responsibility and to take decisions. By contrast, it can be argued that very many Minority World children are overcontrolled and overprotected by parents and by society (Huggins & Wickett, 2017), even though they may have more freedom within schools and classrooms. Thus it may be that Majority World ECEfS needs to draw upon and harness these qualities and experiences in order for children to become comfortable in using them in educational, social and political contexts. This strongly suggests that EfS cannot be a narrow matter of classroom input but must be a wider process of interaction with families and communities based upon shared understandings and goals, once again emphasising the role of discussion and negotiation.

A further source of difference will be that some of the major areas of concern and action for ECEfS in the Minority World may currently have lesser relevance for Majority World countries. An example is that of sustainable lifestyles. A significant element in Minority World EfS, as Sterling and Orr (2001) have argued, is teaching children about the dangers of overconsumption, of consumerism and of advertising-driven demand shaping their health and their developing sense of personal worth and social acceptability. Until recently in a Majority World country like Ethiopia this has been much less important, as very many families have not had access to sufficient disposable income to buy much more than the basic staples of life such as food and housing, and limited access to medical care and education. A far greater concern in Majority World countries has been to address poverty and prevent further environmental devastation, driven by an understandable sense of being victims of global changes, outsiders to the benefits that increasing wealth has brought to the Minority World, yet suffering disproportionately in terms of climate change, food shortages and environmental pollution. These issues should still be a central aspect of Majority World ECEfS. However, with the economic growth described earlier, and with rapidly increasing ownership of TVs and mobile phones, education about advertising-driven consumerism is gaining importance.

A similar pattern can be seen in relation to the rapidly growing concerns in the Minority World about the levels of unfitness and obesity of the population, involving increasing numbers of children. For example, in the UK the recent research of Elliott (2015) suggests that the lack of exercise resulting from the overuse of TV and elec-tronic devices, as well as parental restrictions of unsupervised activities outside the home, may be leading to children in the UK becoming amongst the most unfit in the world, with rapidly increasing concern about the impact of this upon their immediate schooling and their long-term health. Thus there is a growing pressure upon ECE settings to work with both children and families/societies to alert them to this danger. But by contrast, very young children in Majority World countries such as Ethiopia have had little or no access to such electronic devices as yet and are physically very active; as long as they have sufficient nutritious food and access to clean water, they are frequently fit and healthy. This might suggest that Majority World ECEfS has little need to be concerned with these issues, but again, the situation, especially in many private, urban preschools, is beginning to mirror that of the Minority World.

Similarly, until recently there has been little need to promote the 7 Rs of Sus-tainability (Siraj-Blatchford & Huggins, 2015) in many Minority World commu-nities. In Ethiopia, for instance, recycling, repair and reuse have of necessity been central to the way of life, just as described by Varga et al. in their earlier chapter on Hungarian kindergartens. Most children have not expected to play with shop-bought toys; instead, they have played traditional games like Mancala, using peb-bles in a pattern of hollows scooped out in the dust, have constructed hoops and wheeled toys from discarded wire, have made footballs from plastic bags stuffed with rags and tied with string, all providing much in terms of experience of pro-blem-solving, innovation and creativity (Gupta, 2001). In classrooms in Ethiopia, Ghana and The Gambia I have observed teachers becoming increasingly creative in providing teaching resources from recycled materials – for example, using bottle tops from local bars for counting, sorting and pattern-making, sacking for posters, sticks for mark-making and small locally made blackboards and chalk to save paper. Most Majority World countries and communities are minimal contributors to the current international concerns about ocean pollution from the discarding of plastic bottles and containers; in Ethiopia these are usually carefully saved, used and reused for a variety of purposes. In terms of sustainability, the use of low-cost, locally resourced materials is hugely powerful, rather than hoping for donations from the Minority World to buy expensive equipment that may be culturally inappropriate, may not be replaceable and so sometimes may be considered as too precious to use.

From the 'external' perspectives of the EfS movement, and of the Minority World threatened with a potential requirement to reduce global consumption and so to restrict affluent lifestyles, these patterns may be seen as positive developments. It is tempting for the Minority Word to promote EfS as a way of persuading the Majority World to hold back from developments such as industrial processes that were the basis of Minority World prosperity (and arguably of the global crises of climate change, pollution and environmental damage). There is therefore a danger that EfS in the Minority World becomes an inward-looking debate concerned largely with defence against threats to an existing way of life, characterised by telling people what to do based on Western experiences and attempting to prevent legitimate development in order to preserve their own lifestyles. It must be appreciated that these families and communities gradually working their way towards affluence may not see the reuse and recycling, the limited, if healthy diet, the improvised playthings, the avoidance of consumerisms, as positives, but as the result of disadvantage and poverty, and that they may aspire to have the consumerist lifestyle that the Minority World increasingly now sees as a significant part of the sustainability problem. The ambitions of very many parents are for their children to have access to ECE so they can have a more affluent, comfortable lifestyle than previous generations, gaining a professional qualification to open up career opportunities, not necessarily to become a well-rounded global citizen (Huggins & Siraj-Blatchford, 2015) or to support sustainability.

It is important to recognise their ambitions and their sense of entitlement as valid whilst looking to counter and to minimise the potential negative consequences of ignoring EfS. This is becoming an urgent matter. The economies of many Majority World countries are growing quickly, putting affluent lifestyles within reach of an increasing number of people. Last year, in a small regional town in Ethiopia, I saw a good number of young Ethiopian women wearing current Western fashions and hairstyles, rather than traditional dress, young men buying locally made copies of the latest Arsenal, Chelsea and Manchester United football shirts, and the establishment of toy shops! Much of this has been made possible by the enormous spread of the internet and mobile phone technology which has made young people increasingly aware of, and covetous of, the lifestyles of Minority World affluence. And, for the first time, I encountered several obese Ethiopian children. This trend is not going to diminish or disappear.

The SDGs and the consequent considerable expansion of ECE have therefore made it more urgent for decisions about appropriate patterns of EfS in Majority World countries. Many Ministries of Education are compiling ECE curricula and establishing teacher education programmes for Early Years teachers, but so far there are few signs of sustainability being embedded from the outset. For instance, in Rwanda, the Competence-Based Curriculum for pre-primary to secondary (REB, 2015) has a 'Curriculum for Sustainable Development' logo on the cover, and close reading reveals some references to aspects of EfS. However, the pre-primary guidance is very limited; it merely states that by the end of pre-primary the children should be able to show awareness and respect for the environment and interact peacefully with others. Arguably, educators need to work hard to incorporate more substantial aspects of ECEfS into such new curriculum approaches; but given the different Majority World contexts, and so differing priorities, it must be reiterated that importing wholesale Minority World approaches offers no solution. As UNESCO (2010) points out, its current knowledge base does not have the answers but this in no way justifies a wholesale rejection of EfS because it is defined as a wholesale Minority World product. It is not. But I would argue that it is potentially from the Majority World itself that many solutions will emerge, and thus it is only through dialogue and collaboration that we may learn to improve all our lives.

This would suggest that a two-pronged approach would be beneficial. One is that from within the schooling system itself those responsible for young children, in both the Minority and Majority Worlds, need to engage in wider analysis of what constitutes ECEfS, as advocated by Huggins and Evans in their Introduction. This will demand some significant changes in their approaches to classroom teaching and learning, as well as identifying, strengthening and supporting those aspects of their existing practice which are important in developing in children the beliefs, attitudes, values and dispositions which will prepare them to contribute towards and to shape sustainable development in their communities and their countries. Yet the traditional and conservative culture within schools does not easily support any such changes in emphasis. Even now, Ethiopian students coming into the profession find it hard to express opinions in the Teacher Training Colleges, as their schooling has not encouraged them to do so (Tigistu, 2013). Yet these students and teachers are the role models we need children to look to for learning about sustainability. As Dyment et al. (2014) argue, based upon their experiences in Australia, professional development on EfS is necessary to ensure that it is valued, understood and implemented in ECE; this may be even more the case in African countries.

The second approach must acknowledge that successful and meaningful ECEfS needs to be rooted in the everyday lives of families and communities, yet I have identified in this chapter several ways in which parents and local communities may not currently share in the sustainability agenda. In many Majority World contexts (and indeed in many Minority World communities), local traditions and ways of passing knowledge on to future generations about how to live sustainably and within the resources of the local environment are in danger of being marginalised by the cultural impositions of Western ways of thinking and neoliberal values. It is therefore vital for poorer communities to be enabled to engage in the debates, not as victims, but as informed participants in the necessary future developments. Here, too, schools and teachers have important parts to play. One is indirect. In the Minority World there is evidence that including approaches to sustainability in ECE curriculum and practice does result in many children influencing their own families towards sustainable approaches (Davis, 2015). Another is that schools can directly communicate and explain to parents and the wider community their approaches and the reasons behind them, with the intention of securing a consensus about an appropriate curriculum and pedagogy for sustainability. This role is currently problematic in Ethiopia, where there remains a powerful belief that schooling is the teachers' business, and structures for consulting and involving parents are minimal, not least because of the demands of the usually very large classes. But without creating a consensus, what schools and teachers can achieve is likely to be limited.

Education in emergencies

In the Minority World, such major educational decisions (in the broadest sense of education) are usually part of a stable political and social process. In the Majority World they are more often impacted upon and distorted by sudden and unexpected situations, such as civil unrest in Nigeria, the 2010 earthquake in Haiti and the current drought in East Africa. These potentially compromise and so undermine the educational plans of some low-income countries to expand their ECE in response towards the SDGs, which in turn impacts upon any pattern of ECEfS.

Currently, agencies such as UNICEF (2006) and Save the Children (2015) are actively promoting Education in Emergencies (EiE), working to standards set by the INEE (2010). A fundamental aspect is the continuing provision of basic literacy and numeracy teaching, which will give the children skills for life and aid their employability. More immediate is the establishment of school as a refuge and a place of stability, offering a predictable routine in a life that may be chaotic due to war or to living in a refugee camp, or due to the consequences of drought, flood or famine having severely disrupted their homes, communities and way of life, and led to uncertain economic/financial support. Furthermore, it is recognised that the schoolteacher may be in a position to offer young people psychosocial support – for instance, by giving children opportunities to share their experiences through storytelling, drawing and small-group discussion in order to help them make sense of what is happening in their lives. But such provision requires that these schools become more child-friendly. In countries where schooling tends to be very formal and didactic this can once again be difficult, as it shifts the power relationship and changes the role of the teacher, a change which some adults may consider a challenge to their authority. But if the school is more child-friendly, the children will be likely to have stronger motivation to come to school, even when under pressure in home and community.

EiE reinforces the argument of ECEfS that any related curriculum must be shaped by the realities of the local context. For instance, such a curriculum may very well include, especially with older children, teaching about Disaster Risk Reduction (DRR), since drought and famine emergencies are likely to reoccur and children can be taught strategies of what to do in such situations. It may also include information about climate change, sustainable lifestyles, ways to prevent or minimise such disasters in the longer term and, particularly in areas that are affected by conflict, how to keep oneself safe in times of change. But, perhaps most

significantly, it does allow for the possibility of considering what customs (religious/
social) it may be permissible in an emergency not to comply with – for example,
clothes, religious observations, overriding the conservatism of families and
communities, as has so often been the case in the past.

All this constitutes a powerful short-term response to crisis. Yet longer-term it
throws up serious issues about the roles and responsibilities of teachers, schools and
schooling systems in the Majority World. Might such aspects need to be considered
a regular part of the curriculum in such areas as Eritrea, Somalia or South Sudan?
Might there need to be a greater emphasis in such regions upon child-friendly
classrooms and schools? What the EiE initiatives throw up in relation to EfS is the
possibility that in order to educate for sustainability schools may need to move
away from the current narrow brief to deliver an academic curriculum and simply
to achieve certain 'standards', with teachers as skilled 'technicians' with limited
responsibilities. Instead they may look towards being sites of dialogue, giving voice
to children, providing places of safety and encouragement, with adults learning
alongside the children about coping in their changing world, and giving the children
a pedagogy of hope for the future, where they feel they have some control, as
advocated by Warwick et al. in Chapter 3 of this text.

Conclusion

In this chapter, I have discussed the place and status of ECEfS in the Majority
World, drawing substantially upon my experience in Ethiopia. I argue that as
provision for ECE, driven by the SDGs, is currently in its infancy in many areas of
the Majority World such as Sub-Saharan Africa, now should be the time to consider how EfS can be embedded in ECE from the outset and to define what it might
look like in practice, since EfS is widely acknowledged to be a key indicator of quality
educational provision.

I suggest that some of the approaches of Indigenous Education should shape
provision, balanced by acknowledgement of more widely held beliefs about young
children's learning, but that there also needs to be explicit teaching about sustainability
issues, recognising the role of schools and teachers in encouraging positive dispositions, both in the children they teach and in families and the local community.
We need to be more conscious of the understandable resistance of many in the
Majority World to Minority World attempts to restrict or prevent their enjoyment
of the benefits of increasing affluence in the name of sustainability, whilst seeking
to protect against the repetition of the huge past mistakes made by people in the
Minority World.

I would also argue that such efforts cannot be left until later in the children's
schooling. If EfS is embedded from the outset in the Early Years, there is a better
chance that those children's beliefs, values and attitudes, and so their subsequent
behaviours and actions, can be influenced when they are very young. In thirty to
forty years' time, many will be the teachers, the health professionals, the scientists,
the entrepreneurs, leading and shaping changes in the Majority World, which by

that time may well have become economically and politically powerful in the world. To influence them, today's teachers need to be helped to become increasingly critical thinkers, innovators, challengers of taken-for-granted patterns of schooling and enablers of new ways of thinking in the children they teach. Given that currently the overwhelming majority of such teachers are women, often working in cultures that devalue and depower their abilities and their contribution, this is likely to be an even more uphill struggle, and it may need considerable support from Minority World governments and agencies to bring about change.

But we have seen that such support can itself be fraught with dangers of self-interest, of colonialist perspectives, of intercultural insensitivity, of arrogant presumptions about the superiority of the Minority World approaches and more. I would therefore suggest five 'lessons' that those supporting the establishment of ECEfS in Majority World contexts might like to take to heart in guiding their involvement.

First, and most obvious, there can be no one simple ECEfS model, fix-it-all pattern and curriculum, and so any such patterns that have been previously constructed in relation to Minority World contexts, needs and perceptions will at the very least need to be adapted in a Majority World situation. Second, we need to be constantly alert to the dangers of promoting a 'colonialist' agenda when working in Majority World contexts, and any appropriate and effective Minority World contribution to local Majority World EfS needs to have been planned, agreed and constructed in close consultation with the local community, which has previously been encouraged/enabled/supported in putting forwards a clear and powerful statement of its own needs/wishes. This is an enormous and daunting agenda, impossible to achieve in totality, but it is important to embark upon it to set the parameters and the responsibilities of EfS. Once this pattern of local direction has been established, Minority World expertise can make a very valuable contribution.

Third, in setting up such consultation, serious consideration must be given to ensure a level playing field and an appropriate power balance in the structure of the negotiations by taking the following steps:

- Ensuring in advance that all interested parties have been identified and invited to be involved and appropriately represented.
- Organising balanced representation – for example, not a single token women nor a lack of parent representatives nor an overweighting with politicians and businesspeople.
- Appointing a chairperson with authority and reasonable independence.
- Considering aspects of local languages, including translation arrangements where appropriate, in order to make it possible for all parties to have a full understanding of the debate, and to make a full contribution to the process.

Following on from this, for any proposed scheme of ECEfS the nature and level of its resourcing, including the administration of regional and national government financial support and of any local contributions, should be established and agreed in advance of implementing the scheme.

Fourth, it is clear that the development of ECEfS will be impossible without very considerable expansion and enhancement of teacher training. The Sustainability agenda and the EiE projects both require that the teacher's role and expertise has to expand well beyond its current definitions and levels. Nevertheless, such expansion will have to counter entrenched conservatism in both education theory and practice. It will also face difficulties in any country, such as Ethiopia, which currently has no government provision and resourcing for schooling four- to six-year-olds or which has only introduced such provisions very recently, because of a lack of ECE expertise. Here too there can be an important role for Minority World input, provided that once again, it is organised in full consultation with local stakeholders, within the context of local priorities, and delivered by experts with humility and sensitivity, based upon their intercultural capabilities, to enable them to match their inputs to local needs.

Finally, all concerned at local, national and regional levels will need to work towards a consensus of what schooling can offer to the promotion of sustainable lifestyles and to the development of 'global citizens'. This will necessitate ways of engaging on the nature of 'a good life', about what this might involve in practice and so about how we might best prepare children to achieve it (Siraj-Blatchford & Huggins, 2015). This will require ECEfS to lift its vision above the sometimes cosy, self-justifying satisfaction with the worthwhileness of its current provision, and not only to confront the immediate negative aspects of individualism, consumerism and globalisation, but also to consider how best to prepare its young children to deal positively with whatever the future will throw at them, from how best to create social structures to support growing numbers of centenarians to confronting apocalyptic scenarios such as climate change, natural disaster and limited nuclear warfare. Any serious consideration of EfS, even in the very Early Years, now forces upon us as professionals the requirement to take a future perspective upon our practice and our responsibilities.

Questions for you to consider

1. What unfamiliar ideas in this chapter have impacted upon your thinking about ECEfS? Why?
2. If you were involved in developing ECEfS in a particular community, how would you find out what the beliefs and aspirations for this were amongst the parents and other key stakeholders?
3. How far would you feel justified in attempting to influence or change these beliefs and aspirations?

Further reading

The Young Lives project offers invaluable data from their longitudinal research projects on children's lives in four Majority World countries. They produce a range of useful reports, which includes the following:

Woodhead, M., Rossiter, J., Dawes, A., & Pankhurst, A. (2017). *Scaling-up early learning in Ethiopia: Exploring the potential of O-class* (Working Paper 163). London: Young Lives. [Online resource.] Available at: www.younglives.org.uk/sites/www.younglives.org.uk/files/YL-WP163-Woodhead%20(2).pdf. Accessed 10 January 2017.

Trudell, B. (2016). *The impact of language policy and practice on children's learning: Evidence from Eastern and Southern Africa.* Nairobi: UNICEF. [Online resource.] Available at: www.unicef.org/esaro/UNICEF(2016)LanguageandLearning-FullReport(SingleView).pdf

This review of the impact of language policy and practices on children's learning in 21 countries in Eastern and Southern Africa adds to the debate about what constitutes 'quality' early childhood education. It also highlights the tensions between using mother tongue and/or an international language as the language of instruction.

References

AAI (2015). *State of Education in Africa Report 2015.* New York: The Africa-America Institute. Available at: www.aaionline.org/wp-content/uploads/2015/09/AAI-SOE-report-2015-final.pdf. Accessed 23 March 2017.

Awopegba, P. O., Oduolowu, E. A., & Nsamenang, A. B. (2013). *Indigenous Early Childhood Care and Education (IECCE) Curriculum Framework for Africa: A focus on context and content.* Addis Ababa: UNESCO. [Online resource.] Available at: www.iicba.unesco.org/sites/default/files/Fundamentals%20of%20Teacher%20Education%20Development%20No6.pdf. Accessed 24 February 2017.

Awopegba, P. O., Oduolowu, E. A., & Nsamenang, A. B. (2016). Fundamentals of teacher education development: (No. 6). Indigenous Early Childhood Care and Education (IECCE) Curriculum Framework for Africa: A focus on context and contents (Policy Brief). Addis Ababa: UNESCO. [Online resource.] Available at: www.iicba.unesco.org/sites/default/files/sites/default/files/Policy%20B.Funda.%206.pdf. Accessed 24 February 2017.

Ball, J. (2010). Afterword. In A. Cleghorn & L. Prochner (Eds.), *Shades of globalization in three early childhood settings: Views from India, South Africa and Canada.* Rotterdam: Sense.

Bollier, D. (2017). *Think like a commoner: A short introduction to the life of the commons.* Gabriola Island, BC: New Society Publishers.

Dahlberg, G., Moss, P., & Pence, A. (2007). *Beyond quality in early childhood education and care: Languages of evaluation* (2nd ed.). Abingdon: Routledge.

Davis, J. (Ed.) (2015). *Young children and the environment: Early education for sustainability* (2nd ed.). Port Melbourne: Cambridge University Press.

Davis, J., & Elliott, S. (Eds.) (2014). *Research in early childhood education for sustainability.* Abingdon: Routledge.

Dyment, J. E., Davis, J. M., Nailon, D., Emery, S., Getenet, S., McCrea, N., & Hill, A. (2014). The impact of professional development on early childhood educators' confidence, understanding and knowledge of education for sustainability. *Environmental Education Research, 20*(5), 660–679.

Elliott, S. (2015). Children in the natural world. In J. M. Davis (Ed.), *Young children and the environment: Early education for sustainability* (2nd ed., pp. 32–54). Melbourne: Cambridge University Press.

Friedman, T., Schwantner, U., Spink, J., Tabata, N., & Waters, C. (2016). *Improving quality education and children's learning outcomes and effective practices in the Eastern and Southern Africa Region: Report for UNICEF ESARO.* Camberwell, VIC: ACER Press. Available at: www.unicef.org/esaro/ACER_Full_Report_Single_page_view.pdf. Accessed 21 April 2017.

Gupta, A. (2001). Children's toys from Africa exhibition. Paris: UNESCO. [Online resource.] Available at: www.arvindguptatoys.com/arvindgupta/africantoys.pdf. Accessed 27 March 2017.

Huggins, V., & Siraj-Blatchford, J. (2015, Summer). Education for sustainable development through international partnerships. *Early Education*, 76, 9–11.

Huggins, V., Tadesse, T., & Tadesse, T. (2015). Supporting the expansion of pre-primary education in Ethiopia: A collaboration between an Ethiopian and a UK Higher Education institution. In B. Cozza & P. Blessinger (Eds.), *University partnerships for community and school development* (pp. 61–79). Bingley, UK: Emerald.

Huggins, V., & Wickett, K. (2017). Very young children learning outdoors: Its place in the schooling system. In S. Waite (Ed.), *Children learning outside the classroom* (pp. 69–81). London: SAGE.

INEE (2010). *INEE minimum standards for education: Preparedness, response, recovery – A commitment to access, quality and accountability.* New York: INEE. [Online resource.] Available at: www.ineesite.org/en/minimum-standards. Accessed 04 March 2017.

Nega, A., & Merry, E. (Eds.) (2012). *Ethiopia Policy Brief 2: Why public investment in pre-school education is needed to boost cognitive and school outcomes for the poorest children.* Oxford: Young Lives.

OECD (2015). *Starting strong IV: Monitoring quality in early childhood education and care.* Paris: OECD Publishing. doi:10.1787/9789264233515-en. Accessed 27 March 2017.

OECD (2016, May). *What are the benefits from early childhood education?* Paris: OECD Publishing. [Online resource.] Available at: www.oecd-ilibrary.org/docserver/download/5jlwqvr76dbq-en.pdf?expires=1490620589&id=id&accname=guest&checksum=0FF8F51F9D3E238E5DCFB3322AE80904. Accessed 27 March 2017.

Penn, H. (2010). Development and learning. In L. Brooker & M. Woodhead (Eds.), *Culture and learning.* Milton Keynes: Open University.

REB (2015). *Competence-based curriculum: Summary of curriculum framework pre-primary to upper secondary 2015.* Kigali: Republic of Rwanda Ministry of Education. [Online resource.] Available at: www.tcop.rw/file/2041/download?token=T398Bm6a. Accessed 18 February 2017.

Save the Children (2015, August). *Education in emergencies: A showcase of Save the Children's work over the last decade to provide education in emergencies.* Fairfield, CT: Save the Children. [Online resource.] Available at: https://savethechildreninternational.exposure.co/education-in-emergencies. Accessed 04 March 2017.

Serpell, R., & Nsamenang, A. B. (2014). *Locally relevant and quality ECCE programmes: Implications of research on indigenous African child development and socialization.* Paris: UNESCO. [Online resource.] Available at: http://unesdoc.unesco.org/images/0022/002265/226564e.pdf. Accessed 14 March 2017.

Siraj-Blatchford, J., & Huggins, V. (2015, Summer). Sustainable development in early childhood education and care. *Early Education Journal*, 76, 3–5.

Sterling, S., & Orr, D. (2001). *Sustainable education: Re-visioning learning and change.* Dartington, UK: Green Books.

SWEDESD (2008). *The Gothenburg recommendations on education for sustainable development.* Gothenburg: SWEDESD. [Online resource.] Available at: www.desd.org/Gothenburgl%20Recommendations.pdf. Accessed 24 February 2017.

Tigistu, K. (2013). Professionalism in early childhood education and care in Ethiopia: What are we talking about? *Childhood Education*, 89(3), 152–158.

UN (2015). *The Millennium Development Goals Report 2015.* New York: United Nations. [Online resource.] Available at: www.un.org/millenniumgoals/2015_MDG_Report/pdf/MDG%202015%20rev%20(July%201).pdf. Accessed 27 March 2017.

UN (2017). *Sustainable Development Goals.* New York: United Nations. [Online resource.] Available at: www.un.org/sustainabledevelopment/sustainable-development-goals/#pretty Photo[gallery4884]/0/. Accessed 18 February 2017.

UNESCO (2010). *Early Childhood Care and Education Regional Report: Africa.* Dakar: Regional Bureau for Education in Africa. [Online resource.] Available at: http://unesdoc.unesco.org/images/0018/001894/189420e.pdf. Accessed 21 April 2017.

UNESCO (2012). *Shaping the Education of Tomorrow: 2012 Report on the UN Decade of Education for Sustainable Development, abridged.* Paris: UNESCO. [Online resource.] Available at: http://unesdoc.unesco.org/images/0021/002166/216606e.pdf. Accessed 24 February 2017.

UNESCO (2016). *Global Education Monitoring Report 2016. Education for people and planet: Creating sustainable futures for all.* Paris: UNESCO. [Online resource.] Available at: http://unesdoc.unesco.org/images/0024/002457/245752e.pdf. Accessed 04 March 2017.

UNICEF (2006). *Education in emergencies: A resource tool kit.* New York: UNICEF. [Online resource.] Available at: www.unicef.org/rosa/Rosa-Education_in_Emergencies_ToolKit.pdf. Accessed 04 March 2017.

UNICEF (2014). *Building better brains: New frontiers in early childhood development.* New York: UNICEF. Available at: www.unicef.cn/en/uploadfile/2015/0319/20150319103627793.pdf. Accessed 24 March 2017.

UNICEF (2017). *Water, sanitation and hygiene.* New York: UNICEF. [Online resource.] Available at: www.unicef.org/wash/. Accessed 27 March 2017.

UNICEF (n.d.). *Convention on the Rights of the Child.* New York: UNICEF. [Online resource.] Available at: www.unicef.org/crc/. Accessed 7 January 2017.

Westbrook, J., Durrani, N., Brown, R., Orr, D., Pryor, J., Boddy, J., & Salvi, F. (2013). *Pedagogy, curriculum, teaching practices and teacher education in developing countries.* London: Department for International Development. [Online resource.] Available at: www.gov.uk/government/uploads/system/uploads/attachment_data/file/305154/Pedagogy-curriculum-teaching-practices-education.pdf. Accessed 21 April 2017.

Woldehanna, T. (2016). Inequality, preschool education and cognitive development in Ethiopia. *International Journal of Behavioral Development,* 40(6), 509–516.

Woodhead, M., Rossiter, J., Dawes, A., & Pankhurst, A. (2017). *Scaling-up early learning in Ethiopia: Exploring the potential of O-class* (Working Paper 163). London: Young Lives. [Online resource.] Available at: www.younglives.org.uk/sites/www.younglives.org.uk/files/YL-WP163-Woodhead%20(2).pdf. Accessed 10 January 2017.

World Bank (2017). *Ethiopia Economic Overview.* Addis Ababa: World Bank. [Online resource.] Available at: www.worldbank.org/en/country/ethiopia. Accessed 27 March 2017.

9

THE CONTRIBUTION OF FOREST SCHOOL TO EARLY CHILDHOOD EDUCATION FOR SUSTAINABILITY

Sara Knight and Paulette Luff

(WITH PARTICIPANTS IN THE FOREST SCHOOL AND EDUCATION FOR SUSTAINABILITY WORKSHOPS RUN AT THE FOREST SCHOOL ASSOCIATION CONFERENCE, 2014, IN DANBURY, ESSEX)

Introduction

Forest School is a familiar and popular feature of early years education in the UK and, increasingly, in other developed countries. By contrast, across a wide spectrum of early childhood care and education in England there is still a limited awareness or knowledge of Sustainability. As Forest School is well-accepted within the sector, we would argue that it is very promising as a means of promoting and developing aspects of Early Childhood Education and Care for Sustainability (ECECfS). Forest School is important as an initiative to promote awareness of natural, woodland environments and to instil the 'sense of wonder' advocated by nature writer and pioneering environmentalist Rachel Carson (1965) and so can make a particular contribution to the environmental dimensions of ECECfS. But it is more than this. The aims, principles and pedagogy of Forest School are also aligned with the wider values and approaches of ECECfS and so are full of potential both as a means of fostering understandings of sustainability amongst early years educators and young children and as a powerful example of embodying sustainability in the practice of ECEC.

To this end, the first part of this chapter will offer an appraisal of the role of Forest School in fostering ECECfS. The focus for this will be a comparison between the aims and pedagogy of Forest School and those of ECECfS. The second part of the chapter is based upon findings from two workshops on Forest School and Education for Sustainability run at the Forest School Association Conference 2014 in Danbury, Essex, at which the participants (Forest School trainers, trainees or practitioners running Forest School sessions for young children) discussed the '7Rs of Sustainability: reduce, reuse, repair, recycle, respect, reflect and responsibility' as proposed by Pramling Samuelsson and Kaga (2010, p. 59). During the dialogues that took place in the workshops, Forest School actions and activities for ECECfS were identified. These are described and discussed to exemplify each of these 7Rs in practice.

Forest School and Early Childhood Education for Sustainability: aims and principles

Forest School can make a positive contribution to ECECfS through its impact upon the children and adults who participate in Forest School and through its wider influence in the early years sector. Participating in Forest School sessions often fosters a love of and respect for the wooded environment in which it takes place for both children and adults. A possible limitation of such Forest School provision is that for obvious reasons both adults and children may perceive it, consciously or unconsciously, as a 'special', separate environment with its own rules, procedure and behaviours, and so its powerful educational messages may easily be dismissed or ignored outside its boundary fence. The existence of matches between Forest School and Education for Sustainability does not mean that Forest School will necessarily influence the latter; we would wish to argue strongly that it can and should. Circumstantial evidence from visits to settings and discussions with Forest School leaders indicates that, as well as creating an affinity with a particular place, many Forest School experiences also raise awareness of issues relating to environmental sustainability. From observations of settings which participate in Forest School sessions and then go on to increase the amount of recycling and gardening that takes place in the setting as a whole, it would appear that Forest School sessions also have an influence on non-participating members of staff and children in raising environmental awareness. Certainly parents report exhortations from children to increase their engagement with the natural world (Knight, 2013a/2009).

As explained in the Introduction to this book, the overall aim of ECECfS is to enable the youngest citizens to make decisions, solve problems and learn to act in ways that improve quality of life without compromising the resources of Planet Earth. Environmental concerns are important, as are broader values of democracy, equity, social justice, peace and ethical responsibilities in local and global contexts. The principles of ECECfS are presented in different ways by various authors and organisations, using several different frameworks. We have taken ideas and inspirations from Davis et al. (2008), Siraj-Blatchford et al. (2010) and Davis (2015). The aims and principles of Forest School in the UK are published on the Forest School Association website (FSA, 2011). There are many parallels that can be drawn between the two sets of principles but we would like to highlight three common concerns for ECECfS and Forest School: children's agency; communication and cooperation; and concern for equity. For example, all participants are viewed as 'equal, unique and valuable' and 'entitled to develop positive relationships with themselves and other people' as well as strong relationships with 'their natural world' (FSA, 2011).

In the first place, ECECfS is grounded on the notion that children are competent, active participants in their own lives and learning (Davis et al., 2008). This recognises the rights of children and the agency of the child in making choices and decisions. This coheres with the view of the child in Forest School as 'competent to explore and discover' and 'entitled to choose, and to initiate and drive their own learning and development' (FSA, 2016) in order to fulfil their potential. This is a vital principle for EfS, as young children who have opportunities to influence their environment and create change are more likely to become adults who believe that they can make a difference in the world (Davis, 2015; Siraj-Blatchford et al., 2010) and will act to do so.

Secondly, ECECfS is not just about promoting the agency of individuals but emphasises interdependence and the importance of communication and cooperation, relating to one another and taking collective responsibility. Forest School, too, is about the development of positive relationships between people, the management of conflicts and the creation of communities for learning. Children have opportunities to develop and display pro-social behaviours through playing together, working on group tasks and sharing tools and materials. This also extends more widely to include the participation of families and the development of local community links (Knight, 2016; O'Brien & Murray, 2006).

Thirdly, relationships and collaborations cannot work well without shared values and respect for differences. ECECfS has a brief to challenge unfairness and inequalities and to work to break down segregation and to promote inclusion. One example of this is gender equality and the concern for parity of rights and opportunities afforded to boys and girls (Davis et al., 2008; Engdahl & Ärlemalm-Hagsér, 2008). Similarly, a principle of Forest School is that all participants are 'equal, unique and valuable', and in Forest School gender stereotypes and biases are confronted – both girls and boys may dress in gender neutral outdoor clothing and wellington boots and are encouraged to engage in physical activities with all children 'entitled to experience appropriate risk and challenge' (FSA, 2011). The ways that Forest School leaders act and dress can also offer role models for both boys and girls that differ from those that they are used to and so can lead them to question dominant social messages about gender. Sara Knight's (2011a) book *Forest School for All* contains many examples of implementing inclusive practices through Forest School with different groups and in a variety of contexts.

Pedagogical approaches

Uniting all the shared aims of Forest School and EfS is the belief that ECEC is important and can make a difference. Sara Knight discussed the relationship between Education for Sustainable Development (ESD) and Forest School in 2011 (Knight, 2011b) and explored it further in 2013 (Knight, 2013b). The UNESCO ESD guidelines, updated in 2016 following the publication of the Sustainable Development Goals (SDGs), state that 'education is essential for the success of all sustainable development goals' (UNESCO, 2016). Moreover, UNESCO recommends participatory teaching and learning methods that motivate and empower learners to change their behaviour and take action for sustainable development.

This fits with the learner-centred pedagogy of Forest School where the emphasis is on facilitating children's choices and following their interests; these concepts are also central to traditional pedagogical approaches in early childhood education. This should come as no surprise, given that Forest School pedagogy was developed from a synthesis of early years pedagogies in Scandinavia and England.

Central to Forest School pedagogy is the regularity of sessions and repetition to reinforce learning. Regular experience of Forest School and the process of being outside and engaged holistically with the natural world, over time, develops responses such as awareness of the environment and has potential to create citizens who are more engaged with environmental sustainability. Many Forest School practitioners believe that a sense of awe and wonder engendered through engagement with natural spaces seems to enhance emotional and even spiritual responses to Forest School sessions, especially where there are trees. Jung (1967) identified the special effect that trees have on the human spirit, an effect that is reflected in the symbolism of trees in so many world religions. In many Forest School sessions the children select a tree to be the gatekeeper of their space, whose permission they ask as they arrive and thank as they leave. This provides an immediate focus on both the living nature of all things in the space and the need for respect for other living entities. Such awareness and respect translates easily into ECEC practice in both settings and the wider community.

The identification of significant markers such as gatekeeper trees and the delegation to the children of the task of acknowledging their responsibility to them is one part of the way in which even very young children can take, or at least share, control of the Forest School space. They will remind the adults as well as other children if the site is not left as it should be or if damage is done by anyone. The freedom for children to initiate and lead action that is central to good Forest School sessions is especially empowering where children are otherwise overly subject to the controlling influences of the adults around them. Children who find their confidence and self-esteem boosted by their Forest School experiences have been shown to transfer those skills back into their settings (Knight, 2013a/2009, p. 122).

The training that Forest School leaders undertake helps them to guide children to be respectful of the natural world and to see themselves as a part of that world. A key word identified by practitioners is 'ownership'. This element of ownership relates, in part, to the regularity of Forest School sessions that enables children to feel that the space they use is their space. This is identified by social geographers as a sense of place and is recognised by Erickson (cited in Louv, 2010) as being one form of attachment. Secure and appropriate attachments are key to mental health, and a review of research into the outcomes of Forest School sessions highlights the benefits to children's well-being (Gill, 2014). We are aware that mental health issues are affecting some of our youngest children and that stress inhibits learning (Jakins, 2012); linking feelings of peace, calm and reduced stress with being outside may strengthen a bond with the natural world that will lead to positive attitudes towards sustainability. This concept of a sense of place is the focus of much new thinking in the outdoor education sector as leaders move from many practices that use nature as a resource to more that embrace nature as an immersive entity to respect and protect.

Forest School activities are often creative as children build dens and shelters in different ways, make homes for smaller creatures in their space or represent their findings in mud, pictures or with photographs. Children are encouraged to be resourceful and flexible in how and what they use and to be open to various ways of pursuing ideas, making discoveries and completing tasks. This entails sensitive leadership by the practitioners who will watch for times where the children's interests offer opportunities to further their skills or knowledge. At these points they are taught the correct ways to use tools to achieve their aims as well as dis-cussions about which are the most appropriate tools. In this way skills build up slowly as the practitioner matches developing abilities with children's expressed needs and desires. For example, when learning about fire-lighting, several weeks may be spent on establishing agreed safety rules around the fire pit and on identi-fying burnable materials. Discussions about what is needed for a successful fire are always accompanied by instructions about successfully extinguishing the same fire. This engages the children as active decision-makers whilst ensuring their safety and well-being, and reflects another important element of ECECfS, in fostering flex-ibility and critical thinking, to enable the next generation to be prepared for the unknown challenges that they may have to deal with in an ever-changing world.

The delivery style, the repetitions, sense of place, and fostering of creativity and flexibility are main points of contact between ECECfS and Forest School but not the only instances where the holistic pedagogical approaches of Forest School resonate with ECECfS. The links between Forest School in its widest applications and sustainability can be further explored on the Forest School Association website (www.forestschoolassociation.org) and the pedagogy of Forest School is summarised in *Forest School in Practice* (Knight, 2016, see Chapter 8). Nevertheless, as with much of early years practice, education for sustainability is often implicit within Forest School practice and the links could be made more explicit in both directions.

Implementing the 7Rs of sustainability through Forest School

With the aim of analysing and illustrating how ECECfS may be made more overt through Forest School, we go on to describe some actions in Forest School that match the 7Rs (Pramling Samuelsson & Kaga, 2008, 2010). At an international workshop in Göteborg, Sweden, on the role and contribution of ECEC to a sus-tainable society, it was proposed that as an alternative to education that exists only to promote the 3Rs of reading, writing and arithmetic, there should also be a focus upon 7Rs of education for sustainable development, defined by Pramling Samuelsson and Kaga (2008, p. 12) as reduce, reuse, recycle, respect, repair, reflect and refuse. These 7Rs have been widely cited, discussed and at times modified. For example, in 2011, the Organisation Mondiale pour l'Éducation Préscolaire (OMEP) project about ESD in practice linked the 7Rs to the three pillars of sus-tainability: with respect, reflect and *rethink* related to the social pillar; reduce and reuse to the environmental pillar; and recycle and *redistribute* to the economic pillar. The words in our italics indicate that *rethink* and *redistribute* replaced *repair* and *refuse* in this OMEP project.

At the 2014 FS Association Conference participants in two workshops were invited to discuss a third version, where *responsibility* replaces refuse as the 7th R (Pramling Samuelsson & Kaga, 2010, p. 59). They were presented with the following definitions:

Reduce	Decreasing consumption of food, materials and resources
Reuse	Using materials many times and for different purposes
Recycle	Awareness of alternatives to discarding rubbish
Respect	Nurturing understanding of and reverence for nature and natural processes and reducing the extent to which they are violated; showing consideration for people and other animals
Reflect	A habit/skill of being thoughtful, asking questions, and wondering about experiences
Repair	Restoring places and things, fixing/mending broken objects
Responsibility	Being trusted to take care of something or to do something worthwhile

and agreed that Forest School encourages all of them. The participants then broke into pairs to think of examples to make each of these elements of ECECfS explicit, and therefore easier to express to others as values of Forest School. A wide range of ideas were generated for each R; these were then discussed in plenary sessions and the findings noted down and summarised as follows.

Reduce

In England and in other Minority World contexts most children are exposed to materialistic values from a very early age and so grow up with a great desire for products and possessions, considerably influenced by marketing messages from the commercial world. ECECfS aims to challenge the resulting overconsumption, to limit waste and to foster environmentally responsible behaviours, as does FS. Many Forest School practitioners provide 'litterless lunches' – in other words, avoiding items in disposable wrappers and using reusable packaging where packaging is necessary and they always emphasise to the children the importance of removing all litter from the site. Participants also suggested ways to consider reduction of waste when purchasing supplies – for example, by buying large pots of raisins to share, not individual boxes. Creating or finding local sites for Forest School sessions, ideally within walking distance, reduces the consumption inherent in transporting children in vehicles.

Reuse

Reuse can be about using items repeatedly. An example cited by Forest School practitioners was using durable tools made from wood and metal rather than plastic alternatives. Plastic items are often inexpensive and disposable and thus associated with waste and with the pollution of oceans and other wildlife habitats. As part of ECECfS, children can use items made with sturdier materials and be shown how to care for tools so that they can be used repeatedly. These were seen to be beneficial for the children, in that they work more effectively, as well as being better for the planet. In play, too, 'loose parts' (see Brown & Patte, 2013, p. 128) that can be rearranged in different ways on many occasions are more creative for play than one-use plastic imitations.

Creative reuse was also seen as central to this R: the notion of changing the way in which we look at objects so that we can reframe them as something different. Examples included using milk cartons as water containers for handwashing. Forest School practitioners were keen to return natural resources back into the environment, too. Ideas ranged from composting to creating minibeast habitats from used sticks and brush. Coppicing appropriately creates materials for sessions, while planting and replanting can create new sites as well as benefitting the environment.

Recycle

Another way of cutting down waste is to convert used materials into something new. Forest School leaders encourage healthy eating of fruit, and this can lead to composting of peelings and provide children with opportunities to look at natural recycling and the processes and benefits of decay. Using fallen tree materials to make dens and fires preserves the living materials and encourages the children to be respectful of them. Young children will inevitably pick up 'treasures' in the woods, found objects to which they attach special significance and which will act as a plaything, a talisman or simply a prompt to memories of a positive experience. These objects may therefore be treasure to some and rubbish to others which can lead to fruitful discussions and expanding awareness of attitudes towards the things that we desire and own.

Respect

The value of respect for self, for other people, other species and for natural places is central to the ethos of Forest School and to ECECfS. This places demands upon Forest School practitioners to show respect for children and to one another and to inspire respectful attitudes.

Forest School leaders encourage children to respect the place where Forest School is held. Sometimes children are expected to ask the forest for permission to enter and play; this might involve identifying a particular tree as the 'Grandmother' and addressing their greetings and farewells to her. Sometimes 'guardians' are appointed for each session to check for litter or damage, and emphasis should always be placed upon leaving the site as it was found. Children are taught to respect other people's creations (e.g. dens and sculptures) when sharing a site, although it may be necessary to dismantle such creations on occasion so as not to do harm to the environment.

Modelling respectful behaviour towards nature involves leaders in considering the impact of their group's footfall on a site and determining when it is advisable to move a 'base camp' area to allow the understory to recover. This provides opportunities for involving the children in discussing why this is important, where would be a good place for a new site, as well as what can be moved (for example, to discuss sitting logs that may have become homes for minibeasts and how to move or replace them). Some leaders suggested that the use of magnifiers can help developing children's understanding of the vulnerability of plants and insects as living things; others felt that developing awareness by focused looking with the naked eye enabled them to take fewer items of non-natural kit into the woods. There was common agreement that children must learn the importance of putting minibeasts back where they came from.

Reflect

In all Forest School sessions, the leaders recognise the importance of respecting children's quiet spaces and giving them the unhurried time that is so often lacking in everyday life. 'Sit spots' are used by many Forest School leaders to create time and place to reflect on surroundings, to listen carefully and to observe closely. Identifying a place to sit and cultivate an awareness of the surroundings by opening all the senses to the natural world is something that all children and adults can do. Some leaders allocate a specific time for doing this, particularly with a new or very young group, in order to support the development of the skill. Others are just sensitive to when participants elect to remove themselves for a period of contemplation. Many groups also organise time to reflect together on experiences at the end of session, sometimes using the device of a stick or symbolic object to signal who has the right to speak. It is important that the adults in the group model reflective practice so that children see its benefits.

One challenge that many settings face is the need for leaders to visit sites used at other times by the general public prior to any sessions. It may be necessary to collect and dispose of the leftovers from drug and alcohol abuse as well as more commonplace litter. Rather than cocooning children from this process, leaders are more accustomed to discussing with the children what they need to do before the site can be used. This often stimulates thoughtful consideration of societal issues in quite young children that can surprise adults who are unaccustomed to the depths of thinking that three- to five-year-olds are capable of.

Back in the indoor setting, photographs can help children to revisit events and discuss them. One of the authors used this method with an early years class in two ways. After the session the children would sit and discuss reflectively on the highs and lows of the day's session with the aid of photographs shown on the class whiteboard linked to the leader's phone. Before the start of the next session a scrolling album of edited photos would be playing on the whiteboard as the children prepared to leave the setting (toileting and dressing), stimulating memories, discussions and planning for the new session ahead.

Repair

A part of developing confidence at Forest School is helping children to take responsibility on occasions when things get broken and to discuss what can be mended or fixed and how this can be done. For example, tent pegs used to put up tarpaulins are easily bent and distorted. Straightening them out again is an easily learned task which children can take charge of. In simple ways experiences at Forest School can help children to understand cause and effect and the consequences of their actions. It is possible to engage all children and adults in the maintenance and care of tools, equipment and the space used. This includes practices such as putting logs back after looking underneath and restoring fire sites to their original state. In addition, supporting children to repair equipment and toys, where that is possible, mitigates in some small way against the influences of mainstream throw-away society.

Responsibility

All of the practices listed above involve taking responsibility. In addition, when visiting most Forest School settings the children carry their own rucksacks containing extra clothes, snacks and drinks, ensuring that they bring all they need into the wood and that they carry it all back out of the wood. This fosters independence as well as personal responsibility, as does assigning tasks to children – for example, caring for a child who is new to the group or carrying a particular item of equipment. Forest School practitioners may also choose one child each week to be the leader into the wood. In this way they are led towards caring for habitats and the environment. Practitioners may also help to create broader connections with the environment, perhaps with stories about a particular tree, or by fostering wider environmental responsibility – for example, by linking wasteful use of paper to the destruction of trees.

Other Rs

In addition to the suggestions for each of the 7Rs, above, some discussion took place about the headings proposed by Pramling Samuelsson and Kaga (2008, 2010). The participants felt that 'refuse' was an R worthy of consideration, particularly given the double meaning of the word, and that 'rethink' would also signal the need for radical action that is critical and political as well as environmental. 'Recover' was proposed as an original addition to the list, signalling a need for restoration of natural environments, return to values of making and mending, and renewal of well-being and of physical and mental health. Readers may reflect on their own amendments to the list of 7Rs, having considered the ideas above and the questions below.

Conclusion

Much writing and research into Forest School (e.g. Knight 2016; O'Brien & Murray, 2006) identifies benefits to children's well-being as well as value for all areas of development. This is, in itself, important for social sustainability as people seek antidotes and alternatives to stressful modern life. But benefits can also be seen in the ways identified above that Forest School may challenge attitudes towards environmental issues, encouraging children and adults to see themselves as part of nature, and be a sentient part, one with responsibilities to protect and maintain other species and ecosystems. Establishing this positive caring awareness in the early years is an important contribution towards ECECfS.

In summary, it seems vital for early years educators to see the potential of Forest School in contributing to ECECfS, even if they themselves are not direct participants in the Forest School sessions. In turn, Forest School leaders and practitioners need to recognise that their roles and responsibilities can go far beyond offering child-centred learning experiences in natural environments. Inevitably this may require more training. Many early years degree courses do now include sustainability as a theme and an introduction to outdoor learning as part of the curriculum; and all level three Forest School training involves an amount of learning about child development. These can only be starting points, and both sets of practitioners may need to reflect on whether additional training would increase their understanding of the potential for Forest School to enhance wider ECECfS with young children. In the meantime, through Forest School, young children can acquire and practice skills, knowledge, attitudes and values that are necessary for a worthwhile present and the shaping of a sustainable future.

Questions for you to consider

1. Are you familiar with Forest School? If so, do you agree with this assessment of the contribution of Forest School to ECECfS?
2. Can you add examples of your own to the ways in which the 7Rs of ECECfS are followed in Forest School?
3. What more could Forest School practitioners do to promote ECECfS and raise awareness of environmental issues elsewhere?
4. How can Forest School experiences be integrated with policies and practices for sustainability in early years settings?

Further reading

Harris, F. (2017). The nature of learning at Forest School: Practitioners' perspectives. *Education*, 45(2), 3–13.

This paper raises questions about the role of Forest School practitioners in promoting ECECfS.

Knight, S. (2016). *Forest School in practice*. London: SAGE.

This text includes excellent sections on nature provision for very young children and Forest School opportunities for three- to five-year-olds.

References

Brown, F., & Patte, M. (2013). *Rethinking children's play*. London: Bloomsbury Academic.

Carson, R. (1965). *The sense of wonder*. New York: Open Road Integrated Media.

Davis, J. M. (Ed.) (2015). *Young children and the environment: Early education for sustainability* (2nd ed.). Port Melbourne: Cambridge University Press.

Davis, J. M., Engdahl, I., Otieno, L., Pramling Samuelsson, I., Siraj-Blatchford, J., & Valladh, P. (2008). *The Gothenburg recommendations on education for sustainable development*. Gothenburg: Swedish International Centre for Education for Sustainable Development (SWEDESD).

Engdahl, I., & Ärlemalm-Hagsér, E. (2008). Swedish preschool children show interest and are involved in the future of the world. In I. Pramling Samuelsson & Y. Kaga (Eds.), *The contribution of early childhood to a sustainable society* (pp. 57–61). Paris: UNESCO.

FSA (2011). Full principles and criteria for good practice. [Online resource.] Available at: www.forestschoolassociation.org/full-principles-and-criteria-for-good-practice/. Accessed 17 July 2016.

FSA (2016). What is Forest School? [Online resource.] Available at: www.forestschoolassociation.org/what-is-forest-school/. Accessed 17 July 2016.

Gill, T. (2014). The benefits of children's engagement with nature: A systematic literature review. *Children, Youth and Environments*, 24(2), 10–34.

Jakins, A. (2012). Learning and teaching styles. In P. Beckley (Ed.), *Learning in early childhood* (pp. 150–162). London: SAGE.

Jung, C. G. (1967). *Memories, dreams, reflections*. London: Fontana.

Knight, S. (Ed.) (2011a). *Forest School for all*. London: SAGE.

Knight, S. (2011b). Forest School as a way of learning in the outdoors in the UK. *International Journal for Cross-Disciplinary Subjects in Education (IJCDSE)*, Special Issue 1(1), 590–595. [Online resource.] Available at: http://infonomics-society.org/wp-content/uploads/ijcdse/published-papers/special-issue-1/Forest-School-as-a-Way-of-Learning-in-the-Outdoors-in-the-UK.pdf. Accessed 17 July 2016.

Knight, S. (2013a/2009). *Forest School and outdoor learning in the early years*. London: SAGE.

Knight, S. (2013b). Forest School and education for sustainable development. In S. Knight (Ed.), *International perspectives on Forest School* (pp. 9–11). London: SAGE.

Knight, S. (2016). *Forest School in practice*. London: SAGE.

Louv, R. (2010). *Last child in the woods* (revised and updated edition). London: Atlantic Books.

O'Brien, L., & Murray, R. (2006). *A marvellous opportunity for children to learn*. Farnham, Surrey: For Res. [Online resource.] Available at: www.forestry.gov.uk/pdf/fr0112forestschoolsreport.pdf/$FILE/fr0112forestschoolsreport.pdf. Accessed 17 July 2016.

Pramling Samuelsson, I., & Kaga, Y. (2008). *The contribution of early childhood to a sustainable society*. Paris: UNESCO. [Online resource.] Available at: http://unesdoc.unesco.org/images/0015/001593/159355E.pdf. Accessed 17 July 2016.

Pramling Samuelsson, I., & Kaga, Y. (2010). Early childhood education to transform cultures for sustainability. In L. Starke & L. Mastny (Eds.), *State of the World 2010: Transforming cultures from consumerism to sustainability* (27th ed., pp. 57–62). London & New York: Worldwatch Institute.

Siraj-Blatchford, J., Smith, K. C., & Pramling Samuelsson, I. (2010). *Education for sustainable development in the early years*. Gothenburg: OMEP.

UNESCO (2016). *Sustainable Development Goals for Education*. Paris: UNESCO. [Online resource.] Available at: http://en.unesco.org/sdgs/ed. Accessed 17 July 2016.

10

SUSTAINABLE LEADERSHIP IN THE EARLY YEARS

Jan Georgeson

Introduction

Recently I was leading a session on 'Sustainable Leadership in the Early Years' as part of a UK professional development day. I was speaking to a mixed audience of practitioners from schools, private day nurseries and community preschools in the after-lunch slot on a hot day at the end of the school year. In the hope of prompting more audience participation as energy levels dropped, I asked for comments on how they might respond if members of staff, who had been funded by their organisation to attend training, were to leave their post taking their newly acquired expertise with them (why this might be of interest in the context of sustainable leadership should become apparent later). This certainly woke the audience up but produced such opposing and irreconcilable views that the happy end-of-term atmosphere was temporarily shattered. The manager of one private day nursery was adamant that those who received training from an organisation should either work on long enough so that the organisation benefited from their investment or repay the cost of training, whereas a community preschool manager was horrified by this attitude; she considered staff development to be an integral part of what her setting was aiming to achieve for the community and could not countenance asking staff for money to recover the setting's outlay on their training if staff left. Other members of the audience were left feeling uncomfortable because they could see both points of view; training is expensive and settings need to budget carefully, but it is nonetheless important to instil in staff a positive attitude towards lifelong learning. My observation that what might be appropriate in one context might not fit somewhere else did not help to resolve the underlying dilemma over where to place one's priorities – sustaining the workforce or sustaining the business. However, I did make my point that taking a lead on sustainability issues in an early years setting is not always straightforward and decisions about such issues will not always be unanimous.

It is possible to identify three aspects of sustainable leadership in the early years: managing resources, leading the curriculum and sustaining people (Georgeson, 2015). The first two aspects appear regularly in project evaluations; for example, Davis (2008), reporting on a 'whole setting' sustainability project, describes

> a synthesis of interlocking components – *housekeeping and management practices* committed to reducing the centre's 'ecological footprint'; *curriculum and pedagogical practices* underpinned by belief in the capacity of children to be informed learners and environmental activists, right now.
>
> *(Davis, 2008, p. 22, my emphasis)*

Davis goes on to add 'community interactions that embrace parents and the wider community', thereby introducing the need to consider people's involvement in the project and extending the sustainability agenda beyond the setting. But, while agreeing with the importance of making connections outside the setting, Hargreaves and Fink (2004) emphasise the need for leaders to sustain people *inside* the setting too. Leaders need to inspire staff teams (Hargreaves & Boyle, 2014); working towards sustainability, while undoubtedly rewarding, can take effort and one of the functions of the leader is to remind people why the effort is worth it.

In this chapter I would like to highlight some of the issues and tensions concerning the first two aspects – resources and curriculum – which can arise for leaders seeking to promote a sustainable ethos in their early years setting, before turning to the broader literature on sustainability and leadership to consider how concerns for sustainability can, and indeed should, be applied to sustaining the workforce. This will include consideration of the compatibility of sustainability and entrepreneurialism in the context of early years settings, a debate which resonates with the particular issues that emerged during the professional development session discussed above and which might offer, albeit belatedly, some comfort to my confused and disgruntled audience as well as to others wrestling with similar concerns.

Managing resources

Some leaders may feel overawed by the task of putting sustainability on to the agenda in an early years setting. I suggest that an obvious starting point is to encourage staff to carry out an environmental audit, either designing your own within the setting or using an existing checklist – for example, the Go Green Rating Scale (Boise, 2007). Early years leaders in Australia offering advice to colleagues suggest that leaders who feel overawed by this responsibility should

> [e]stablish a starting point: a self-assessment or an audit conducted by someone else will help to identify what you already do. It will also help to establish a baseline for your use of resources. How much electricity, water and gas do

you use? How many paper towels and tissues? And what cleaning chemicals? How much garbage do you throw away? How much recycling?

(NQS PLP, 2013, p. 2)

Taking an overview of what is happening in the setting's physical environment, in terms of use of energy and resources, can lead to the development of a sustainable resourcing policy. Although taking a lead by initiating this kind of activity might appear relatively straightforward, hidden tensions and surprising levels of resistance can lurk to subvert the endeavour. The key to avoiding disagreements and disgruntlement is openness and clarity about *why* the setting is adopting a sustainable approach; if this is kept to the foreground during discussions over a particular resourcing decision, solutions can be found that everyone at least understands. Putting the sustainable (and perhaps cheaper) option into practice, however, can alter the balance between acting in accordance with one's principles and keeping the work manageable; going 'paperless' for staff meetings reduces paper consumption but requires checks that everyone can access materials circulated by email. Careful planning is needed to fit new processes or resources into routines, to minimise inconvenience and to keep everyone on board.

Early years practice has a long tradition of sustainable resourcing – for instance, using found objects and packaging instead of or in addition to art materials and construction toys, which has the added benefit of offering children opportunities to develop symbolic function, whereby one thing can stand for another. There are, however, possible tensions between early years practice and sustainable resourcing; opening doors to encourage children to move freely between the inside and outside areas can impact energy bills, especially in settings which were not designed with the maintenance of an easy inside–outside interface in mind. Free-flow play and energy conservation are not mutually exclusive, but might mean that the children playing inside have to wear their coats as well as the children outside.

Foodstuffs, such as trays of cooked spaghetti for tactile play or interesting shapes of pasta for collage, need careful consideration in the context of a sustainable resourcing policy. These activities can send out confusing messages to children; we shouldn't waste things but here we are playing with something that is a scarce resource for some people who don't have enough to eat. Issues such as this should be discussed in staff meetings and all decisions taken about whether such activities fit in with the setting's ethos should be explicitly supported by clear reasoning which justifies the use (or otherwise) of foodstuffs in play. These decisions will vary with the cultural context; the North American Association for Environmental Education (NAAEE), for example, has produced guidelines that consider that:

> it is important to recognize differences in families regarding attitudes toward their child's handling certain insects or creatures and their reverence toward some animals or plants in nature. Corn or maize is revered in traditional Mexican culture. Similarly, in certain cultural groups – especially in West Africa – using foods such as rice, beans, or other vegetables in art projects is

viewed as wasteful. Using alternative materials to food is advisable. […] One nature-based preschool allows food for play only if it ends up as food for the school animals or outdoor wildlife. Dried corn in the sensory table feeds the chickens, for instance. Potatoes are not used for prints because they cannot be eaten afterwards. Such respect for food is part of this school's cultural value and reflects the values of the families they serve.

(NAAEE, 2010, p. 13)

Md-Yunus (2009) discusses the position of food play in the context of a multi-cultural classroom and suggest ways to help teachers adopt culturally appropriate practice (Md-Yunus, 2009). Children who come from families where there is a strong cultural belief 'in conserving food and not wasting it' or where 'there is a certain amount of reverence given to food' (Md-Yunus, 2009, p. 4) may not feel like they belong in their early years setting, something which can be a particular concern during transition from home to setting, or between settings and school (O'Connor, 2013, p. 56). Md-Yunus suggests that by '[m]odelling respect for their own food – as well as for the beliefs of others about food' can help teachers to avoid mismatches over attitudes towards the conservation of food in their settings (Md-Yunus, 2009, p. 8).

Leading the embedding of sustainability into the curriculum

This is not, as is sometimes thought, largely a matter of finding relevant sustainability content and activities for the children. Rather there are several general concepts, such as sufficiency, fairness and care, which underpin a sustainable approach and which provide the basis for helping staff embed sustainability principles into the curriculum. Considerations of *sufficiency* – whether there is enough to complete a bounded task or whether there is enough for everyone to take part – are connected with the cognitive processes of self-monitoring and control, processes that underpin children's development of the capacity for self-regulation (Whitebread, 2014). The emergence of children's concern that there should be enough for everyone is also related to the development of the concept of fairness and awareness of the needs of others. This kind of thinking requires a theory of mind, again something that is needed for the development of higher mental function (Astington & Hughes, 2013; Fernyhough, 2008). Leaders can therefore support their staff to see how embedding the sustainability principles of sufficiency, fairness and consideration for others promotes the development of children's dispositions for effective learning in general, as well as their personal and social development and their ability to understand more complex aspects of sustainability in practice.

Opening up the possibilities of embedding sustainability in the curriculum can also help staff to see the connections with specific areas of learning within the early years curriculum, such as the development of children's awareness of the physical properties of objects, and of their own body with its strengths, needs and limitations. The connections between sufficiency and the mathematical functions of sharing, estimating and measuring are clear, while finding more sustainable alternatives often requires creative thinking and consideration of design principles. Language skills of explaining, arguing and reasoning are needed to encourage other people to agree to a more sustainable solution, and listening will enable children to find out about other people's needs.

This approach can be applied even more broadly. The UNESCO workshop on the contribution of Early Childhood Education to a Sustainable Society, documented by Pramling Samuelsson and Kaga (2008), goes beyond the recruitment of sustainability to support other areas of the curriculum, and proposes the inclusion of the following:

- Context sensitive and culturally relevant content
- Content that fosters caring attitudes and empathy towards the natural environment and people living in other parts of the world
- Learning about respect for diversity
- Learning about gender issues and equal rights
- Learning basic life skills
- Learning for life
- Activities built around the 7Rs: reduce, reuse, repair, recycle, respect, reflect and refuse (Pramling Samuelsson & Kaga, 2008, p. 15)

Most early years leaders are likely to find that the first five elements are consistent with the ethos of their settings and in facilitating the professional development of their staff they are clearly supporting the sixth point of lifelong learning. The setting may also offer training and learning opportunities to parents, thereby establishing for children that taking part in learning opportunities is a normal part of life for everyone. However, to achieve the final point to promote the 7Rs, leaders may consider delegating someone in the setting to identify activities and routines appropriate to the setting which appeal to both children's and adults' interests.

Sustaining people

Early years practice depends on the powerful commitment of staff to work for the benefit of children and their community and, while a professional culture of giving more to the job – over and beyond set hours – also exists in other areas of work, in early years this extra commitment tends to go well beyond the level of remuneration. Setting leaders know this very well and need to act responsibly to manage human resources in such a way that they do not deplete people's store of goodwill – but still manage to balance the books.

Careful and sensitive use of people's individual skills and experience, the personal resources that they bring to the job, can help to match individuals to roles and positions in the setting through identifying and developing particular talents and interests. This can be achieved through thorough and insightful use of opportunities provided during recruitment, induction and supervision. Setting leaders can identify and nurture individuals' strengths and enthusiasms; people work best when they are doing what they like to do.

Leading sustainably involves knowing how to 'feed' goodwill; it is, however, also important to recognize when one might be in danger of exploiting those very enthusiastic members of staff, the ones who volunteer for everything. It is tempting to ask them to take something on because they readily and pleasantly say yes; however saying yes to everything can result in overcommitment and ultimately in exhaustion. Burnout is an increasing problem in caring professions, particularly during times of financial austerity (Rekalidou & Panitsides, 2015), and the need to promote and preserve the emotional well-being of early years staff is now receiving more attention (Buettner & Jeon, 2016; Maggiolini et al., 2016). Systems for early years provision appear to depend on the goodwill and physical and emotional labour of a dedicated few to keep running, as Andrew (2015) suggests:

> The societal reluctance to value early childhood work highly is an attempt to keep in place systems of power which have seen women and the less economically privileged made responsible for the care and emotional well-being of others, whether in the paid work of nursing, eldercare or childcare, or the unpaid work of mothering … Burnout and staff turnover are responses, I suggest, to the intractability of a system that values early childhood work so poorly.
>
> *(Andrew, 2015, p. 361)*

Enthusiastic and accommodating staff need to be cherished, not worn into the ground; their loss will be felt keenly if they are forced to take time off to recover from doing too much to the detriment of their health.

Such an approach challenges the pervasive managerialist discourse of efficiency and effectiveness. Bottery (2016, p. 61) urges leaders to move further away from considering staff as resources, because this perpetuates arguments about staff performance based on economic efficiency. Just as outlined above when embedding sustainability in the curriculum, leaders should adopt a sufficiency approach to staffing. Squeezing every drop of energy out of a machine might sound efficient, but squeezing every drop of energy out of staff members leaves them drained and unable to fulfil the many physical and emotional demands that their job makes on them. Instead, Bottery argues, leaders need to guard against heading up 'greedy' organisations (Gronn, 2003) that treat staff as resources to be deployed as efficiently as possible to ensure targets are met, and instead see each member of the workforce as 'ends in themselves, where their care and well-being are fundamental concerns, irrespective of their utility' (Bottery, 2016, p. 61).

All staff should therefore be encouraged to maintain a healthy work–life balance. This was once the focus of a UK government initiative, the Work-Life Balance Challenge Fund, launched October 2000 to help businesses develop work–life balance policies. This cause was pursued at a European level (European Commission, 2015), but in the economic and political climate of the UK, job scarcity and a discourse of 'hard-working families' has made it more difficult to implement in practice.

Some staff members prefer to keep home and work separate, while others may find it helpful to share their home lives in the workplace; indeed, early years staff whom I have interviewed about their work mention the camaraderie and companionship of their colleagues as one of the main reasons for working in an early years setting (Georgeson, 2006). Again this requires sensitivity from the setting leader to recognise when there might be a tipping point – 'a moment of critical mass, the threshold, the boiling point' when little things can make a big difference (Gladwell, 2000) – that needs careful consideration rather than a more superficial response to a perceived dip in practice. Although it might appear professionally inappropriate, it might sometimes be the snatched conversations over the children's heads in the playground that are sustaining hard-pressed staff to keep turning up to work. A solution here might be to suggest that these staff members take over sorting the bike shed while someone else interacts with the children on the slide, and to arrange a time to talk to them later to see if support needs to be put in place to help them through a difficult time in their home life.

The concept of sustainability is closely associated with the concept of 'finiteness' and the limitations on our own and our planet's resources. Some people might not be comfortable with thinking too deeply about the finite nature of their own ability, energy, working life and especially lifespan. A sensitive leader needs to be aware that staff members might have different ways of dealing with 'finiteness' and be clear about the boundaries between the setting's ethos and private beliefs. Nonetheless, leading for sustainability entails moving towards the realms of spirituality – not the private spirituality bound up with religious belief but 'workplace spirituality', a particular way of thinking about self, work and organisations (Hicks, 2003). Consideration of ethical business practice has introduced workplace spirituality as a new area of study and the connections with sustainability are clear. Rhodes (2006) identifies 'emphasising sustainability' as the first of his six 'Characteristics of a Spiritual Workplace', and includes within this characteristic awareness of limited resources and the possible negative impact of decisions made by leaders of organisations on individuals, communities and the environment.

Adopting a sustainable approach to workplace ethos can also help with the tricky decisions over investing in staff development that caused such disquiet in the training session I described at the beginning of this chapter. Leadership for sustainability involves thinking more globally, beyond the level of one's own context; investing in the training of anyone in the early years workforce means that children will benefit from this investment, perhaps in one's own setting but perhaps in the future elsewhere. And what goes around comes around; leaders who look beyond their own setting and become involved in local and national networks are likely to benefit from recruiting new staff who have developed their skills in other settings.

Keeping up to date with local and national policy developments through involvement in professional networks can also help leaders to 'insulate' staff from some of the changes caused by constant shifts in policy. As early years provision has risen to the top of government agendas over the last twenty years, this has been accompanied by waves of changes in policy, funding and regulation. Leading within a system that keeps changing can feel like wasted energy; as Hargreaves and Fink (2004, p. 10) point out, 'If change is to matter, spread and last, sustainable leadership must also be a fundamental priority of the systems in which leaders do their work.' Leaders can find themselves deciding which policy changes require wholesale revision of practice, and which can be managed by more superficial changes that allow the setting to continue to develop good practice along established and successful lines.

Insulating staff members from frequent policy change is demanding work, especially if leaders are also monitoring practitioners' well-being, containing their fears and supporting their professional development. Leading sustainably therefore also entails taking care to sustain one's self, recognising and accepting one's own limitations. This includes leaders accepting their personal fallibility (Bottery, 2016, p. 63), perhaps acknowledging that in hindsight another decision might have been more appropriate but accepting that predicting the precise working of complex systems is not humanly possible. Leading sustainably means recognising that both leaders and their staff must be trusted to act on the basis of well-informed professional judgment. If something goes wrong, attribution of blame wastes time and emotional energy; learning lessons for the future is more important. Leaders can also share their learning with others in similar situations; in this way knowledge about how to manage complex situations, such as provision for children with particular needs, can be built up to support others in the future. Local and national networks can also help to share the emotional burden of change and reduce the need for constant horizon scanning to anticipate new policies, initiatives and sources of funding.

Hargreaves and Fink (2004) argue that one of the most important aspects of sustainable leadership is the realisation that, from the first day of leadership, leaders should be planning for their succession. This involves spotting potential future leaders within (and beyond) the staff team, but avoiding the resentment that can accrue towards someone apparently favoured as the successor. Distributing leadership, so that everyone feels they are trusted to take responsibility for particular aspects of provision, can help to dissipate antagonism towards a single 'anointed successor' – who might leave for another setting anyway before leaders themselves move on. The concept of intergenerational awareness should go hand in hand with the development of a sustainable ethos; if everyone in the setting is already accustomed to thinking about the needs of the next generation and planning how to meet these needs, then thinking about who will next take on the work of the leader should not come as too much of a surprise.

Distributed leadership, while helping to share responsibility, can nonetheless make demands on people's time and energy, including 'the work of all individuals who contribute to leadership practice, whether or not they are formally designated or defined as leaders' (Harris & Spillane, 2008, p. 31). Staff members have different ideas about what is worth sustaining, but everyone's voice should be heard when decisions have to be made. Sustainable leaders therefore establish and support transparent and democratic processes for decision-making. Even if unanimous agreement on every decision is not possible, everyone should at least understand the thinking that underpins it.

Motivations for sustainable leadership

Leaders who seek to promote an ethos of sustainability in their settings may not all act with the same understanding of sustainability issues or indeed the same underlying motivation for adopting a sustainable approach. Bottery et al. (2012) note the shift towards greater consideration of moral purpose in understanding of leadership, but also point out that this is likely to be associated with a wider range of ontological and epistemological positions and an awareness of the complexity and interconnectedness of educational issues (Bottery et al., 2012, p. 228). It is possible that some in leadership positions in education settings, as elsewhere, might seek to promote a sustainable ethos for instrumental rather than ideological reasons; switching lightbulbs off saves money and achieving 'green' awards can improve a the setting's profile. Bottery et al. (2012) show, however, that even headteachers of schools with outstanding reputations for sustainability can demonstrate striking differences in motivation, understanding and leadership strategy in relation to how they seek to promote sustainability in their schools. One head drew on his own subject knowledge and deep concern for action to overturn the ecological crisis and argued that his personal moral framework changed the way he was leading, away from a distributed leadership model to something more authoritarian. The second headteacher in Bottery's study did not share the same subject knowledge base and had arrived at her approach to promotion of sustainability because of her particular take on distributed leadership. For her, sustainability is much broader than the curriculum and resource management; it is more like an underpinning theme to her approach to education in general and her foregrounding of relationships. Surprisingly, though, she also saw the need for some regulation, something top down, to ensure that the sustainability agenda is promoted everywhere.

Flexibility and consistency

Bottery (2016) argues that the complexity of many of the problems facing global leaders in general, and educational leaders in particular, means that neat and certain solutions are not possible; there are no 'magic bullets', no simple 'evidence-based' strategies to roll out to meet the complex challenges currently faced by leaders in schools and other educational contexts. Decision-making becomes more difficult as resources become stretched and demands increase. Hargreaves and Fink (2004), in setting out their seven dimensions of sustainable leadership, stress the importance of developing environmental diversity and capacity. They argue that learning from diverse practices makes it easier for people to adapt to increasingly complex environments. Schools that are innovative foster and celebrate this diversity, but standardisation, they warn, is 'the enemy of sustainability'.

Complex problems need flexible solutions, informed by relevant local knowledge built up through networking (Hargreaves & Fink, 2004). If leaders are to avoid standardisation and the unthinking application of 'what works' to a problem regardless of context, a certain creativity and agility of mind is likely to help. The importance of these particular qualities suggest that sustainable leaders might benefit from recent thinking about entrepreneurs' contribution to the discovery of sustainable solutions (Wyness et al., 2015). At first glance, this might seem like an unlikely collaboration, because of the depiction of entrepreneurs as exploiters of business opportunities and, by association, as promoters of consumerism. But just as business leaders move towards considerations of sustainability as they grapple with the idea of workplace spirituality, so can leaders seeking to promote sustainability learn from contemporary conceptualisations of entrepreneurs as agile, horizon-scanning, creative niche-finders. Entrepreneurs can be considered to have particular strengths in innovating and bringing about social change (Wyness et al., 2015, p. 835), both of which are likely to be necessary if we are to meet the global challenges of climate change and the local challenges of an overregulated education sector. Flexibility, agility and creativity have been identified as crucial to address the needs of a diverse client group, and personal co-configuration between service/goods providers and customer is increasingly recognised as essential (Victor & Boynton, 1998). Many early years settings in the private, voluntary and independent sector in the UK recognise the importance of this approach; they need to provide a service that matches parents' needs as closely as possible and to maximise opportunities to access funding to balance the books. They need to become serial entrepreneurs to survive in a highly competitive childcare market.

Providing a service that responds to diversity and addresses many different needs does not necessarily create the most comfortable conditions for staff members. Leaders can find they are faced with a dilemma over the need to insulate their workforce from too much change while still responding to shifts in the market and political agendas. Hargreaves (2016) acknowledges that employees crave consistency, but argues that this can be achieved through consistency between the goals of leadership (what leaders are leading for) and the ways in which leaders lead. This entails identifying and clarifying with the staff team what are the fixed points, the non-negotiables, and what are the flex points, where there is room for negotiation. Nuttall and colleagues, in their study aimed at identifying systemic tensions hindering efforts to promote staff development, also highlight the importance of consistency for early years leaders. They report that early years leaders displayed an 'underlying desire … for a sense of collective cohesion' in their settings, where everyone was 'on the same page', while at the same time relying on 'individualized models of development' (Nuttall, Thomas & Henderson, 2016). They argue for

> a shift from conceptions of leadership based in individualized solutions (too often resulting in burnout) to thinking about leadership as work that influences the collective cultural norms of the entire field.
>
> *(Nuttall et al., 2016)*

This call echoes the emphasis on networking endorsed by Hargreaves and colleagues – but which can prove difficult to achieve in a sector not noted for the 'collective autonomy of an agentic profession' (Edwards, 2015, p. 783).

Conclusion

Leading for sustainability in the early years is much more than carefully managing resources and embedding the principles of sustainability into the curriculum. Consistency is needed between sustainable goals and a style of leadership concerned with sustaining workforce well-being. Early years leaders, acting as buffers between the setting and the outside world and choosing which messages to let through, must maintain a coherent ethos while also monitoring opportunities to ensure the financial sustainability of the enterprise. The work of the early years sector is by its very nature future-orientated – we are supporting the development of the citizens of the future. The challenge of current complexities can, however, make leading for a more sustainable world for these future citizens a rather lonely endeavour. The sector has a coherence of purpose but limited opportunities to share the burden of these challenges. Networking, both locally and globally, can provide the emotional support and information to make the position of early years leader more sustainable.

Questions for you to consider

1. In protecting staff against external pressures, leaders can be in danger of transferring the load onto themselves and absorbing the impact of change and worry. Is this a sustainable strategy? If not, how would you look to remedy the situation?
2. Consider one change that you might introduce to make your environment more sustainable. How would you introduce this to your colleagues? Are there practical barriers to overcome? What benefits might accrue?
3. What do you feel about using foodstuffs in play? Should everyone in the setting follow your lead or is this a matter of individual choice?

Further reading

Andrew, Y. (2015). What we feel and what we do: Emotional capital in early childhood work. *Early Years*, 5(4), 351–365.

Andrew discusses the emotional load on early years educators, arguing that building up emotional capital for supporting children and families can provide them with resources to promote their own well-being and that of their colleagues, leading to a more resilient workforce 'with the emotional insight to challenge the inequalities of the system'.

Bottery, M. (2016). *Educational leadership for a more sustainable world*. London: Bloomsbury.

In his wide-ranging book, Mike Bottery argues that a failure to appreciate the complexity of educational systems means we don't generate appropriately complex responses. He goes on to explore how adopting sustainable values and principles can help educational leaders both locally and globally.

References

Andrew, Y. (2015). What we feel and what we do: Emotional capital in early childhood work. *Early Years*, 5(4), 351–365.

Astington, J. W., & Hughes, C. (2013). Theory of mind: Self-reflection and social understanding. In P. D. Zelazo (Ed.), *Oxford Handbook of Developmental Psychology* (Vol. 2, pp. 398–424). New York: Oxford University Press.

Boise, P. (2007). *Go Green Rating Scale for Early Childhood Settings Handbook*. St. Paul, MN: Redleaf Press.

Bottery, M. (2016). *Educational leadership for a more sustainable world*. London: Bloomsbury.

Bottery, M., Wright, N., & James, S. (2012). Personality, moral purpose, and the leadership of an education for sustainable development. *Education 3–13*, 40(3), 227–241. doi:10.1080/03004279.2010.512563

Buettner, C., & Jeon, L. (2016). What predicts early childhood teachers' social and emotional wellbeing? Examining teachers' relationships within childcare settings. Presentation at the 26th EECERA Annual Conference, Dublin, Ireland, 3 August to 3 September, 2016.

Davis, J. (2008). What might education for sustainability look like in early childhood? A case for participatory, whole-of-settings approaches. In I.Pramling Samuelsson & Y. Kaga (Eds.), *The contribution of early childhood education to a sustainable society* (pp. 18–24). Paris: UNESCO.

Edwards, A. (2015). Recognising and realising teachers' professional agency. *Teachers and Teaching*, 21(6), 779–784.

European Commission (2015). *Roadmap. New start to address the challenges of work-life balance faced by working families*. Brussels: European Commission (DGs Justice and Consumers and Employment, Social Affairs and Inclusion and Health).

Fernyhough, C. (2008). Getting Vygotskian about theory of mind: Mediation, dialogue, and the development of social understanding. *Developmental Review*, 28(2008), 225–262.

Georgeson, J. (2006). *Differences in preschool culture: Organisation, pedagogy and interaction in four selected settings*. Unpublished doctoral thesis, University of Birmingham.

Georgeson, J. (2015, Autumn). Leading for sustainability: Resources, curriculum and people. *Early Education Journal*, 77, 9–11.

Gladwell, M. (2000). *The tipping point: How little things can make a big difference*. Boston: Little, Brown.

Gronn, P. (2003). *The new work of educational leaders: Changing leadership practice in an era of school reform*. London: Paul Chapman.

Hargreaves, A. (2016). *The consistency of leadership*. Keynote presentation at the European Educational Research Association annual conference in Dublin, 24 August 2016.

Hargreaves, A., & Boyle, A. (2014). *Uplifting leadership: How organizations, teams, and communities raise performance*. San Francisco, CA: Jossey Bass.

Hargreaves, A., & Fink, D. (2004). The seven principles of sustainable leadership. *Educational Leadership*, 61(7), 8–13.

Harris, A., & Spillane, J. (2008). Distributed leadership through the looking glass. *Management in Education*, 22(1), 31–34.

Hicks, D. (2003). *Religion and the workplace: Pluralism, spirituality, leadership*. Cambridge, UK: Cambridge University Press.

Maggiolini, S., Zanfroni, E., & D'Alonzo, L. (2016). *Understanding the risk of burn out in early childhood care professionals: Setting the stage for wellbeing*. Presentation at the 26th EECERA Annual Conference, Dublin, Ireland, 3 August to 3 September, 2016.

Md-Yunus, S. (2009). Rice, rice, rice in the bin: Addressing culturally appropriate practice in early childhood classroom. *Childhood Education*, 86(1), 27–32. [Online resource.] Available at: http://thekeep.eiu.edu/eemedu_fac/36.

NAAEE (2010). *Early childhood environmental education programs: Guidelines for excellence.* Washington, DC: North American Association For Environmental Education. [Online resource.] Available at: http://resources.spaces3.com/c518d93d-d91c-4358-ae5e-b09d493a f3f4.pdf. Accessed 03 October 2016.

NQS PLP (2013). Talking about practice: Embedding sustainable practices. *National Quality Standards Professional Learning Programme e-Newsletter, 67,* 1–3.

Nuttall, J., Thomas, L., & Henderson, L. (2016). Formative interventions in leadership development in early childhood education: The potential of double stimulation. *Journal of Early Childhood Research.* doi:10.1177/1476718X16664555

O'Connor, A. (2013). *Understanding transitions in the early years: Supporting change through attachment and resilience.* London: Routledge.

Pramling Samuelsson, I., & Kaga Y. (Eds.) (2008). *The contribution of early childhood education to a sustainable society.* Paris: UNESCO.

Rekalidou, G., & Panitsides, E. A. (2015). What does it take to be a 'successful teacher'? Universities' role in preparing the future early-years workforce. *Early Years, 35*(4), 333–350. doi:10.1080/09575146.2015.1080231

Rhodes, K. (2006). Six components of a model for workplace spirituality. *Graziadio Business Review, 9*(2).

Victor, B., & Boynton, A. (1998). *Invented here: Maximizing your organization's internal growth and profitability.* Boston: Harvard Business School Press.

Whitebread, D. (2014). The importance of self-regulation for learning from birth. In H. Moylett (Ed.), *Characteristics of effective learning: Helping young children become learners for life* (pp. 15–35). Maidenhead: Open University Press.

Wyness, L., Jones, P., & Klapper, R. (2015). Sustainability: What the entrepreneurship educators think. *Education + Training, 57*(8/9), 834–852.

11

DESIGNING ENVIRONMENTALLY SUSTAINABLE MULTIMODAL PROVOCATIONS FOR EARLY YEARS LEARNING ENVIRONMENTS

Sandra Hesterman

Introduction

ESD is not a particular programme or project, but rather an umbrella for many forms of education, those promoting human effort to rethink lifestyle challenges that relate to environment, society, culture and economy (Dyment et al., 2014; UNESCO, 2016). The United Nations Education, Scientific and Cultural Organization (UNESCO) provides the following definition of ESD and specifies its status:

> Education for Sustainable Development (ESD) is a vision of education that seeks to empower people to assume responsibility for creating a sustainable future.
>
> *(UNESCO, 2011)*

> Citizens of the world need to learn their way to sustainability. Our current knowledge base does not contain the solutions to contemporary global environmental, societal and economic problems. Today's education is crucial to the ability of present and future leaders and citizens to create solutions and find new paths to a better future.
>
> *(UNESCO, 2016)*

While the aims of ESD are diverse, they are fundamentally twofold:

1. To foster through education, training and public awareness, the values, behaviour and lifestyles required for a sustainable future.
2. To make decisions that balance and integrate the long-term future of the economy, the natural environment and the well-being of all communities, near and far, now and in the future (UNESCO, 2010).

To facilitate ESD across the education spectrum, UNESCO (the lead agency for the United Nations' Decade of Education for Sustainable Development, 2005–2014) recommends a renewed emphasis on participatory teaching and learning methods that can motivate and empower learners to take action for sustainable development. Integral to achieving ESD aims is the promotion of competencies such as critical thinking, imagining future scenarios and making decisions in a collaborative way to motivate eco-citizenship. The eco-citizen recognises their obligations and responsibilities towards sustaining the global environment and shares a civic concern for the implications of their individual actions on the environment (UNESCO, 2016; Wolf, 2007).

The momentum for ESD in the early years of childhood is founded on the following beliefs:

- Young children have capacities to be active agents of change through small, individual actions.
- Early childhood is a natural starting point for learning about ESD.
- Early childhood educators can play a significant role in shaping children's attitudes, knowledge and actions to promote eco-citizenship behaviour (Dyment et al., 2014).

This chapter examines one higher education eLearning initiative aimed at facilitating authentic connections between educational theory and practice for pre-service teachers who were these studying Australian early childhood learning environments. More specifically, these students were required to create an environmentally sustainable 'provocation' suitable for an early learning environment. A provocation (which can take many forms) provokes thought, discussions, questions, debate, interest, collaboration, creativity and ideas. A provocation that is environmentally sustainable will promote resource conservation and provoke ideas of how to live, work and play sustainably (Elliott & Young, 2006). Significantly, the higher education assignment within this project aimed to expose pre-service teachers – while they were working in the online environment – to the same learning processes that they were promoting for young children; the online assignment was essentially an environmentally sustainable provocation in a higher education environment (Johnston, 2013).

Before proceeding to the discussion of the higher education initiative, it is important that the reader is familiar with ESD in relation to the Australian National Quality Framework (NQF), to a pedagogy of multiliteracies and to higher education provocations for ESD that have relevance to early childhood education. Following the review of relevant literature, the integral relationship between these educative processes as enacted in an Australian higher education context is examined to show how these processes have promoted ESD in early childhood education.

The National Quality Standard and EfS

Established in 2012, the NQF aims to raise quality in the provision of Australian early childhood education and care and to provide momentum for continuous improvement and consistency in education for young children (ACECQA, 2011a). A key component of the framework is the 'National Quality Standard' (ACECQA, 2013). The NQS applies to most long day care, family day care, preschools and kindergartens (collectively providing for children aged birth to five years) and focuses primarily on seven domains/quality standards that are considered central to the planning, implementation and assessment processes underpinning quality Early Childhood Education provision. A review of the NQS shows that ESD is embedded in 'Quality Area 3: Physical Environment', which focuses on ensuring that early learning centres are safe and age-appropriate in design, and that they provide a diverse range of experiences that promote children's learning and development. The following Quality Area 3 statements are relevant to ESD:

- The service takes an active role in caring for its environment and contributes to a sustainable future.
- Sustainable practices are embedded in service operations.
- Children are supported to become environmentally responsible and show respect for the environment.

According to the national standards, the early years learning environment should cater for children's different learning capacities and learning styles and invite children and their families to contribute ideas, interests and questions. Educators will assist children to appreciate the natural world and develop an awareness of the impact of human activity on the environment. They will also provoke thinking on ways in which children can contribute to a sustainable future. The ECE program and environment will support each child's learning about ESD in relation to their identity as an eco-citizen, will enable the formation of connections with their community and will ensure opportunities for them to become effective communicators 'around sustainability issues and topics related to their own lives' (Davis, 2009, p. 6).

While the standards pertaining to ESD can be readily identified in accessible documents, the challenge for course coordinators working in higher education is deciding how to facilitate pre-service teachers' understanding of methods for embedding ESD naturally in early childhood centres. A further challenge is deciding how to support pre-service teachers to share their ESD knowledge and to build connections between early childhood educational theory and practice in a higher education and an online learning environment. This challenge was met by the author as the coordinator of a university course that aimed to enact a pedagogy of multiliteracies while providing pre-service teachers with an opportunity to work collaboratively on an authentic task to learn about ESD.

Education for sustainability through the lens of a pedagogy of multiliteracies

The importance of dialogue

The strongest and most stable ecosystems are those that are the most diverse: 'diversity contains the potential for adaptation whereas uniformity can endanger a species (including the human species) by providing inflexibility and unadapt ability' (Baker, 2001, p. 281). It follows that cultural and linguistic diversity in humanity can offer the possibility to maximise human endeavour to inspire new ways of thinking about ESD (St Clair, 2001). For example, if ECE fully engages with sustainability, then children's points of view will be heard in order to strengthen sustainable practices, and their participation and input will be valued (Robinson & Vaealiki, 2015). Similarly, educators will be able to reflect critically on how they can provide greater latitude for children's individual expressions of ESD meaning and initiative and children will be more likely to understand what is important in relation to their own environment based on their own experiences (Arpi, 2010). Terralingua provides these crucial insights:

> Through a diversity of cultural traditions and practices, in a great variety of natural environments, human communities have acquired invaluable knowledge of how to achieve harmony with nature.
>
> *(Terralingua, 2015a)*

and

> Monocultures of the mind have the same end result as monocultures in nature: they make our planet more fragile and vulnerable to both natural disasters and human-made crises.
>
> *(Terralingua, 2015b)*

Former UN Secretary-General Kofi Annan (2001) asserted that 'Our biggest challenge in this new century is to take an idea that seems abstract – sustainable development – and turn it into a reality for all the world's people.' At the heart of ESD are provocations that can stimulate conversations and innovations and that can improve the capabilities of people to address environment and development issues (UNESCO, 2005). Rinaldi (1998) reminds educators that children are rich in resources, are strong and competent and are protagonists of their own learning. Emblematic of democratic dialogue with children (and families and the broader community) is *a pedagogy of listening* – children and adults searching for meaning and understanding through listening to each other that allows for their experience to be shared and debated (Rinaldi, 2012). The accommodation of negotiation, experimentation and the interrelation of alternative mindsets are evident in ECE when there is openness to diversity and the application of children's own ideas and experiences to foster their awareness of what ESD means (Pramling Samuelsson, 1996). The research described in this chapter illustrates how provocations, when embedded in a pedagogy of multiliteracies, can support ESD in ECE through intercultural dialogue and interdependent efforts.

A pedagogy of multiliteracies

The term 'multiliteracies' embraces the notion that there are multiple 'modes of representation [that communicate meaning] much broader than language alone' (Cope & Kalantzis, 2000, p. 5). A pedagogy of multiliteracies 'encourages a broader perspective of the student as a learner and values diverse ways of knowing, thinking, doing and being' (O'Rourke, 2005, p. 10). Underpinning a pedagogy of multi-literacies is the theory of multimodalities that asserts there is a '… multiplicity of ways in which children make meaning … [a] multiplicity of modes, means and materials' for self-expression (Kress, 1997, p. 97). This theory postulates that from birth, a child actively seeks to make and understand 'messages and meanings' in accordance with their interests and using available resources that include visual, aural, gestural, spatial and linguistic communications (New London Group, 1996).

The epistemology underpinning a pedagogy of multiliteracies is consistent with theoretical perspectives that view knowledge as 'relative to time and space' and language as 'relativist in stance' (Patton, 2002, p. 100). ESD knowledge and language are open to varied interpretation and change by participants with different life experiences and alternative worldviews. In the context of ESD, a pedagogy of multiliteracies, multimodal theory and multiple modes of meaning all expand humanity's meaning-making enterprise, which could be described as the generation and exchange of knowledge and solutions: 'every meaning exchange is cross-cultural to a certain degree' (Cope & Kalantzis, 2015, p. 3). A pedagogy of multi-literacies relevant to early childhood recognises children's individual readings of the world and acknowledges that there are multiple modes of meaning they can use to communicate their knowledge of how to live sustainably.

Certainly, a pedagogy of multiliteracies embedded in an ECE multidisciplinary and transdisciplinary curriculum has rich potential to support ESD. A multidisciplinary curriculum provides children with opportunities to integrate and study relationships across two or more subjects as a whole; a transdisciplinary curriculum focuses on child-initiated questions and projects related to real-life contexts and connected to real-life experiences (Drake & Burns, 2004). In ECE, both types of curricula are relevant to ESD: time, space and resources are needed for children to marry subject content with their ideas and questions about sustainability by exploring both indoor and outdoor provocations. Davis (2013) notes that ESD in the early years is not a shift of responsibility from adults to children; it is not 'asking them to fix the problems we [adults] leave behind' (p. xiii). Rather, ESD focuses on the explora-tion of human capabilities to support the growth and development of a sustainable world in diverse ways. In a similar fashion, Chalofsky (2005, p. 55) observes that '[i]n the knowledge era … there are not only multiple ways of viewing reality, but also multiple ways of knowing (learning). Indeed, diversity is a stimulant to learning because it forces us to confront different perspectives.'

Initiating higher education ESD tasks in early childhood education

Since 2000, the Australian government's approach to ESD has included raising the profile and effectiveness of community education and to position it as an essential component of national policy on the environment and sustainability (Commonwealth of Australia, 2009). The aim of the Australian government's 'National Action Plan for Education for Sustainability' is to equip all Australians with the knowledge and skills required to live sustainably. In other words, to harness the 'community spirit to act' to improve community access to ESD knowledge and tools (Commonwealth of Australia, 2009, p. 5). It is envisaged that the collaboration of many diverse providers of education (including higher education) will support research to improve understanding of ESD issues, attitudes and behaviour. It is with this mantra of the 'community spirit to act' that the author sought to build the capacity of higher education students studying ECE to explore provocations for sustainability.

In 2015, a new university course, Early Childhood Education Learning Environments, was offered to students enrolled in Early Childhood Studies. These students needed to become familiar with the national standards to raise quality and ensure continuous improvement of Australian early childhood learning environments. Forty pre-service teachers from across the nation enrolled in the course, which was offered only to learners outside the university. One course assessment item required students to work online in a group to design an environmentally sustainable provocation that could be integrated in an ECE environment to stimulate learning about ESD and that would include learning processes associated with the following concepts:

Constructivism	The idea that human beings actively construct their knowledge and do not simply absorb or reproduce reality.
Social constructivism	The idea that human beings learn through interactions with more competent 'others', who provide feedback to help new ways of thinking about the world.
Discovery learning	The idea that human beings can learn through their own exploration, experience and enquiry.
Multiliteracies	The idea that human beings can create and express meaning and messages using multiple modes of representations.

At the commencement of the course, the students were assigned to a university online group discussion forum for the purposes of providing one another with informal support during the course and discussing the design of their online group project. The course readings, visits to recycling centres/websites and observations conducted at two early childhood learning environments (located in each student's local community) had exposed students to a range of real-life play ideas with accompanying design considerations. The group task involved designing a presentation using Prezi (a cloud-based presentation software application). The Prezi software enabled students to communicate their ideas using motion, zoom and spatial relationships and to embellish their presentation with audio features. The presentation (consisting of twenty slides) required specific design elements:

- A self-explanatory title for the environmentally sustainable provocation.
- Images of the provocation made from recycled materials that could be integrated into a real-life early childhood learning environment. Using computing skills, students could superimpose and scale an image of the 'virtual' provocation onto a photograph showing its intended integration in an indoor and/or outdoor environment.
- A list of recycled materials used to construct the provocation (including photographs).
- Identification and elaboration of the relevance of NQS ('Quality Area 3: Physical Environment') to the design of the provocation (i.e. safety issues, maintenance, sufficient space, ensuring it invites open-ended interactions, etc.).
- Commentary on the relationship between environmental sustainability and ECE learning environments relevant to the group's provocation, including keywords and metaphors used by Ceppi and Zini (2001) to describe the quality of environmental features.
- Accompanying music inspired by nature, to be played throughout the presentation.
- A summary reflection on each member's personal learning that occurred while completing the assignment, making direct reference to group members' practical experiences in relation to key educational theories.

During the course, the students were able to contact a university IT specialist for support. All presentations were uploaded to the learning platform at the end of the course for other groups to review, thus enabling expansion of the students' repertoires of ESD learning provocations and further promoting knowledge and understandings of ESD in relation to ECE theory and practice.

Designs for ESD provocations in early childhood education

> True learning involves figuring out how to use what you already know in order to go beyond what you already think.
>
> *(Bruner, 1983, p. 183)*

Each online group had four members who were selected at random by the course coordinator (the author) to form the group. Group members did not know (nor live in close proximity to) one another. In the assignment reflections, students commented on the difficulties that 'distance' posed – but noted that it had also provided a unique opportunity to extend their understandings of sustainability with others across the nation: students were able to make connections between ideas and to construct shared meaning in association with their own experiences of sustainability (Nelson Laird et al., 2005):

> The process of this group assignment has certainly challenged me in ways that have allowed me to learn and grow. I realised that there are many ways in which I can improve my sustainability practices at my family day care centre.
>
> *(Student Reflection)*

Students recognised that communicating with others in diverse locales was invaluable:

> We learnt how a combination of negotiation, patience, questioning, organisation, exploration/discovery, knowledge and skills of multiliteracies and multimodalities can combine to achieve an outcome (our provocation).
>
> *(Student Reflection)*

The challenges of creating a sustainable planet require human interdependence through establishing new partnerships and seeking community engagement. While there were initial feelings of vulnerability and inadequacy (with students questioning whether their individual ideas were 'good' or 'bad'), students were keen to hear feedback from others on different ideas about sustainability in ECE. The completion of the project was a mandated task. Members had to 'push' themselves to work together to problem-solve and conduct research on how to provoke children's thinking about sustainability. This in turn provoked their own learning about ESD:

> This provocation helped me construct my knowledge when we were throwing around ideas for our topic as well as creating a lot of excitement about using them in my own classroom. I found this collaborative assignment to be like a provocation for myself.
>
> *(Student Reflection)*

Group members shared a range of knowledge and understandings on ESD when designing their provocation and agreed that the collaborative construction of knowledge enabled 'greater learning' than if they had completed the assignment on their own. Whilst not a course requirement, some groups elected to construct a real-life rather than a virtual ESD provocation to be used in an early years learning environment that they had visited during course fieldwork. This was a rewarding experience for these students, who – spurred by intellectual curiosity to design a provocation – were encouraged to extend their group's creative and critical thinking:

We were fortunate to be able to set up our provocation in a real-life [early years learning] centre ... I felt proud and happy ... This was a valuable experience for me to see how children would engage and explore with our provocation ... this collaborative, hands-on experience extended my own creativity.

(Student Reflection)

It is not within the scope of this chapter to provide detailed information regarding the actual provocations designed, but there was evidence of significant diversity that included (but was not limited to): exploring sand (building); clay (printing); water (water pump stations and becoming 'water warriors'); gardens (sensory and edible); chickens (designing coops, caring for chickens, study of chicken life cycle, and using eggs in cooking); cities and countries (focus on cars and buildings, conservation of energy); oceans (focus on the impact of boats and the fishery industry); designing and constructing play furniture and musical instruments utilising recycled materials; exploring animal habitats and natural resources in the environment; bringing nature (pebbles, shells and leaves used to create images) into the classroom (Figure 11.1); and discovering scrapstores and recycling industrial discards from shops and factories.

At the end of the course, when the online presentations were accessible to all groups, there was considerable interest in the range of ECE environmentally sustainable provocations that groups had generated. One student stated: '... developing provocations using sustainable, recycled materials opened my eyes to

FIGURE 11.1 Bringing nature into the classroom

plenty of new learning and teaching possibilities for the future'. All provocations addressed the national standards for sustainability, referenced keywords and metaphors (Ceppi & Zini, 2001) and were age-appropriate and playful for young children. Each provocation provided a stimulus for conversations and efforts related to sustainability in the early childhood learning environment. An example of one group/team assignment (with student consent) can be accessed using the following link: https://prezi.com/lkoskxbbvsme/copy-of-team-5/

The students made strong connections between the educational theories presented in the course content and real-life experiences. They experienced educational processes involving constructivism, social constructivism, discovery learning and multiliteracies, both on a personal level and on a group level (Figures 11.2 and 11.3). Importantly, the online group assignment extended students' knowledge and understandings of ECE for sustainable development through research and innovation. Nelson Laird et al. (2005, p. 4) comment that 'deep learning' in higher education can tap students' full learning potential when learner-centred environments necessitate 'integrating and synthesizing information with prior learning in ways that become part of one's thinking and approaching new phenomena and efforts to see things from different perspectives'. Figures 11.2 and 11.3 illustrate that an online learner-centred environment was provided and different perspectives were evidenced.

The requirements of the higher education assignment posed authentic tasks to 'parallel real-life practices with multiple solutions, require collaboration and support from a variety of sources and resources, and are multidisciplinary [and transdisciplinary]' (Leppisaari et al., 2014, p. 215). Moreover, the tasks made it possible for the students to experience making integrated solutions work for education for sustainable development (UNESCO, 2005).

Reflections

- Piaget's constructivist theory of learning suggests that children are more able to construct their own understandings through 'hands on' learning experiences. In relation to completing this assignment the self directed research/discovery learning has helped us to reflect on and develop our own personal understandings of how recycled materials can be genuinely used and incorporated into early childhood learning environments as purposeful provocations.
- We have also realised the significance of Vygotsky's social constructivist theory of learning. Whilst we all attempted to actively participate in the creation of our teams presentation and tried to communicate with each other, the lack of actual spoken dialogue and physical interaction was frustrating. On reflection I think we now appreciate that 'hands on' experiences alone, are not necessarily enough to provoke learning. Social interaction is a key learning tool.

FIGURE 11.2 Student reflection on educational theories

Multiliteracies   Reflections   ??
?
?

- We learnt how a combination of collaboration, negotiation, patience, questioning, organisation, exploration and discovery, knowledge and skills of multiliteracies and multimodalities can combine to achieve an outcome (our presentation).

- To bring our provocation to life we used a combination of multimedia (Learning Management System, email, digital photography, the electronic presentation tool). This meant that we needed to use our multiliteracy knowledge and skills to produce our presentation. We used the symbol system of the presentation tool (☺) to add content (text, photographs, YouTube clips, music, colour and templates), and drew on experiences with text (print and electronic), digital cameras, the internet, and multiple modes of communication (linguistics, auditory, visual and design); our presentation was born.

- Although different for each of us, learning occurred through the different ways to create the visual layout (what worked best), what to include; the flow of the presentation, and how to use and navigate our way around the presentation tool. For some this proved more challenging than they would have liked and further learning is still needed.

FIGURE 11.3 Student reflection on multiliteracies

Discussion

Reflecting on the UNESCO definitions of the nature and the status of ESD in higher education, it seems logical that an Australian teacher education course should include content and assessment items related to ESD – particularly when the course focuses on early childhood learning environments. As stated previously, it was the author's contention that in the field of higher education (focused on early childhood education), a pedagogy of multiliteracies (New London Group, 1996) would guide students' collaborative construction of knowledge to achieve different sorts of learning – including ESD in ECE. A review of the students' online group assignments showed that they successfully made meaningful connections with ESD in the delivery of content and diversity of interpretation:

> The major thing I learned in completing this assignment on sustainability with my group members is that we all read and interpret information, instructions and messages in different ways – hence the need for communication and multiliteracies is paramount to the effective completion of group work.
>
> *(Student Reflection)*

The higher education project also fostered students' awareness that working towards a sustainable future requires the ability to communicate in diverse multi-modal ways to secure multiple understandings of ESD. This diversity contains the potential for adaptation (Baker, 2001). The contribution of families and communities was recognised as part of the ESD learning journey:

> The group assignment encouraged me to seek active family and community input – and this is transforming my program's approach in environment and sustainability practices and hence making the children's learning far more meaningful.
>
> *(Student Reflection)*

There was also an appreciation of intercultural dialogue and interdependent efforts. This is reflective of the world's mutual dependence to constructively address present and future global challenges and create more sustainable societies (UNESCO, 2009).

> My learning was an active, constructive process linking new information with my prior knowledge. It was a totally new experience for me which led to discovery learning. My group consisted of students with different experiences, backgrounds and environments – problem-solving was vital. I learnt that each individual has strengths and talents and could be beneficial when working as a team.
>
> *(Student Reflection)*

Notably, the group assignment engendered an enthusiasm for ESD learning, developed critical thinking and fostered independent and collective learning for a diverse student population in higher education (Goodling, 2014; Hung & Chen, 2001). A pedagogy of multiliteracies supported this process; students engaged in a range of multimodal literacies and shared environmental knowledge: they communicated their diverse understandings of education for sustainability. The pedagogy of multiliteracies facilitated students' achievement through these methods:

- Discussion on ESD in an early childhood learning environment.
- Application of ESD understandings relevant to an early childhood learning environment.
- Development of provocations to stimulate conversations related to ESD.
- Awareness that the students themselves could perform a leadership role in supporting each other's learning by providing appropriate feedback and prompting critical and creative thinking about ESD ideas and issues.

Whilst challenging, the project assisted the pre-service teachers in recognising that people learn in different ways – an important consideration when working with children in an early learning environment.

Conclusion

This chapter has described one higher education initiative broadly aimed at facilitating meaningful connections between educational theory and practice for students who were studying Australian early childhood learning environments. More specifically, an online group assignment challenged students to design an environmentally sustainable provocation that empowered them to be contributors to ESD and designers of ECE experiences to forge children's strong identity with the environment and develop understanding that issues, attitudes and behaviour regarding the environment matter. As ESD is deemed an integral component of quality ECE programs and quality physical environments, educators have a responsibility to assume an eco-citizen leadership role in modelling sustainable practices – *sustainability in action* – and contributing to a sustainable future by providing the children in their care with time, space and resources to stimulate thought, discussion, questions, debate, interest, collaboration, creativity and ideas on resource conservation and on how to live, work and play sustainably.

The development of ESD higher education provocations can provide diverse stimuli for a child-initiated and emergent curriculum (multidisciplinary and transdisciplinary) which includes a range of key learning processes. These can be used by educators and children to examine what is already known in order to go beyond and extend collective knowledge and understandings on ESD. As demonstrated in this chapter, a pedagogy of multiliteracies has rich potential to transform education: to inspire new ways of thinking about curriculum; to enable exploration of ESD participatory teaching methods; to facilitate the use of various modes of meaning in order to develop deep learning of sustainability discourses which include cultural and linguistic diversity; and to deliver steady improvement in finding a myriad of paths to a better and sustainable future.

Questions for you to consider

1. Cope and Kalantzis (2015, p. 3) assert that 'every meaning exchange is cross-cultural to a certain degree'. Using a pedagogy of multiliteracies, how can educators facilitate children's 'meaning exchange' about their knowledge of how to live sustainably?
2. How can conversations with young children accommodate their different types of thinking about sustainability – their reasoning, imagining, predicting and recalling of experiences and facts of sustainability in action?

Further reading

Cope, B., & Kalantzis, M. (Eds.). (2015). *A pedagogy of multiliteracies: Learning by design.* South Yarra: Palgrave Macmillan.

This edited text provides a range of examples of the application of the pedagogy of multiliteracies.

Sneddon, S., & Pettit, A. (2016). *Sustainability in action in early childhood settings.* Blairgowrie: Teaching Solutions.

A very useful resource from Australia for practitioners who are taking their first steps into embedding sustainability into their early years settings.

References

ACECQA (2011a). *National Quality Framework*. Sydney: Australian Children's Education and Care Quality Authority. [Online resource.] Available at: http://acecqa.gov.au/national-quality-framework/

ACECQA (2013). *Guide to the National Quality Standard*. Sydney: Australian Children's Education and Care Quality Authority. [Online resource.] Available at: http://files.acecqa.gov.au/files/National-Quality-Framework-Resources-Kit/NQF03-Guide-to-NQS-130902.pdf

Annan, K. (2001). Sustainable development: Humanity's biggest challenge in the new century. Speech by the United Nations Secretary-General Kofi Annan at the International Conference Centre, Dhaka, Bangladesh, 15 March 2001.

Arpi, T. (2010). Early childhood education important for sustainable development. Gothenburg: University of Gothenburg. [Online resource.] Available at: www.gu.se/english/about_the_university/news-calendar/News_detail//early-childhood-education-important-for-sustainable-development.cid948671

Baker, C. (2001). Review of Tove Skutnabb-Kangas 'Linguistic genocide in education – or worldwide diversity and human rights? *Journal of Sociolinguistics*, 5(2), 279–283.

Bruner, J. S. (1983). *In search of mind: Essays in autobiography*. New York: Harper & Row.

Ceppi, G., & Zini, M. (Eds.) (2001). *Children, spaces and relations: Metaproject for an environment for young children*. Modena, Italy: Reggio Children.

Chalofsky, N. (2005). Reshaping the way we view the world. *ProQuest Educational Journal*, 5(11), 54–58.

Commonwealth of Australia (2009). *Living sustainably: The Australian government's national action plan for education for sustainability*. Canberra: Department of the Environment, Water, Heritage and the Arts. [Online resource.] Available at: www.environment.gov.au/system/files/resources/13887ab8-7e03-4b3e-82bb-139b2205a0af/files/national-action-plan.pdf

Cope, B., & Kalantzis, M. (Eds.) (2000). *Multiliteracies: Literacies learning and the design of social futures*. South Yarra: Macmillan.

Cope, B., & Kalantzis, M. (Eds.) (2015). *A pedagogy of multiliteracies: Learning by design*. South Yarra: Palgrave Macmillan.

Davis, J. M. (2009). Revealing the research 'hole' of early childhood education for sustainability: A preliminary survey of the literature. *Environmental Education Research*, 15(2), 227–241.

Davis, J. M. (2013). Transformative approaches to sustainability. *Bedrock*, 18(1), 14–15.

Drake, S. M., & Burns, R. C. (2004). *Meeting standards through integrated curriculum*. Alexandria, VA: ASCD.

Dyment, J. M., Davis, J., Nailon, D., Emery, S., Getenet, S., McCrea, N., & Hill, A. (2014). The impact of professional development on early childhood educators' confidence, understanding and knowledge of education for sustainability. *Environmental Education Research*, 20(5), 660–679.

Elliott, S., & Young, T. (2006). *EEEC environmental sustainability policy for early childhood*. Alphington, VIC: Environmental Education in Early Childhood. [Online resource.] Available at: www.eeec.org.au/downloads/EEEC_Policy.pdf

Goodling, L. B. (2014). The multiliteracy turn in higher education: On teaching, assessing, valuing multiliteracies. *Pedagogy*, 14(3), 561–568.

Hung, D. W. L., & Chen, D. T. (2001). Situated cognition, Vygotskian thought and learning from the communities of practice perspective: Implications for the design of web-based e-learning. *Educational Media International*, 38(1), 3–12.

Johnston, L. F. (2013). Higher education for sustainability: Cases, challenges, and opportunities from across the curriculum. *Management Information Systems Quarterly*, 28(1), 75–105.

Kress, G. (1997). *Before writing: Rethinking the paths to literacy*. London: Routledge.

Leppisaari, I., Kleimola, R., Herrington, J., Maunula, M., & Hohenthal, T. (2014). Developing more authentic e-courses by integrating working life mentoring and social media. *Journal of Interactive Learning Research*, 25(2), 209–235.

Nelson Laird, T. F., Shoup, R., & Kuh, G. D. (2005). *Measuring deep approaches to learning using the national survey of student engagement*. Paper presented at the Annual Meeting of the Association for Institutional Research, Chicago, IL, 14–18 May 2005. [Online resource.] Available at: http://nsse.iub.edu/pdf/conference_presentations/2006/AIR2006DeepLearningFINAL.pdf

New London Group (1996). Pedagogy of multiliteracies: Designing social futures. *Harvard Educational Review*, 66(1), 60–92.

O'Rourke, M. (2005). *Multiliteracies for 21st century schools* (ANSN *Snapshot*, 2). Lindfield, NSW: The Australian National Schools Network Ltd.

Patton, M. Q. (2002). *Qualitative research & evaluation methods* (3rd ed.). Thousand Oaks, CA: SAGE.

Pramling Samuelsson, I. (1996). Understanding and empowering the child as a learner. In D. Olson & N. Torrance (Eds.), *Handbook of education and human development: New models of learning, teaching and schooling* (pp. 565–589). Oxford: Basil Blackwell.

Rinaldi, C. (1998). Projected curriculum constructed through documentation – Progettazione: An interview with Lella Gandini. In C. Edwards, L. Gandini, & G. Forman (Eds.), *The hundred languages of children: The Reggio Emilia approach-advanced reflections* (2nd ed., pp. 113–126). Greenwich, CT: Ablex Publishing Corporation.

Rinaldi, C. (2012). The pedagogy of listening: The listening perspective from Reggio Emilia. In C. P. Edwards, L. Gandini, & G. Forman (Eds.), *The hundred languages of children: The Reggio Emilia approach in transformation* (pp. 233–246). Santa Barbara, CA: Praeger.

Robinson, L., & Vaealiki, S. (2015). Ethics and pedagogy at the heart of early childhood education for sustainability. In J. Davis (Ed.), *Young children and the environment: Early education for sustainability* (pp. 103–123). Port Melbourne: Cambridge University Press.

St Clair, R. N. (2001). Review of Robert Phillipson (Ed.) *Rights to Language: Equity, Power, and Education. Language Problems & Language Planning*, 25(1), 99–103.

Terralingua (2015a). 'Protecting biocultural diversity – The true web of life'. Vancouver, BC: Terralingua. [Online resource.] Available at: http://terralingua.org/#sthash.M8jziomz.dpuf

Terralingua (2015b). The loss of diversity. Vancouver, BC: Terralingua. [Online resource.] Available at: http://terralingua.org/biocultural-diversity/the-loss-of-diversity/

UNESCO (2005). *UNESCO and sustainable development*. Paris: UNESCO. [Online resource.] Available at: http://unesdoc.unesco.org/images/0013/001393/139369e.pdf

UNESCO (2009). *United Nations decade on education for sustainable development (2005–14): International implementation scheme*. Paris: UNESCO. [Online resource.] Available at: http://unesdoc.unesco.org/images/0014/001486/148654E.pdf

UNESCO (2010). *Teaching and learning for a sustainable future*. Paris: UNESCO. [Online resource.] Available at: www.unesco.org/education/tlsf/extras/desd.html?panel=2#top

UNESCO (2011). *Education for sustainable development (ESD)*. Paris: UNESCO. [Online resource.] Available at: http://portal.unesco.org/geography/en/ev.php-URL_ID=14132&URL_DO=DO_TOPIC&URL_SECTION=201.html

UNESCO (2016). *Education for sustainable development (ESD)*. Paris: UNESCO. [Online resource.] Available at: www.unesco.org/new/en/education/themes/leading-the-international-agenda/education-for-sustainable-development/

Wolf, J. (2007). *The ecological citizen and climate change*. Paper prepared for the European Consortium for Political Research (ECPR) Joint Sessions 2007, Helsinki, 7–12 May 2007. [Online resource.] Available at: https://ecpr.eu/Filestore/PaperProposal/c9ae934f-f308-4612-95c7-67c9da8d882f.pdf

12

LOOKING FORWARD

The future development of ECECfS in the context of the Sustainable Development Goals

Lucien Georgeson

Introduction

From my perspective as a geographer and as a member of the Board of Trustees of an education charity that works in East Africa, I consider the Sustainable Development Goals (SDGs) for Early Childhood Education and Care, as well as the growing international appreciation of the contribution of ECEC to sustainable development, as potentially representing a 'window' of agreement. Policy studies have suggested the temporary existence of such 'windows' (Aberbach & Christensen, 2001), which may present an opportunity for disruptive new definitions, such as of ECECfS. So the SDGs can contribute to the development of global access to early childhood education, and engagement with a broad definition of sustainable development can help to shape visions of early childhood education.

Such moments of global agreement are rare (Caprotti et al., 2017), and such a window may be brief. As many contributors note, the new focus on ECEC because of the SDGs is very welcome. Therefore we need a compelling way to present the concept of Early Childhood Education and Care for Sustainability in order to move development-related education debates away from compliance with measuring progress towards the SDG target for ECEC, and towards a new holistic approach that demonstrates the contribution of ECECfS to the environment, to sustainable development and to society. This task is an urgent one for early years educators.

The SDGs can shape ECECfS

The future of ECECfS exists within the broader context of what could be fifteen years that transform global understandings of both sustainable development and education. The difference between the simple Millennium Development Goal target on education ('Ensure that, by 2015, children everywhere, boys and girls alike, will be able to complete a full course of primary schooling') and the subsequent SDG 4 target ('Ensure inclusive and equitable quality education and promote lifelong learning opportunities for all', and includes seven substantive targets and three implementation targets) is a very important one and could significantly affect global efforts for ECECfS. In addition to a growing understanding of the importance of education for sustainability, this field will develop over the 15 years of the SDGs within the context of a much broader, more holistic and more quality-focused understanding of education within sustainable development.

There are individual SDG targets on (paraphrased) *'completion* of free, quality primary and secondary for all boys and girls', 'quality early childhood development, care and pre-primary', 'technical, tertiary and vocational education, technical and vocation skills for youth employment, childhood and adult literacy', and 'education for sustainable development that covers sustainable lifestyles, human rights, gender equality, peace, global citizenship, cultural diversity and culture's role in sustainable development' (United Nations, 2015). The move away from a narrow focus on 'access to primary' under the MDGs to 'quality education from early childhood through primary, secondary, tertiary and adult learning' under the SDGs will fundamentally change the context in which early years practitioners work. The development of ECECfS should be shaped by both the SDG target for all children to have access to quality early childhood development and care and the SDG target for holistic education for sustainable development.

But the transformative potential and contribution to sustainable development must be defined and made explicit, and ECEC researchers and practitioners must have a stake in this process, or, as with the MDGs, the national-level implementation of the SDGs could largely be driven by a simple drive to meet the indicators for each target, which follow a narrow quantified approach. Implementation of the MDGs demonstrated that there are benefits from the quantification of the global goals, but such a process also involves simplification, reification and abstraction (Fukuda-Parr et al., 2014), which can have significant (unintended) consequences for what actually happens on the ground. There will have to be a concerted effort to minimise or avoid such unintended consequences with the SDGs. For example, it appears that the indicators for SDG 4.2 on ECEC do not fully address the broader intent of Education for Sustainable Development (ESD):

> 4.2.1 Percentage of children under 5 years of age who are developmentally on track in health, learning and psychosocial well-being. (Disaggregations: sex, location, wealth (and others where data are available))
> 4.2.2 Participation rate in organised learning (one year before the official primary entry age)
>
> *(United Nations Statistical Commission, 2016, p. 19)*

If ECEC under SDG 4 is narrowly linked to improving participation in organised learning for one year prior to primary, and if the definition of developmentally on track in learning consists of a narrow 'readiness for primary' assessment, then the outcomes may not resemble what the contributors to this volume and many early years practitioners would consider high quality, holistic ECECfS.

This happened in several cases with the MDGs (Fukuda-Parr, 2014; Satterthwaite, 2003), and studies have suggested that there is a complex and reflexive relationship between policy design and performance management (Bjørnholt & Larsen, 2014; Hood, 2012). Setting targets is a valuable part of the process, but a limited tool (Fukuda-Parr et al., 2014). Once set, targets can change the interpretation of the original goals themselves, meaning that they must either be sufficiently broad or treated as indicators of broader progress, not the sole means of deciding if a particular SDG target is 'achieved'. One non-governmental organisation observer stated in an intervention during the SDGs' international negotiations, we should measure what matters, not do what is measurable (Blanken, 2015). Therefore, practitioners and researchers must contribute to shaping what measuring 'ready for primary' (Target 4.2) and 'developmentally on track' (Indicator 4.2.1) means in terms of ECECfS and the SDGs. They must avoid a narrow definition of 'readiness' by including critical thinking and developing children's capabilities as agents for change, as identified by Siraj-Blatchford and other contributors to this volume, including Huggins and Evans, Ärlemalm-Hagsér and Pramling Samuelsson and Hesterman. Moreover, as Huggins stresses in her chapter, such definitions must be based in and reflect the local context in which each is working.

However, there is significantly more recognition of such issues within the SDGs' framework; many delegates in the intergovernmental negotiations noted the importance of disaggregation of data by a number of categories of potential discrimination (such as gender, ethnicity, age, religion). Along with an increased focus on subnational authorities and cities through the New Urban Agenda of Habitat III (United Nations, 2016), this could contribute to ensuring more situationally appropriate approaches. However, both of these potential developments still present significant technical and political challenges.

Linking SDGs from policy to practice

As Huggins stresses in her chapter, provision of ECEC is relatively new in many national contexts. As a further example, Kenya enacted a law in 2014 to provide early childhood education for all, administered through the county governments, following similar policies to expand free provision of primary and secondary education in previous years. However, there is no significant history of publicly provided early childhood education; there is therefore a powerful and timely need for the perspectives in this volume to inform current understandings of how educators and administrators around the world can begin achieving SDG 4.2 for access to quality early childhood education.

In a more recent development, Kenya is aligning its education policy to the education targets of SDG 4 and mainstreaming ESD (Wakaya, 2017). This is one such example of how the SDGs, despite being global goals of ambition (Scott & Lucci, 2015), will shape national and even local education policy (education in

Kenya is largely devolved to the county governments). However, there is a significant need not just to align policy to the SDG targets but also to align practice to the content and spirit of the SDGs. Education, including early years, needs to reflect the shared, global vision of the SDGs, and the SDGs should not simply give quantitative targets for education. It is important to remember that the SDGs are universal (Long, 2015), unlike the MDGs, and are intended to apply to all countries equally. Therefore, in the future development of ECECfS, and EfS more broadly, it must be recognised that ESD can apply to all countries, not just those in the Majority World frequently considered to need 'development'. This should also influence how ECECfS policy and practices are developed in the future, in each case again reflecting the local context.

As contributions to this volume have begun to map out, we must continue to emphasise how education is key to achieving sustainable development. As Ärlemalm-Hagsér and Pramling Samuelsson note, cultures of sustainability must evolve, and development of capability (Sen, 2000, as cited in Siraj-Blatchford & Pramling Samuelsson, 2016) should be key to how we understand quality education under the SDGs. As Warwick et al. point out, questions need to be asked around what kind of education is necessary; future collaboration is required between researchers, practitioners and policymakers from both early childhood education and development.

Reconnecting the environment and the socioeconomic worlds

As Huggins and Evans note in their Introduction, reviews of the literature have suggested that EfS may be moving from a narrower, environment-focused definition to a broader approach. Although the historical approach of EfS seems to have had a greater focus on the environmental, to truly grow an environmentally and socially sustainable ECECfS framework there needs to be further elaboration of ECECfS as it relates to all 17 SDG areas and as it may be more broadly defined.

The 17 goal areas together represent a complex, interconnected development agenda, not 17 'silos'. An inclusive approach that considers early years education and care together can further demonstrate the potential contributions of ECECfS to an interconnected SDG agenda and a transformational approach to global development under the SDGs. In particular, ECECfS is highly related to SDG 2 (nutrition and hunger), SDG 3 (health), SDG 5 (gender equality) and SDG 16 (peace, justice and inclusive societies). The contributions of Ärlemalm-Hagsér and Pramling Samuelsson, Folque, Georgeson, Huggins and Warwick et al. all include examples of how this volume points towards important avenues for further research and reflection in broadening the understanding of sustainability, sustainable development and the SDGs in ECECfS.

We may also consider the ongoing debate relating to the Anthropocene: the growing view within geography, geology and other disciplines that humanity is now the driving force behind planetary change (Monastersky, 2015). Although there is significant disagreement over the start of the Anthropocene, the emerging consensus is that we can identify it as a new 'era' of the earth's timeline, and this has major implications for how we teach sustainability. Contrary to 500 years of scientific discovery that has emphasised human investigation and understanding of the complexity and size of the planet and universe, humans must now acknowledge that they are not passive observers of the planet but are actively central to its development and future (Lewis & Maslin, 2015). Thus, critical thinking allied to problem-solving, systems thinking and active reflection on the role that we can and do have as individuals and collectives in influencing social and environmental change are all central to the role of ECECfS.

Perhaps the imperative for sustainability education here is developing the skills and approaches for inquiry that recognise that we live in a world of interrelatedness and complexity, and accelerated, human-induced change. This also requires laying the foundations for an understanding that we are all 'part' of the environment and of a globalised socio-economic system, and that we affect these two interconnected systems. Teaching understanding and engagement with the natural world in ECECfS, while a crucial element as our lives become forever further removed from 'nature', cannot alone give children the skills they need. Many contributors note the importance of critical thinking and better understanding of interactions with the 'non-human'. As Siraj-Blatchford and others in this volume note, ECECfS should be a critical and transformative exercise; ECECfS needs to prepare the way for engagement with all the decisions that we will have to make and a better understanding of how we may solve problems.

Conclusion

A future vision and future policies for ECEC must include a broader understanding of sustainability and sustainable development. That the SDGs include specific global goals for ECE and ESD is ambitious in itself, and this will positively affect the attention and resources flowing towards these two things. It will also, hopefully, mean that ECECfS is working within and feeding into a system of education that will also be focusing on similar issues and aiming to deliver the same aims.

Therefore, ECECfS needs to develop young children's capabilities and under-standing in relation to a broad range of social, environmental and even economic challenges, both local and global. With governments and development agencies having to consider the provision and quality of all forms of education, not just access to primary, ECECfS should not shy away from its role as the foundation for a new approach to education globally under the SDGs. The next step must be to build on the findings of this volume through further collaboration to understand what this might look like, both globally and in different national and local contexts. However, taking this step is a matter of urgency for all ECEC practitioners. Time is short.

Questions for you to consider

1 Looking across the range of SDGs and their targets, identify ways in which ECECfS relates to, and supports, the achievement of at least two other goals.

2   With reference to the indicators for measuring SDG 4, can you suggest how
    current approaches to measurement and reporting in your setting could be
    improved to reflect the broader, holistic goals of ECECfS?

Further reading

Chasek, P. S., Wagner, L. M., Leone, F., Lebada, A.-M., & Risse, N. (2016). Getting to
    2030: Negotiating the post-2015 Sustainable Development Agenda. *Review of European,
    Comparative & International Environmental Law*, 25(1), 5–14. doi:10.1111/reel.12149

This article provides a useful background and commentary on the intergovernmental process
of negotiating and finalizing the Sustainable Development Goals.

Fukuda-Parr, S., Yamin, A. E., & Greenstein, J. (2014). The power of numbers: A critical
    review of Millennium Development Goal targets for human development and human
    rights. *Journal of Human Development and Capabilities*, 15(2–3), 105–117. doi:10.1080/
    19452829.2013.864622

This article provides a useful critical review of the targets of the Millennium Development
Goals and the impact that they had on development actions, providing a basis for considering
what the impacts of the targets of the Sustainable Development Goals may be.

UNESCO (2014). *Roadmap for implementing the Global Action Programme on Education for Sustainable
    Development*. Paris: UNESCO.

This influential report is an important resource for understanding education for sustainable
development at the international level, and probably influenced the content of the Sustainable
Development Goals.

References

Aberbach, J. D., & Christensen, T. (2001). Radical reform in New Zealand: Crisis, windows
    of opportunity, and rational actors. *Public Administration*, 79(2), 403–422.
Bjørnholt, B., & Larsen, F. (2014). The politics of performance measurement: Evaluation use
    as mediator for politics. *Evaluation*, 20(4), 400–411.
Blanken, E. (2015). *Statement by Elles Blanken of VSO Papua New Guinea at the March inter-
    active dialogue with major groups and other stakeholders*. New York: VSO. [Online resource.]
    Available at: www.youtube.com/watch?v=y1zjC9iGUAY. Accessed 20 July 2017.
Caprotti, F., Cowley, R., Datta, A., Castán Broto, V., Gao, E., Georgeson, L., Herrick, C.,
    Odendaal, N., & Joss, S. (2017). The New Urban Agenda: Key opportunities and challenges
    for policy and practice. *Urban Research & Practice*, 0(0), 1–12.
Fukuda-Parr, S. (2014). Global goals as a policy tool: Intended and unintended consequences.
    Journal of Human Development and Capabilities, 15(2–3), 118–131.
Fukuda-Parr, S., Yamin, A. E., & Greenstein, J. (2014). The power of numbers: A critical
    review of Millennium Development Goal targets for human development and human
    rights. *Journal of Human Development and Capabilities*, 15(2–3), 105–117.
Hood, C. (2012). Public management by numbers as a performance-enhanced drug: Two
    hypotheses. *Public Administration Review*, 71(S1), S85–S92.
Lewis, S. L., & Maslin, M. A. (2015). Defining the Anthropocene. *Nature*, 519(7542), 171–180.
Long, G. (2015). The idea of universality in the Sustainable Development Goals. *Ethics &
    International Affairs*, 29(2), 203–222.

Monastersky, R. (2015). The human age. *Nature*, 519(7542), 144–147.

Satterthwaite, D. (2003). The Millennium Development Goals and urban poverty reduction: Great expectations and nonsense statistics. *Environment and Urbanization*, 15(2), 181–190.

Scott, A., & Lucci, P. (2015). Universality and ambition in the post-2015 Development Agenda: A comparison of global and national targets. *Journal of International Development*, 27(6), 752–775.

Sen, A. (2000). *Development as freedom*. Oxford: Oxford University Press.

Siraj-Blatchford, J., & Pramling Samuelsson, I. (2016). Education for Sustainable Development in Early Childhood Care and Education: An introduction. In J. Siraj-Blatchford, C. Mogharreban, & E. Park (Eds.), *International research on Education for Sustainable Development in Early Childhood* (pp. 1–15). New York: Springer International Publishing.

United Nations (2015). *Transforming our world: The 2030 Agenda for Sustainable Development*. New York: United Nations.

United Nations (2016). *New Urban Agenda*. New York: United Nations.

United Nations Statistical Commission (2016). *Report of the Inter-Agency and Expert Group on Sustainable Development Goal Indicators: Note by the Secretary-General Rev.1**. New York: United Nations.

Wakaya, J. (2017, 21 March). Kenya aligns education objectives with SDGs. *Capital News*. [Online resource.] Available at: www.capitalfm.co.ke/news/2017/03/kenya-aligns-education-objectives-sdgs/. Accessed 27 March 2017.

AFTERWORD

David Evans

In editing this volume in the TACTYC series 'Research informed professional development for the Early Years' we have been fascinated to compare and contrast the ideas and insights of our expert contributors from across the world, enjoying and being stimulated by the variety and differences. But in doing so we have become conscious of the emergence of four overarching themes, or broad assertions. We are confident that they would endorse them, and so we offer them for your consideration.

Firstly, Education for Sustainability (EfS) does not constitute a 'subject' or 'field of study' to be taught, with narrow outcomes to be specified and assessed. Rather, it constitutes an approach in educating young people, future-oriented, leading towards the goal of a sustainable world, arguably an approach that should underpin all education provision in the 21st century. From this understanding we propose that Early Childhood Education for Sustainability (ECEfS) and Early Childhood Education and Care for Sustainability (ECECfS) must look to provide a 'foundation' for the youngest children's understandings and actions towards a sustainable future. It therefore demands a wider focus than a curriculum/programme of study narrowly defined in terms of knowledge, skills and activities; it must substantially involve the development of attitudes, values and predispositions. Moreover, it is not restricted within the bounds of schooling but demands that practitioners adopt a holistic approach involving family, social relationships, health and the concerns of the wider community.

Secondly, appropriate ECEfS has therefore to be based in and responsive to the local contexts of community, region and country. There can be no universal 'blueprint' or set curriculum for ECEfS to be advocated and imposed, no sense of the unquestioned superiority of Minority World approaches. Instead, the approach must be constructed by educators through respectful processes of consultation with the local communities and stakeholders, but also, crucially, with representatives/ advocates of important understandings and practices about young children and their learning that have been established by the enormous body of theory and international research findings. EfS must always be a balance between the range of interests, wishes, beliefs and knowledge. Asserting this fundamental principle identifies an appropriate role for Minority World expertise in contributing to EfS in Majority World contexts. But, challengingly, it also demands that similar negotiations take place within regions and local communities of Minority World countries.

Thirdly, the development of EfS will make enormous demands upon Early Years practitioners. As so often, they cannot define their professional role as that of 'technicians' delivering and assessing a predetermined programme of study. Rather, they must be thoughtful and critical analysers and innovators, responsive to rapid change and able to identify the principles of EfS and apply them in practice They must be well-trained, knowledgeable, confident and, arguably, willing to be 'political'. The professional development of Early Years practitioners may well prove to be a vital element in developing ECEfS.

Fourthly, and crucially, time is running out. By 2030, at the end of the period of the Sustainable Development Goals, the children currently in ECE provision will be entering and engaging in adult life. How well will they have been prepared by EfS to undertake their roles and responsibilities as adults, as members of their communities and as global citizens? Can we afford to delay?

INDEX

Note: Page numbers in **bold** refer to tables and page numbers in *italics* refer to figures.